John Barry

A Life in Music

John Barry
A Life in Music

Geoff Leonard
Pete Walker
Gareth Bramley

Sansom & Company

First published in 1998 by Sansom & Company,
81g Pembroke Road, Bristol BS8 3EA

British Library Cataloguing in Publication Data.
A catalogue record for this book is available from The British Library

ISBN 1 900178 86 9

Designed and typeset by Bristol City Media.
Printed by WBC Book Manufacturers, Bridgend.

CONTENTS

*J*NTRODUCTION

John Barry is arguably Britain's best known composer of film music. He emerged at a time when the score of a movie was seldom recorded for the album market, and when the musical arranger, for all his importance to the end product, was a comparatively anonymous part of the film-making process. Barry's career has spanned the years in which there has been this increasing awareness of the importance of this role. The expansion of the record industry in the 1960s; the growing recognition of the impact of a memorable main theme on box office receipts; a wider acceptance of film music as a serious art form; all have helped ensure that securing the services of a 'name' composer is now almost as important as hiring the star actors. Musicians from all walks of life have entered the fray, but only the most talented have survived.

John Barry has not only survived but prospered spectacularly, and the aim of this book is to make sense of the route he has taken to win the position of pre-eminence he holds today. In doing so, we set out to give his international following, as loyal as it is diverse, as complete a record of his musical achievements as possible. Until now, no such project has been undertaken. We make no apologies for making the discography section a central feature of the book, because it serves numerous purposes. It states precisely what Barry has accomplished throughout his career, while eliminating inaccuracies that have crept in over the years through rumour and lack of information. It is also an invaluable reference for the inquisitive musicologist who wishes to sample Barry's prolific output; and finally, it may induce the record industry to re-evaluate what has become an internationally popular back catalogue.

Barry himself remains an enigma. He guards his privacy as resolutely as a top goalkeeper protects his penalty area. We respect him for that, so have focused on his career as a musician. In the first part of the book we have tried to show how he burst on to the music scene by researching his formative years as one of Britain's foremost pop personalities. We have talked to people who worked with him and who helped shape his career. These early years as performer, producer, arranger and writer add up to a formidable body of work, and provide fascinating insights into a man whose ultimate ambition was always to work in films. We tell how he reached that goal, after which the music itself takes centre stage. The picture content spans his entire career and contains hitherto unpublished photographs, along with many that have not been available in any form for a number of years.

One has only to glance through the sketchiest John Barry discography to appreciate the remarkable diversity and quality of his output. Stretching over a career now spanning forty years, Barry's musical canon takes many different forms and so means different things to different listeners, depending on how they first heard his work. Film enthusiasts will no doubt home in on his Oscar-winning scores for *Born Free*, *The Lion In Winter*, *Out Of Africa* and *Dances With Wolves* as his major creative achievements. Chart aficionados, on the other hand, are likely to point to his commercial successes with 'Hit And Miss' (adopted as the theme for BBC TV's *Juke Box Jury*) and 'The Persuaders' (the theme from the ITV series of the same name). Rock 'n' rollers are likely to consider the John Barry Seven as one of the most innovative pioneers of the pre-Beatles British music scene, while pop historians would probably highlight his distinctive pizzicato string arrangements for Adam Faith's phenomenally successful records as the definitive John Barry sound. Whichever way you look at it, Barry's back catalogue is impressively eclectic, while being stamped throughout with a highly individual personal touch.

Chapter 1
Early Years

John Barry Prendergast was born on November 3rd, 1933 in York, the youngest of three children. His great-grandfather fought professionally just before boxing became a legal sport, and was known as Professor Jack Sullivan. The art of boxing was not continued down the family line. Barry's father Jack owned a small chain of cinemas in the north of England, so it is perhaps fair to say that JB was born into the film industry. Music was also an early influence, as his mother had been an accomplished concert pianist. At a very early age the young lad could be found acting out scenes from battles with the aid of Dinky toys, to the accompaniment of classical music from the family gramophone. This precocious love of music developed further when he was nine, at which point he began to take piano lessons from Mrs Baird, a white haired old teacher who lived not far away. Barry, as he was always known to his father, recalls being struck across the fingers with a stick whenever he struck a wrong note. It was perhaps not surprising that in his teens he decided to take up the trumpet: 'When I was 15 I met totally different music. My brother Pat, ten years older, was crazy about swing – Goodman, Ellington, Herman, the Dorseys, Harry James and the rest. I was horrified. Then secretly fascinated. Then openly fascinated. James became my idol. I bought all his records and he triggered my interest in the trumpet.'

Former neighbour Mrs Jean Allison vividly recalls her father Fred Gibson teaching Barry at his house. The boy's favourite tune of the time was 'The Sheikh Of Araby'. At the same time, Barry was learning to operate his family's cinemas, and at the age of 14 he could look after a projection room on his own. It was about this time that he saw the film *A Song To Remember*, starring Paul Muni. It was about the life and death of Chopin, and he vividly remembers this as his first great inspiration towards composing music for films. Other early favourites were *The Treasure Of Sierre Madre*, with a Max Steiner score, and *The Third Man*. He recently told fellow composer David Arnold for *Mojo*: 'Anton Karas's score to *The Third Man* killed me. It's the most extraordinary score ever, played on one instrument (the zither), the ultimate lesson in simplicity and character.'

Apart from owning and managing cinemas, his father also put on local concerts, and according to another near neighbour, Barry was always to be seen at the Rialto with his friends Paul Duffield and Kevin Cowling. On one occasion Stan Kenton was the big-name star of the show, and his band played what must have been the first performance of a John Barry arrangement. He was only 15 at the time, so the work was rather basic; nevertheless, Kenton publicly forecast a big future for him and called him up on stage. Barry, still very shy, refused.

After leaving school – which he hated, apart from music lessons under the master of York Minster, Dr Francis Jackson – he worked full time for his father while playing trumpet most evenings in a local jazz band, the Modernaires. This agreeable state of affairs lasted three years, until he was called up for National Service. The obligatory period was two years, but Barry, seeing the chance of joining a musical regiment, enlisted for three with the famous Green Howards. He spent much of this time in Malta and Cyprus, where he was able to persuade his musical colleagues to experiment with all kinds of arrangements. At the same time he took a correspondence course with Bill Russo, then a noted arranger for the Stan Kenton band in America. Returning to York he continued to experiment with arrangements, sending them to Johnny Dankworth, Ted Heath and Jack Parnell, then among the biggest British bandleaders of the day. He clearly believed in starting at the top. Dankworth was very encouraging and broadcast one or two, while Jack Parnell suggested that he should form a band of his own. It was one night during one of his stints with the Modernaires that he took the plunge and followed Parnell's advice. He gathered some ex-army colleagues together with others and formed John Barry and the Seven.

Ken Golder remembers his introduction to the band. He was playing drums with the Blue Mariners dance band at the Spa in Scarborough, a big band that included his friends the guitarist Ken Richards and bass guitarist Fred Kirk. At that time, early in 1957, John Barry would go to dances at the Spa with his girl friend Barbara Pickard, who knew the band. They would chat during intervals, and eventually Barry asked the three of them if they would break from the Mariners to join a band with him and two saxophone players from York, Derek Myers and Mike Cox. The idea was they would rehearse on Sunday mornings at the Rialto. The last of Barry's friends to join was Keith Kelly, who played rhythm guitar and had a small solo spot singing with another local group. He recalls Barry rushing into the shoe shop where he worked and insisting that he should leave immediately to become one of the Seven; he must have been very persuasive, because Kelly duly obliged. The Seven's first full line-up, then, was John Barry (vocals & trumpet), Mike Cox (tenor-sax), Derek Myers (alto-sax), Ken Golder (drums), Fred Kirk (bass guitar), Ken Richards (lead guitar) and Keith Kelly (rhythm guitar).

The Sunday morning rehearsals became a part of their life, and were often watched by Barry's father Jack from a seat in the stalls. Not only was he able to offer the band their first professional engagements at the Rialto; he also lent his son £5,000 to set himself up when the band moved to London – and that was a lot of money in 1957.

John Barry and the Seven cut a couple of demos in London and sent them to Jack Good, the producer of the BBC's new youth programme *Six-Five Special*. At first

An early portrait of John Barry.

they were turned down because they were thought to be too similar to a regular band on the show, Don Lang and his Frantic Five, who coincidentally also had roots in Yorkshire. Undaunted, the group made their professional debut on Sunday, March 17th, 1957 back at father's Rialto in York, where they were a supporting act to Mitchell Torok and Cy Laurie's Jazz Band. They were billed as a 'brand new rock 'n' roll group which also features calypsos'. The Seven had been a minor sensation at a 'snap' try out at the theatre earlier in the week, and Val Parnell had offered them an ITV audition; but their real break came when they were spotted at the Rialto by the London agent Harold Fielding, who gave them a summer season with the top-of-the-tree Tommy Steele in Blackpool. From nothing to weeks of high-profile work by the sea in no time at all; it was a sensational start for the Seven.

An early shot of the John Barry Seven around 1957. From the left: Mike Cox, Derek Myers, Fred Kirk, Ken Golder, John Barry, Ken Richards, Keith Kelly.

They rehearsed all day at an eighteenth-century barn, determined to make the most of their big break. They were kitted out in light grey suits and a choreographer taught them some basic dance steps – a routine made famous by the Shadows, and the kind of regimentation eventually ridiculed by the Beatles and other groups of the Mersey Beat era. John Barry soon turned against it, too. For a short time during this season Ken Golder was under contract to the big band in Scarborough and had to be replaced on drums by Don Martin, from Torquay. They were so well received and immaculately turned-out in Blackpool that not only did the BBC change their mind about an appearance on *Six-Five Special* but ITV stepped in to snap them up for their first TV appearance – on the ultra-conventional Teddy Johnson's *Music Box*. Golder is convinced that their polished performances – together with their ability to accompany almost any other act – was what attracted such influential rock TV producers as Jack Good and Josephine Douglas.

Their first visit to the *Six-Five* studio was preceded by a concert appearance at

A portrait of John Barry in 1958 by Landseer.

London's Royal Albert Hall on Sunday, September 8th. *The Top 20 Hit Parade All-Star Show* also featured Lonnie Donegan, Bob Cort, Russ Conway, Nancy Whiskey, Russ Hamilton and the King Brothers, a fair cross-section of British pop talent in 1957. The skiffle king Don Lang had topped the charts twice in the year, with 'Cumberland Gap' and 'Gambling Man'. Nancy Whiskey and the Chas McDevitt group had been in the Top Twenty for months with 'Freight Train', and on the weekend of the show Russ Hamilton was riding high with his massive hit 'We Will Make Love'. The compères were actor John Fraser and Radio Luxembourg DJ Keith Fordyce.

The concert was put on in association with the *New Musical Express*, which reported that 'another solid rock success was the John Barry Seven. Reminiscent of Freddie Bell and the Bellboys, this British unit certainly had the vast hall jumpin' with some all-out beat music, spiced with vocals and precision movements. John Barry himself proved a true leader and shone in solo work, climaxing with "Three Little Fishes".' The act obviously made a big impression with the *NME*, as they also printed what is probably the first photo of the group in action, captioned: 'They came, you saw, they conquered! Yes, it's the John Barry Seven, who took London by storm with their exciting music at Sunday's Royal Albert Hall concert'. The following week the paper noted – inaccurately, in the case of Barry – that both the JB7 and new discovery Marty Wilde had been signed by Philips records, and first sides would be cut within ten days. There had been fierce bidding for Barry's signature, it noted, and two other major record groups had made offers. In fact Harold Fielding

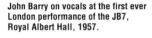

John Barry on vocals at the first ever London performance of the JB7, Royal Albert Hall, 1957.

★ ★ ★ ★ PROGRAMME ★ ★ ★ ★

THE 'TOP ALL-STAR POP' SHOW

COMPERED BY
REG THOMPSON
Direct from the Tommy Steele Show

THE GORGEOUS LOVELIES
MARGO and JUNE

★

MARGO and JUNE

LAUGHS GALORE WITH YOUR COMPERE
REG THOMPSON

★

DYNAMIC SINGING STAR OF THE 6-5 SPECIAL
DON RENNIE
Songs will include Rock Baby Rock   Volare   Rock-A-Bye
Day That The Rains Came

STARS of COOL FOR CATS and the JACK JACKSON SHOW
THE AVON SISTERS
Songs will include their hits Jerry Lee and Baby Oh

★

THE KING OF THE KEYBOARD, STAR OF RECORDS AND T.V.
RUSS CONWAY
Playing selections from Pal Joey   South Pacific   Party Pops
Blues Medley   World Outside
and many other all time hits

BRITAIN'S SENSATIONAL " ROCKIN " MEN
THE JOHN BARRY SEVEN
with LISA PAGE
Numbers selected from Farrago   Bee's Knees   Rodeo   Saints
Blue Room   Flippin and many other great hits

★

BRITAIN'S FABULOUS TOP TUNE TRIO
THE KING BROTHERS
Selected from Wake Up Little Susie   Oh Babe   Torero
Thank Heaven For Little Girls   Aint Misbehavin'
Leanin' On A Lampost   and many more top tunes

— INTERVAL —

★

NOW ENJOY THE WONDERFUL FIVE-STAR SALES SERVICE
ICE CREAM FRUIT DRINKS POP-CORN NUTS
and a wonderful selection of Confectionery and Cigarettes at the Kiosk

★

SENSATIONAL FINALE

GOD SAVE THE QUEEN

REG THOMPSON WILL CONDUCT THE GRAND DRAW FOR THE DREAM HOLIDAY
Look at your Programme Number on Page 3, your chance for a **FREE HOLIDAY** on the Cornish Riviera at the fabulous
KENEGIE HOLIDAY HOTEL (AND COUNTRY CLUB) **GULVAL, PENZANCE**

PROGRAMME

THE JOHN BARRY SEVEN
FROM I.T.V.'s "OH BOY" SHOW

★

DES O'CONNOR

★

THE HEDLEY WARD TRIO
IN SELECTIONS FROM :—
The greatest feeling in the world
That's the way love goes
Who's sorry now?
My baby's got such lovin' ways
Steamboat rock
Big ears

| INTERMISSION |

MARINO MARINI
QUARTET
★
TOTO .... the electric Guitar
RUGGERO .... the Singing Bass player
ANGELO .... Drummer
MARINO MARINI .... Pianoforte

★

Ciao, Ciao Bambina

Lo Sono il Vento

Volare

Come Prima

Bebe'

Capriccioxa

Marena

I could have danced all night

THIS PROGRAMME IS SUBJECT TO ALTERATION AT THE DISCRETION OF THE MANAGEMENT

John Barry & The Seven in early 1957. Back, from the left: Fred Kirk, John Aris, John Barry, Ken Richards, Keith Kelly. Front, from the left: Derek Myers, Ken Golder & Mike Cox.

had been negotiating with both Philips and Decca, but it had been EMI who had stepped in with the first concrete offer, and that is how the group came to join the Parlophone label in September.

The Seven's first appearance on *Six-Five Special* was on September 21st 1957, and *The Record Mirror* noted that the group would include two new faces for the show, John Aris on vibes and Ken Golder, back from duties at Scarborough. Aris on vibes proved to be a very short-lived experiment. Between them the group made £35 for the live performance, plus a further £14.70 for rehearsals, which lasted a great deal of the Friday and Saturday. Out of this had to come commission paid to Harold Fielding, who was by then their agent – but their foot was in the door, and it was the first of a long string of contracts for BBC TV. On this first show the JB7 played two vocals, a Barry original called 'We All Love To Rock' plus 'Every Which Way'. Further TV appearances followed, and they returned to a seaside show at the other end of the country from their debut gig in Blackpool, in a short season with Frankie Vaughan in Torquay.

Things were moving. The Seven were starting to get regular mentions in the music press, and *The Record Mirror* even recorded that first pre-*Six-Five* television appearance with a small photo of Barry headed 'TV debut for JB7'. It went on to say: 'The JB7 rock 'n' roll group makes its TV debut in the ITV *Music Box* show this Friday, August 30th, at 9 p.m. The Seven, led by 23-year-old trumpeter John Barry, has just finished a four-week season with the Tommy Steele show at Blackpool. They also appeared last week in Bournemouth with Frankie Vaughan, and will do a further week commencing September 2nd at Torquay. In October the group is due to undertake a ten-week tour of music halls throughout Britain with the supporting acts who appeared in the Steele show at Blackpool. Skiffle girl Nancy Whiskey will probably head the bill.' It is a mark of the impact of the Seven that they were being gossiped about in such detail in the music press after such a short time in the business. On September 28th, The *Record Mirror* published a review of the Nancy Whiskey show at The Metropolitan, Edgware Road: 'The first half of the show is closed by the JB7. They are mainly on a rock kick, but if you can stand that, then the act is excellent. They are faultlessly turned out, perform with slickness, precision and abandon. An act produced with professional thoroughness, an object lesson to other youngsters in the business.'

The following week an even longer piece was published, possibly helped by the fact that the editor was a friend of Barry's father. Under the heading: 'Theatre owner's son heads John Barry Seven', it featured a discussion with Jack Prendergast about John: 'I know a good act when I see one, and I won't be influenced by a relationship. I'm convinced my boy is leading a first rate outfit, and I'm sure he'll get along on merit, without any push from me.' Jack Prendergast said he would not have been bothered with the act if it had not been good and professional.

The group's first record for Parlophone – they were billed as John Barry and the Seven – was 'Zip Zip', coupled with 'Three Little Fishes'. The fact that few people can now recall the first and that the second title is usually thought of as a comic song by Frankie Howerd tells all about the disc's impact beyond lead vocalist Barry's home city of York. But at least the JB7 were now recording artists.

The next breakthrough was a guest spot in the film version of *Six-Five Special*. Barry even wrote a song, 'Little Old Fashioned Love', which he hoped to feature in the film, but eventually he sang two others, 'Every Which Way' and 'You've Gotta Way'. Later they formed both sides of his second single, and Larry Page recorded 'Little Old Fashioned Love'. In January, 1958, *Six-Five* producer Jack Good decided to take the show on the road – in fact to Leicester and Hull for a series of performances on Tuesdays and Wednesdays. The BBC took exception to this and sacked him, and it was the beginning of the end of the TV show, which was beginning to show its age, in any event; soon enough other early Saturday evening rock shows would build on its success. The stage version, too, soon waned, not least because of its unpromising midweek dates and venues; but among its achievements it produced the first meeting of two men who would bring a new sound to British pop before the decade was out, John Barry and a teenage newcomer being tried by Good, one Adam Faith.

That winter also brought a massive vote of confidence in the JB7 when it was chosen to tour England backing Paul Anka, EMI's teen wonder whose 'Diana' was topped only by Pat Boone's 'Love Letters In The Sand' as the UK's top-selling disc of 1957. Ken Golder recalls the band auditioning for Anka and his management in a Soho rehearsal room one Sunday morning, when the usually bustling area was quiet. They coped well with 'Diana', along with the other material he asked them to

play, and he was delighted with them. A seven-piece band would be just right for his tour, he said, and they were on the road just before Christmas. Also on the bill was an act the Seven had met at the Royal Albert Hall, the Bob Cort Skiffle Group, in whose ranks was a dazzling new guitarist named Vic Flick. Barry and Flick hit it off straight away, and often found themselves eating, drinking and talking music together on the tour. Vic Flick was very much John Barry's type, combining show-manship with technical brilliance and musical competence. Barry was to remember him later in 1958 when it became clear that changes were necessary in his Seven.

CHAPTER 2

THE EMI YEARS

Towards the end of 1957, Parlophone decided to release an album featuring many of the acts who appeared on *Six-Five Special*. They were recorded 'live' in the studio – but naturally they could include only artists under contract to EMI. This meant that the Seven were obvious choices, and they were given a good showing. They contributed three of the fifteen tracks, all vocal performances, and sales went well; especially good news for Barry was the fact that he had composed two of the songs, so this was the time he began to pick up the first of what would be many album royalties over the coming decades. Ironically, the song that was not written by him, 'Every Which Way', became the top side of the band's second single, released in January 1958. It was backed by Barry's 'You've Gotta Way', another track featured in the film version of *Six-Five Special*.

Barry was among a host of celebrities who attended the movie's première in London on March 30th, but all the hullabaloo was not enough to get his single into the charts, in spite of another favourable review in *The Record and Show Mirror*. The disc was a milestone, however, being the last to feature Barry as a vocalist. From then on the group took the massively important step of relying on an instrumental format alone, both on stage and in the recording studio, and Parlophone were with them all the way. It did not take the company long to release a follow-up – a mere two months, to be precise. It was 'Big Guitar', a pounding instrumental composed by Americans Owen Bradley and Frank Derosa, so catchy that it was covered by four other artists in the UK alone. Not for the first time in those years of endless 'cover versions', this approach was enough to prevent any version from making the charts; doubtless it would have been a big hit by just one band. Barry, however, shrewdly continued his policy of writing the B-side, on this occasion 'Rodeo'. This was his first recorded instrumental composition, and it was good enough to prompt Frank Chacksfield to release his own version of it for Decca.

By now Barry and his group were London-based. John was able to afford a flat in Redcliffe Gardens, after first living in digs in Soho, but the others had to make do with rooms in Shepherds Bush and Chiswick. The Seven were kept constantly busy touring the country, not only in their own right but to accompany a bewildering diversity of acts. It was tiring work, sometimes involving being on stage all evening. In the pre-Beatles days there was still a 'variety' feel about pop artists' tours, and the band found themselves supporting Mike and Bernie Winters, the then largely unknown Larry Grayson and even the big-voiced Edmund Hockridge, as well as the more pop-orientated Jackie Dennis, a Scots youth who sang rock 'n' roll in a kilt, the 'boy next door' Marty Wilde and the penny-whistle man Desmond Lane. Golder recalls that Wilde was occasionally backed by his Wilde Cats, who were not averse to asking for tips on presentation from members of the Seven. He thought they should have started by doing away with their leather jacket image, as Brian Epstein advised the Beatles a few years later. The two groups got on well together, however, and Golder struck up a friendship with his drumming opposite-number, Brian Bennett. They would be watching one another's solo spots, and would compare techniques and be generally supportive.

Soon the records were beginning to make an impact on the local charts. Back in 1958, *The Record and Show Mirror* printed Top Tens based on sales at shops throughout the UK, though primarily in the London area. The band's fourth single, 'Pancho' coupled with 'Hideaway', registered in a few of these charts, without hitting the all-important national scene. This Latin-American-inspired release was the first one on which Barry had written both sides, a sign of the attention and encouragement he was receiving from A & R man Norman Newell, who allowed him the luxury of experimenting in his bid to succeed. Meanwhile, ITV were planning a homespun rock show, *Oh Boy!*, aimed at a youth market growing tired of the Beeb's *Six-Five*, though it was to that programme's Jack Good that they turned to create it. Southern Music's Bob Kingston got together with Good to form a resident band for the show. At one stage Barry was in line to front it, but he was away touring Sweden with the Seven at the crucial moment. They used Harry Robinson instead, and he had great success with the big fat sound of Lord Rockingham's XI.

On their return from Scandinavia the JB7 were recruited to *Oh Boy!* not only as performers in their own right but as a second resident house band to accompany other artists, the likes of the Dallas Boys and Neville Taylor and the Cutters. Barry lost no time on the show to plug their latest release, 'Farrago', which was backed by 'Bees Knees'. This was the closest JB had come to having a hit record at that time. Once again several record shops in the London area recorded it as a Top Ten seller, but despite maximum publicity from EMI, the disc just failed to reach national charts which even in early 1958 included a strong sprinkling of standards and ballads among the emerging rock 'n' roll. Not until Duane Eddy's 'Rebel Rouser' broke through towards the end of the year did the climate change dramatically in favour of the kind of singles Barry had in mind.

John Barry on the set of *Oh Boy!*

Jack Good proved a hard taskmaster on *Oh Boy!*, with constant rehearsals and a very fast-paced show. Only a couple were broadcast for this first series in February, 1958, but there was a guarantee of a later return for a full run. That was good news, but there was also bad news for the JB7, for some serious disagreements were now surfacing in the band. They were getting worn out by the constant and widespread tours, and there was also some resentment towards Barry, who did not have to appear when they were accompanying other artists on the bill. A combination of

The John Barry Seven in 1958. From the left: John Barry, Mike Cox, Jimmy Stead, Ken Golder, Mike Peters, Keith Kelly, Ken Richards.

Above: The John Barry Seven in early 1958.
Right: Studio shots of the JB7 prior to the arrival of Les Reed.

this, some rather poor gigs plus the heavy travelling brought matters to a head. At times work could still be patchy, and some of the lads would often have only just returned to their homes in Yorkshire when the London-based Barry would call them south again for a few more dates.

Derek Myers got an offer to play with a big band in Scotland – regular work which he did not feel inclined to turn down. This came on top of a week of almost constant bickering, with Mike Cox complaining bitterly about the class of jobs they were expected to fulfil. Fred Kirk was the next to go, after spotting the opportunity of a job in aviation; he had once been an aircraft fitter. When Ken Richards announced he wanted to return to Scarborough, Golder, not wishing to be the only one of the original big-band trio left, was also happy to leave. With the departure of the other founder members, he felt, the 'sound' was just not there any more. To this day he maintains that the original band would have lasted much longer if they had not been called on to do the additional work on touring shows. Some of the artists they backed were exasperatingly fussy about their arrangements, and they often spent more rehearsal time on them than on their own act.

John Barry & Lisa Page.

Mike Peters and Jimmy Stead, from Ossett, near Leeds, replaced Kirk and Myers respectively. Peters then introduced Londoner Dennis King in place of the disenchanted Mike Cox, and Stead brought in Dougie Wright on drums, a musician with whom he had played in the big Leeds-based Bill Marsden Band. It meant that with the exception of Barry and Keith Kelly, the original band was a thing of the past. With the departure of lead guitarist Ken Richards, Barry was in urgent need of a replacement. Jack Oliver, also from Leeds, lasted only a week, and it was at this point that Barry approached Vic Flick, then still working with Bob Cort. He jumped at the chance and duly arrived in time to rehearse for another important show at the Metropolitan in Edgware Road. The Seven were contracted to perform a 20-minute act as well as backing several other artists, including Marty Wilde, and the line-up was: John Barry (trumpet), Vic Flick (lead guitar), Mike Peters (bass guitar), Keith Kelly (rhythm guitar), Jimmy Stead (baritone sax), Dennis King (tenor-sax) and Dougie Wright (drums). For a very short time they experimented with a female singer, Lisa Page, the sister of the TV star Jill Day, but this did not prove as successful as they had hoped.

Vic Flick.

Vic's interest in music had started in his early teens, when he joined a band led by his piano-playing father. He remembers the band originally included his brother on saxophone and a neighbour on violin. Although he could already read music and play the piano, he felt the band was missing something and decided to take up the guitar. This was in the mid-fifties, when the guitar was not the universal instrument it has since become; in fact it was really only used in big bands. Vic had just four lessons, but with the added benefit of many hours of listening to records and practising, he soon became good enough to take his place alongside his father and brother in their band. His first attempt at a professional career saw him with Les Clarke and his Musical Maniacs at Butlin's in Skegness. He then spent a winter of nearly six months out of work with just the odd gig to keep his hand in before he decided to link up again with his brother Alan. They agreed to form the Vic Alan Quintet, and successfully auditioned for a summer season at another Butlin's, down south in Clacton. The resident bandleader was a big name indeed, Eric Winstone, and at the auditions he quickly realised that Vic was a rare bird at that time, a young musician who could actually read music.

Before long, Vic found himself working with both bands throughout the engagement at Butlin's, and afterwards he stayed with Winstone for gigs and broadcasts for BBC radio. The turning point in his career, however, came when he joined the Bob Cort Skiffle group, replacing Ken Sykora on guitar. It was almost Christmas, 1957, and the Cort group got a useful break supporting Paul Anka on his nationwide U.K. tour. As we have recalled, also on the bill was John Barry. Eight months later came Barry's call to Vic that was to change his life. It was the classic offer he couldn't refuse, and almost before he had put pen to paper he was deep in rehearsals for that 20-minute spot at the Metropolitan.

The show was followed by a succession of one-night stands in the north of England, and Vic still laughs about the band's visit to Barry's home town of York. His father, obviously keen to help his son's career, had arranged for posters advertising the Seven's latest record to be plastered liberally all over the city and its surrounding villages. The pity of it was that the record was 'Farrago', while the posters were getting very excited about something called 'Farrango'. It was not the first time Jack Prendergast had got his wires crossed. On the night of that famous visit to York Rialto of the American bandleader Stan Kenton, Prendergast was so excited to have finally booked the great man that he announced him as 'Ken Stanton'.

Vic has many memories of recording sessions at EMI's Abbey Road Studios. There was no mixing down afterwards in those days, which meant that they were recording straight on to quarter-inch tape. It was important to be accurate to avoid extra takes that could mean exceeding the laid-down three-hour session time and involve the studio in extra expense. Studio 2 was a regular location, and at times Vic felt he was almost living there, such was the workload flooding in. He has special memories of recording 'Hit And Miss', forever embedded in the minds of all who recall those times as the signature tune to another early Saturday night pop icon, the BBC's *Juke Box Jury*. The rhythm section was arranged along one wall of the studio with the strings just in front of Vic – a daunting experience, as they were all watching him critically, as only musicians can. On the 'Walk Don't Run' session, Barry wanted a guitar sound quite different from the one produced on the American original by the Ventures. To achieve it, Vic was told to use a Bigsby tremolo arm attachment for that distinctive wavering effect. He did not have one, so he borrowed an instrument from the other guitarist on the session, Eric Ford. Vic still feels that the take that was used for the Top Ten success was the one on which he had over-done the tremolo!

Up to this time John Barry had been involved with artists with other recording companies, but EMI decided that it was time they had him on an exclusive basis. Norman Newell came up with a contract that effectively committed him to EMI, and over the next three years both Vic and Barry spent more and more time in Studio 2 at Abbey Road. EMI had originally concentrated purely on Barry's potential as a record seller in his own right, but his TV arrangements and accompaniments for fellow performers were attracting a lot of attention – and as often as not before the new contract, it was to EMI's rivals. In those early days he was reluctant to turn down any interesting work, as he still needed to establish himself; though he was discreet enough to record his 'moonlighting' work under a pseudonym, the Johnny Prendy Orchestra.

March 1959 brought the first release on Decca with a Barry backing. This was by three Tyneside girls who were later backed by him occasionally on BBC TV's *Drumbeat*, the Three Barry Sisters. The Johnny Prendy Orchestra accompanied them on 'Tall Paul', a novelty number which was used regularly on the show and was a popular Walt Disney classic, the flip being 'Till Then'. A second release followed soon afterwards with two more tunes featured on the show, 'Jo-Jo The Dog-Faced Boy' and 'I-Ay Ove-lay Oo-yay'.

In between these two records another Decca single was released, Derry Hart and the Hartbeats, whose 'Nowhere In This World'/'Come On Baby', sold reasonably well without reaching the charts. The credit on this occasion read 'Accompaniment directed by Johnny Prendy'. The Decca label also put out releases by Little Tony, a good-looking young Italian who had been a hit on *Drumbeat* with Barry backing him. The discs give no indication of the backing orchestra, but Barry was involved with at least one Little Tony record – almost certainly a tune he had written himself; a medium-paced rocker called 'Arrivederci Baby'.

Meanwhile, the Seven's own assault on the charts continued with 'Long John' and 'Snap 'n' Whistle', which were again heavily promoted on television. Fledgling pop weekly, *Disc*, together with *The Record and Show Mirror*, expected great things of this latest offering, but in keeping with previous predictions they were proved wrong, and chart success again eluded the band. Parlophone were still spending heavily on promoting the group's records, however, further evidence at this early stage of how highly Barry was regarded. Undeterred, the band continued their punishing touring schedule, managing to fit in their final two singles for Parlophone during the summer of 1959.

CHAPTER 3

DRUMBEAT

John Barry pictured on trumpet in 1960.

John Barry with pianist Les Reed.

It was to fill a spot in their summer schedules that persuaded BBC TV to launch a rival to the popular *Oh Boy!* Knowing Bob Kingston's involvement with the ITV show, producer Stewart Morris approached him and asked for suggestions for a band in his new project, to be called *Drumbeat*. Kingston unreservedly recommended Barry and arranged a meeting between them in his office. Morris duly signed the JB7 to appear in their own right and to back a variety of other artists, just as in the early days of *Oh Boy!* Barry liked the idea, and to ensure they got the booking he decided to introduce a piano into the group as a replacement for Keith Kelly, who had decided to try a solo career as a singer. Vic Flick suggested his flat mate Les Reed, then playing jazz piano in London night-clubs.

After his release from National Service in 1956, Les had started in the music business by playing with big bands and in clubs. He first teamed with Vic at Butlin's in Clacton with the Vic Alan Band, after which he found steady work in the West End with the Harry Singleton Orchestra at the Lido night spot in Swallow Street. That is where he was when Vic contacted him about playing with the John Barry Seven, and he needed little persuading. It would be a great change from playing standards every night, and would give him a valuable insight into what was going on in the pop world

For the first time, John Barry introduced an electric piano into the Seven, heralding it as 'the new sound'. It was produced through a block of wood stuck on the underside of the piano and fed into a speaker also placed under the piano. Nobody made a sound like the JB7's after that . . .

The band auditioned for *Drumbeat* at a pub in Shepherds Bush, and this nearly did not go according to plan. Barry had been making a great play of promoting Reed and his 'new sound' to producer Morris, but Les failed to show on time. Just as Morris was grumbling: 'Where's this bloody "new sound", then?' he rushed breathlessly through the door to join his new colleagues, and all was well.

Morris was keen to hire an unknown but up-and-coming young singer for the show, and asked Barry for help. He recalled working with Adam Faith on that ill-fated Jack Good stage show of *Six-Five Special* and after some early difficulty in locating him, he arranged a successful audition. The trouble was, Faith had already made one unsuccessful attempt at a full-time career as a performer, and he insisted

JOHN BARRY: A LIFE IN MUSIC   **23**

John Barry pictured on trumpet in 1960.

John plays trumpet on the *Drumbeat* set.

on keeping his job as a film cutter until he knew whether or not *Drumbeat* would prove a solid base for a second stab. He need not have worried. Despite some unfavourable comparisons with *Oh Boy!*, the show proved highly lucrative for both Faith and Barry after a meeting on the set with Johnny Worth, a member of the Raindrops vocal group.

Drumbeat opened on April 4th, 1959 with a line-up of Bob Miller and the Millermen, the John Barry Seven, the Kingpins, the Three Barry Sisters, Vince Eager, Roy Young, Sylvia Sands, Adam Faith, Dennis Lotis and compère Gus Goodwin. The theme tune was 'Bees Knees', the recent JB7 single, and on this first show they also included 'Long John', 'When The Saints Go Marchin' In' and 'Jumping With Symphony Sid', on which they were joined by the Millermen. They also accompanied Vince Eager, the Barry Sisters, Roy Young, Adam Faith and guest artist Russ Conway. Barry arranged ten of the numbers – and this was to be the way of the rest of the 21 programmes.

For the first four-week contract the JB7 received £185.50, of which £52.50 went exclusively to Barry as musical director of the group. Rehearsals took place normally at the Carlton Ballroom or the Riverside Studios, the latter being the venue for the live broadcast. All except one of the programmes were live, the exception being the one on July 18th, which was tele-recorded on close circuit two days earlier. During the run of *Drumbeat* the terms of their contract prevented the Seven from appearing on ITV.

As the series went on, Barry became so deeply involved in the arrangements that he was able to negotiate himself another £52.50 every four weeks. This extra work meant he was forced to bring in outside help to produce enough copies of band parts, so he would send out the arrangements to a copier and then put in the bill direct to the BBC each month. It seems that after each performance Barry was in the habit of keeping all these parts for his own future use, but the BBC rapidly caught on to this. After three such bills they politely suggested that in future they would deal direct with the copyist, and keep the parts themselves.

Vic Flick recalls the heat in the studios at Riverside, where there was no air-conditioning – and the pink suits they had to wear made it even hotter. On one show Stewart Morris decided to include 'Guitar Boogie Shuffle', with a solo from Vic, and though all went well at rehearsal, when it came to the live performance Morris decided to place the guitarist on his own, well away from the rest of the band and with a very long cable to his amplifier. This distance made it almost impossible for Vic to follow his own performance or that of the JB7, and it was a confused rendition. Despite the endless arrangements played by the Seven at short notice, not to mention their own spots, Vic can remember only one other major hitch, when he was playing the Barry composition 'Little John'. Momentarily he lost his place completely, which in turn threw the cameraman, who up to that point had been following a strict order of shots. With some prompting from the others he managed to recover himself and finish the number reasonably successfully. This unusual lapse of concentration may have passed off unnoticed by the TV audience, but Morris was

The John Barry Seven on the *Drumbeat* set. From the left: Jimmy Stead, Denis King, Dougie Wright, John Barry, Mike Peters, Vic Flick & Les Reed.

Barry in action on *Drumbeat,* flanked by Denis King, Vic Flick & Les Reed.

Vince Eager is backed by the JB7 on the set of *Drumbeat* in 1959.

John Barry plays for the Barry Sisters on the set of *Drumbeat*.

not impressed and he stormed down from the control room at the end of the show shouting: 'This must never happen again.' It didn't.

Barry's first recording session with Adam Faith, made for the Top Rank label in May, 1959, was the only failure in a long string of successes for the pairing. It came in the midst of the *Drumbeat* series and, as has been recalled, their meeting on the show was anything but coincidental. Adam Faith at that time was still little more than a kid but already he had quite a tale to tell.

John Barry & Adam Faith backstage
at The London Palladium in 1960.

CHAPTER 4

ADAM FAITH

Adam Faith was born Terry Nelhams in Acton, London on June 23rd, 1940, the third of five children. An eleven-plus failure, he went to John Perryn secondary modern school in Acton, but from the age of 12 he was demonstrating his entrepreneurial skills through a series of paper rounds that enabled him to buy his own clothes. This was augmented further when he started selling papers from a pitch to finance more than £100 worth of other 'gear', including a record player and an impressive bicycle, each costing around £8. To many people at that time, £8 was more than a week's pay. All this was achieved before he left school, at which point he took his first full-time job as an odd-job boy for a silk screen printer close to his home.

After only a few weeks with the company he heard of a vacancy for a messenger boy at Rank Screen Services where he was taken on at £3.50 per week. He was determined to win a transfer to the organisation's film studios, but after a year had elapsed without promotion he left to join a company in Soho's Wardour Street, TV Advertising Limited. This was Tin Pan Alley, the heart of the British music scene, and at this period of his life he was among the millions who had been bitten by the skiffle bug. His first great idol was Lonnie Donegan, who inspired him to form his first group with colleagues from work. They called themselves the Worried Men after the skiffle classic 'Worried Man Blues', and according to Faith they played all the Soho espresso coffee bars – Mars, the Cat's Whiskers, Orlando's, the Skiffle Cellar and the daddy-o of them all, the Two I's, where they eventually became resident.

Not surprisingly, Faith was soon close to complete exhaustion. He had been promoted to assistant cutter at TV Advertising, and by this time he was not only performing most evenings but taking managerial responsibility for his group. Apart from anything else, success suddenly seemed to be within their grasp. Jack Good's *Six-Five Special* had a reputation for originality, and one idea was to broadcast a show direct from the Two I's. As the resident band, the Worried Men opened and closed the programme – valuable exposure, and ultimately Faith's first big break.

Good was impressed with his performance, but not with the group as a whole. He invited him back on the show as a solo singer, convinced of his potential as Britain's answer to James Dean. Faith gave up his job as a film cutter, turned professional, won a recording contract with EMI's HMV label on the strength of his TV appearance and was helped by Good to choose the stage name by which he has been known ever since. His début disc, combining '(Got A) Heartsick Feeling' with 'Brother Heartache And Sister Tears', was released in January, 1958. It was given scant publicity, either from the music press or EMI's publicity department, and made not the slightest impression on the charts. Despite all Good's confidence in him, Faith failed to make any immediate impact on television, either, but he was given another opportunity when he was booked to appear in the stage version of *Six-Five Special*. As we know, the John Barry Seven were also on the bill, and this brief first meeting with Barry was later to prove vital. At the time, though, the stage show flopped, and after just four performances Faith found himself looking for a new job.

As ever the survivor, he swallowed his pride and made the painful decision to abandon showbiz and return to the film cutting world. Despite this, HMV released his second single in December, 1958, a cover of Jerry Lee Lewis' 'High School Confidential', backed with 'Country Music Holiday'. Apart from cursory attention in the music press, sparked by the fact that he was covering a song by the high-profile Jerry Lee, it attracted no publicity whatever, and it was not long before Faith found a job as a cutter at the National Studios at Elstree. That is where he was when he took the phone call from John Barry in March, 1959, inviting him to audition for *Drumbeat*. He impressed producer Stewart Morris enough to land a contract for three shows, later extended to the full 22-week run. *Drumbeat* went on air in April, and the following month, Faith, now out of contract with HMV, was again heard on vinyl performing one track – 'I Vibrate' – as part of a six-track EP on Fontana. The label's publicity said the set was 'a direct recording from a BBC telecast'.

Fortune again smiled on Faith when Barry introduced him to his manager, the redoubtable Evelyn Taylor. She was an old hand whose father had been a show-business impresario of some renown, and she was so steeped in the tradition that she had herself been part of a comedy and tap-dancing act during the thirties. Since becoming an agent she had established a reputation for never accepting anything less than the best for her clients, and many an errant theatre manager had felt the lash of her biting tongue. She readily agreed to take Adam on, and immediately set about changing his image and appearance as well as securing him another recording contract, this time with Top Rank. His only record for them, 'Ah, Poor Little Baby' backed by 'Runk Bunk', was released on June 6th, with the top side benefiting from an arrangement and accompaniment by John Barry. Both sides were produced by Tony Hatch, just before his appointment as an A & R manager at Pye/Piccadilly Records. Again the record failed to catch on, but this time Faith had a legitimate excuse; there was a total absence of publicity for it, since its release date coincided with a national printing strike!

That made it a hat-trick of record failures, yet Faith was becoming well known and popular through his *Drumbeat* appearances. Acting still held sway for him, and in August he announced his intention of taking drama and elocution classes to boost his potential. It was about half way through the *Drumbeat* run when he attracted the attention of film producer George Willoughby, who was searching for a young singer to appear in his new film *Beat Girl* then in pre-production stage. Although Faith had enjoyed little record success, Willoughby was struck by his stage presence, and signed him on the strength of it. The script called for him to sing a couple of songs, and as Barry was by then arranging not only his recordings but his live *Drumbeat* material, it came as no surprise when the film company asked him to write the movie score; so we reach John Barry's first steps into the world of film music composing.

Faith's success on *Drumbeat* enabled Eve Taylor to hammer out a better recording contract for him – this time with Parlophone. The quest for suitable material to launch his debut for the label began in earnest, and was eventually resolved out of a friendship built up on the TV show. A study of the *Drumbeat* scripts shows how Faith had at first concentrated on cover versions of up-tempo slices of American rock 'n' roll. A turning point came when he asked to perform his own version of the current Cliff Richard hit 'Living Doll', and it became apparent to Barry that Faith's vocal delivery was more attractive in a gentler mode. From then on he would steer Adam in that direction. Nevertheless, before this first Parlophone single was issued, Faith made his debut on the label on a live *Drumbeat* album – as distinct from the earlier Fontana EP – recorded on May 10th at Abbey Road and released two months later. The rock influence was still to the fore on this, and Faith sang three numbers: 'Say Mama', 'C'mon Everybody' and 'Believe What You Say'. All were accompanied by John Barry.

The album also showcased the talents of Johnny Worth, a member of the Raindrops vocal trio – and he was to become the final piece in the Parlophone back-room jigsaw that catapulted Faith from contender to champion. Worth, born in Battersea on June 21st, 1931, began working as a draughtsman before his two years' National Service. Back in Civvy Street, he was determined to stay out of office work and make his name as a singer, a decision made after listening to a record by the emotional American crooner Johnny Ray; he believed he could imitate him to perfection. His first task was to change his name. John Skordalides, he decided, did not quite have what it takes.

His first work as Johnny Worth was as a semi-professional in pubs, before he managed to land a television appearance. Among viewers was the wife of the bandleader Oscar Rabin, and she was impressed enough to remember his snappy new name and mention it to her husband. As a result he was signed to sing with the Rabin band, and stayed with them for five years, making a number of recordings for Oriole and Columbia before joining the Raindrops. Like many singers, he also aspired to songwriting, though his first three efforts were rejected out of hand by publishers. It was when Faith, striking up a friendship with him on the *Drumbeat* set, asked if he had any material suitable for recording that he dusted down one of these songs and asked the JB7 pianist Les Reed to help him arrange a demo of it. It was called 'What Do You Want?' Barry has always been credited with the idea of using pizzicato

Johnny Worth.

strings, inspired by Buddy Holly's 'It Doesn't Matter Anymore', but according to Worth, the device was entirely his own. Because he was still under contract to Oriole, Johnny felt the need to adopt a pseudonym as a song writer, and so was born Les Vandyke. This was concocted by combining Reed's first name with Worth's London telephone exchange!

CHAPTER 5

WHAT DO YOU WANT?

Barry was impressed enough with the demo to begin working on an arrangement for the song using the pizzicato style; but here the tale gets complicated, because according to music publisher Bob Kingston, he was the man who suggested such an arrangement: 'John and I actually formed a music publishing company at one time, but this was never activated because I changed course and became MD for Southern Music at about the time he moved into film writing. Having just assumed control at Southern, however, I wanted to try to develop British music within the company, and decided to make a recording, using my friend John Barry as arranger/MD. He brought in the lad whose name was changed to Lance Fortune, I booked Lansdowne Studio and used Joe Meek to engineer. Joe and I also had a close business relationship. At Southern we had the Buddy Holly catalogue; I was impressed with the sound on his recording of "It Doesn't Matter Anymore" – the pizzicato strings – and asked John to try to make an arrangement for our recording along these lines. Before its release, however, Norman Newell approached John and asked him to do the backing for the next Adam Faith recording. At the time I was in New York; this was September, 1959, and the Lance Fortune Pye recording was set for January, 1960 release. John phoned me in the States and asked if I would object to his using the same type of string treatment on the Faith recording as we had used for Lance Fortune. Naturally I said no, I didn't object; of course I had no right to resist, anyway. But I asked John to get Alan Freeman at Pye to push forward our release, and the result was Faith at number one and Lance Fortune's "Be Mine" at number four.'

According to Faith, the singing style he adopted for this now legendary recording was based on coaching he received from Roy Young, another *Drumbeat* cast member. Having heard Adam rehearsing it during a shared car journey, he made a number of suggestions, in particular persuading him to alter his pronunciation of 'baby' to 'bay-beh'. The pop industry was much preoccupied with gimmicks at this time, and 'bay-beh' was a master stroke, somehow giving Faith the kind of gawky vulnerability that had endeared Buddy Holly to millions of young teenage girls even before his tragic death had sealed his future as a rock legend. 'What Do You Want?', coupled with 'From Now Until Forever', was recorded at Abbey Road on September 25th, 1959 – a mere month after *Drumbeat* ended. At the same time, Faith was

signed to appear in an episode of Rediffusion's *No Hiding Place* TV series. Norman Newell, Faith and Barry's A & R manager, was unable to be producer at the recording session. Assistant John Burgess took the helm in his absence, and was to do so for the remainder of Faith's EMI career. According to Barry, one EMI executive, on hearing the record, publicly declared his disapproval, vowing that Barry would on no account be allowed to take part in any more sessions. Later, Barry had admitted that before the recording, both he and Faith had been despondent following previous commercial failures. This time they were determined to impose their own personal tastes far more emphatically than they had done previously, and it had worked. Looking back now, it was a gamble, with Faith's raw, youthful voice laid over a slickly commercial backing. At the time, the trend was very much in favour of a smooth, bland sound – the kind of American middle-of-the-road music that was blasted out of the charts by the Beatles. Though a world away from the Fab Four, Faith was staking a place in the Top Twenty for natural, unassuming British sounds three years before 'Love Me Do'.

Despite favourable reviews of 'What Do You Want?' on its October 24th release date in both the *New Musical Express* and *Disc*, manager Eve Taylor still insisted that Faith's future lay in acting. Keith Fordyce, writing in the *NME*, praised Barry's arrangement and choice of instrumentation. Jack Good, columnist in the rival newspaper, applauded the production and tipped chart success on both sides of the Atlantic. EMI, perhaps scenting success, mounted a strong advertising campaign, promoting the single far more vigorously than either of Faith's first two HMV releases. 'What Do You Want?' was also given a considerable boost when it was voted a unanimous hit on BBC TV's *Juke Box Jury*, and when Faith sang it live on an edition of ATV's *Boy Meets Girl*.

On November 14th came its first chart recognition when *The Record Mirror's* 'British artists only' table listed it as a new entry at number nine. Clearly, interest was growing, and it entered the *NME* charts at number 18 the following week. Adam Faith, singer, had clearly arrived, and there was almost as much interest in the musicians behind him. Barry surprised many people by revealing that the orchestral backing consisted of just four strings, with two tenor saxes suggesting the sound of a cello.

By December, Faith was number one in the *NME* charts and confessed to being terrified of becoming just another overnight sensation; he was determined to continue to develop his acting skills through special training at the Royal Court Theatre. Meanwhile, the JB7 were in the throes of releasing their final two singles for Parlophone. The first of these, 'Little John' and 'For Pete's Sake', featured for the first time on record the recent additions to the group, Vic Flick and Les Reed. Both sides were written by Barry, and as usual they were given regular airings on TV and in their stage act, with no obvious impact on the charts. Nevertheless, 'Little John' was voted one of the best instrumental discs of 1959.

Barry's last Parlophone release revived the much-covered 'Twelfth Street Rag', coupled with a new composition, 'Christella'. Quite why 'Twelfth Street' was chosen as a single is not clear, for it had been recorded many times in the past, arguably better on occasions. It seemed a perplexing decision to release something so unoriginal at that point in Barry's career.

A short article in the *NME* of August 7th, 1959 noted that the JB7 had recorded some of the music, including the title song and caption sequence, for the Lonnie Donegan film *The Hellion.* Vic Flick recalls working on this film, whose improbable producer was the TV quiz show king Hughie Green. Barry, on the other hand, has only the vaguest recollection of it, and there is no clue to whether or not he wrote any of the music; but as he later arranged the title song for exposure on *Drumbeat*, it seems safe to assume that he did. The film was held up by financial problems and was eventually remade in 1962. By then, Donegan was past the first flush of youth and not enough in the limelight to carry the film, so Marty Wilde took over his role. The story line was completely changed, and Barry's involvement in the movie ceased; the veteran mouth organist Larry Adler composed the music for the remake.

In late September came the first of many Abbey Road sessions for EMI on which Barry accompanied other artists. On this occasion he was asked to back Parlophone's new signing, Bill and Brett Landis, whose record was a cover of an American novelty song entitled 'Baby Talk'. Barry's A & R man Norman Newell was responsible for the session, but John was required only for the topside. The record was not successful and the Barry accompaniment was little more than a copy of the American original by Jan and Dean, but he had clearly done well enough to be noticed by the other label heads at EMI.

Saga was an independent label owned by would-be singer Larry Page, who was later to form the much more successful Page One Records. In October, 1959, Page recorded six tracks accompanied by Barry, all released as three separate singles, none of which charted. They were billed as 'Larry Page with the Saga Satellites, directed by John Barry' – not, strangely enough, Johnny Prendy. The track titles for the respective releases were: 'Big Blon' Baby'/'I Vibrate'; 'How'm I Doin' Hey, Hey'/'Throw All Your Lovin' My Way'; and 'Little Old Fashioned Love'/'Marilyn'. 'Throw All Your Lovin' My Way' and 'Little Old Fashioned Love' were both John Barry compositions.

Desmond Lane, the *Pennywhistle Man.*

Barry's next accompaniment and direction was for the Penny Whistle Man, Des Lane. On this occasion, he even wrote the B-side, 'Moonbird'. The A-side was the theme from a current and very successful comedy film, *The Night We Dropped A Clanger,* which went under the name of 'The Clanger March'.

The Johnny Prendy Orchestra was back in action again to accompany Lance Fortune on 'Be Mine', the other pizzicato special, coupled with 'Action', which Barry also co-wrote. This Pye single was issued in early 1960, following an article in the *New Musical Express* relating how Fortune secured his recording contract with Pye on the strength of a private disc made under Barry's supervision. As the music publisher Bob Kingston earlier recalled, 'Be Mine' did indeed climb to number four in the British charts. It was actually an English version of the German song 'Alle

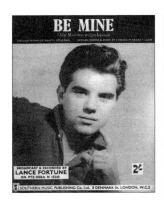

David Jacobs chairing *Juke Box Jury*.

Maedchen Wollen Kussen' (All Girls Like To Kiss). Both sides were engineered by the legendary Joe Meek.

Any one-hit wonder will tell you of the problems of finding a memorable follow-up. Not surprisingly, the Faith management decided to rely on the Worth/Barry team for inspiration, and it was a wise move. At the recording session, John Burgess again took charge of production, since Norman Newell was afraid of upsetting a winning formula. On January 15th, 'Poor Me' was released – with 'What Do You Want?' still at number two in the charts. Originally rejected by several music publishers in its original incarnation as 'Poor Man', it again shot to number one in the UK charts, despite criticism from some Buddy Holly fans, who felt that Faith and Barry were leaning far too heavily on the style of the late lamented singer. The first Faith hit was compared largely with 'It Doesn't Matter Anymore', while 'Poor Me' was likened to 'Heartbeat'. Barry never denied the accusation, although it is probably fairer to say that he adapted rather than copied the style, an individual sound which itself was soon to be widely imitated throughout the popular music scene. A couple of years later, the American Bobby Vee, who had worked closely with the Crickets, was far more a second Buddy Holly than Faith ever was.

February, 1960 was a significant month for Barry, for he joined Faith in the Top Ten with his Columbia debut, 'Hit And Miss', after their joint manager Eve Taylor had arranged a switch from the label's EMI stable mate Parlophone. The JB7 was certainly helped by a chance airing of the disc on BBC TV's *Juke Box Jury*, when it was voted a unanimous hit. What caught the public's imagination even more was when presenter David Jacobs liked it so much that he persuaded his producer to use it without more ado as the show's signature tune; sure enough, the following week, out went 'Juke Box Fury' and in came the infuriatingly catchy tune that gave Barry his first hit after nearly three years of trying. 'Rockin' Already' was on the flip-side, a very original Barry arrangement of the traditional African song 'Wimoweh', which surfaced in several different forms at around this time. These sides were attributed to the John Barry Seven Plus Four, the four being accomplished session violinists playing pizzicato – Bernard Monshin, Sid Margo, Charlie Katz and Alec Firman. Margo was later to act as Barry's 'fixer' for film music recording sessions for many years. The massive TV publicity was a bonus for JB, whose 'Stringbeat' treatment of this and all Faith's early recordings was a key sound of the early sixties.

Having got wind of Barry's arranging sessions for other companies, EMI persuaded him to sign an exclusive three-year contract early in 1960. Under it he was expected to cut an album and three singles a year though by 1962 this was proving difficult because of his increasing film work. This side of his career was just starting to take off; and after completing his score for the Adam Faith film *Beat Girl*, he was instantly hard at work on Faith's second, released as *Never Let Go* but known originally as *Moment Of Truth*. Perhaps the band's new single was inspired by a combination of his work on these films and some recent library music recorded for Chappell. The A side, 'Beat For Beatniks', was virtually identical to a Chappell track entitled 'Mood Three', except for the absence of a guitar solo; the flip-side, 'Big Fella', was also self-penned and jazz-inspired, and both were completely different from anything he had previously tried on record.

The disc drew a rapturous review from the jazz-dominated *Melody Maker*, whose columnist Maurice Burman enthused: 'I put on the record without a lot of interest, and after the first four bars I nearly fell through the floor! The record is like nothing he has done before – it is modern jazz with a fresh approach, tinged with Kentonism. It stamps John Barry as a first-class modern arranger and composer with a daring mind.' Praise indeed, but not everyone was so enthusiastic about its chances of commercial success, and the doubters were proved right. It just about crept into the lower end of the charts, but it simply was not the type of material the record buying public was used to and, despite Burman's and other good notices, it was largely ignored. This was the first time Barry issued a record that did not go out under the name of the Seven. Instead it was credited to the John Barry Orchestra, though JB later admitted that he had simply used the Seven plus established jazz players such as saxophonist Johnny Scott and trumpeter Dicky Hawdon.

Adam Faith signed for a 12-week summer season at Blackpool Hippodrome from June 24th, and he was joined by the John Barry Seven, who had their own spot as well as backing him. They were to accompany him on numerous other occasions over the next couple of years. At a presentation for another silver disc, this time for sales of 'Poor Me', Faith commented at length on John Barry's contribution to his success and did not, at this stage, envisage making records without him. His third Parlophone 45, 'Big Time' and 'Someone Else's Baby', released on April 8th, while 'Poor Me' was still at number 15 in the charts, was advertised as a double A-side in an attempt to demonstrate his versatility. 'Big Time' was a real big band showstop-

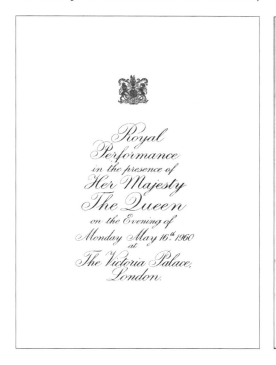

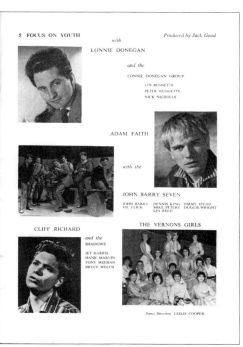

per, taken from Lionel Bart's musical *Fings Ain't What They Used To Be*, showing Faith in quite a different guise. The flip owed more to the usual formula, though on this occasion his pronunciation of 'baby' was even more exaggerated. Needless to say it was another big hit, and Adam was denied his third consecutive number one only by the Everly Brothers' 'Cathy's Clown'.

Just before this, Faith and the Seven were given the ultimate showbiz accolade when they were invited to perform in the Royal Variety Show at the Victoria Palace, London on May 16th – the first of those shows to be televised (on May 22nd). Faith, dressed completely in white, sang 'What Do You Want?' and 'Play It Cool', and then changed into top hat and tails for the grand finale. He was more favourably received than Cliff Richard and Lonnie Donegan, but it must be said that the 20-guineas-a-head audience, whose idea of letting their hair down was listening to the Crazy Gang being mildly cheeky to the Royal Family, did not really get much out of the 'teenage spot' in the show.

'When Johnny Comes Marching Home', Faith's song from *Never Let Go*, was recorded on May 25th, when he and the JB7 travelled to London from gigging in Shrewsbury to lay it down. Three days later, *Never Let Go* won favourable reviews in the music press, anticipating its premiere on June 2nd at the Leicester Square Odeon. Faith's second film starred Peter Sellers in a rare villainous role, alongside Richard Todd and Elizabeth Sellars. Faith played Tommy Towers, a small-time tearaway, and his only musical contribution was to sing 'Johnny' over the end titles.

John Barry rehearses Adam Faith prior to recording 'Someone Else's Baby' at Abbey Road Studios.

Barry adapted the traditional American folk song while Lionel Bart, oddly credited as John Maitland, updated the lyric. At this point, *Beat Girl* was still waiting in a queue of X certificate films to be released.

'Made You'/'When Johnny Comes Marching Home' was released on June 17th, 1960, a week after Faith turned down an offer to act in *Irish Jade*, another George Willoughby production. Both sides of the new release made the Top Ten, despite a BBC airplay ban on 'Made You', on the grounds of its 'lewd and salacious' lyric. It was indeed quite an explicit song for its time, a young man asking his girlfriend for sex in a more or less open way, with its title line and complaint about 'never making first base'. It was a world away from other innocuous songs in the charts at the same time, the likes of Michael Cox's 'Angela Jones', Brian Hyland's 'Yellow Polka Dot Bikini' and Rolf Harris's 'Tie Me Kangaroo Down, Sport'. EMI moved quickly to issue the soundtrack album of *Beat Girl*, from which 'Made You' came; but when the movie was eventually released, it was instantly clear that Barry's music for it stood head and shoulders above the rest of the production. [Full details can be found in the film section of this book]

Norman Newell, Johnny De Little and John Barry at Abbey Road Studios in 1961.

CHAPTER 6
WORKING WITH OTHER ARTISTS

Barry never denied that his first few Faith releases were influenced by Buddy Holly, but for later discs he produced a sound that was very much his own, though it was in turn soon copied widely. Norman Newell's assistant John Burgess, the talisman still taking all the Faith recording sessions, quickly grew to admire JB's work. He admitted recently that he used Barry to back his other artists as often as he could, and other A & R men were queuing for his services. Naturally, many of Barry's backing sessions were for Parlophone and Columbia, and he specialised in debut discs for artists handled by Newell.

One such example was the recording by new boy Johnny Gavotte, released in February 1960, of 'Can't Forget' coupled with 'It's Not Too Late'; it made no impact. Other February releases involving Barry were a début disc from the England Sisters, 'Heartbeat' and 'Little Child', and a Danny Williams single, 'Youthful Years'/'It Doesn't Matter'. 'Heartbeat' was a sparkling update of a Buddy Holly song that at that time had recently been only a minor chart success. Sisters Betty, Julie and Hazel came from Goole in Yorkshire, and were discovered by their manager Paul England after they had won a talent competition at Butlin's in Filey, one of Vic Flick's first stamping grounds. Apparently they sang the harmonies of 'Heartbeat' down the phone-line to John Barry, who wrote an arrangement around it! The record was issued on the day Prince Andrew was born, and 'Little Child' was intended to be a topical main side. Unhappily, it was all too sickly and sentimental, and airplay soon switched to 'Heartbeat'. It caused a flurry but failed to break through, possibly because it was too soon for a revival.

The Danny Williams disc was surprising for two reasons. First, Geoff Love had always accompanied Williams previously, and second, the flip side was an out-and-out rock number, completely out of character for the gentle-voiced South African. Maybe recording manager Norman Newell felt Barry was better suited to handling a beat number, or possibly their recent association on TV was an influence; whatever the reasoning behind it, the record attracted little air play and produced very poor sales. Now it is one of the rarest Barry-accompanied singles around.

Johnny Worth did not write solely for Adam Faith, and Barry's next job for EMI

was to back a Worth song written for the Dallas Boys, an act especially popular on stage at the time and one of the first to be turned to whenever a pop touring bill was being put together. They could sing, they could play the fool and their routines were slick and exciting. The number 'Boston Tea Party' was coupled with an up-tempo revival of 'Ramona', and both were recorded in late March. The topside was a novelty number sung to a marching beat, but Barry was not finding it easy to recapture his success with Adam Faith when it came to backing other artists, as his next assignment perfectly illustrated, when he accompanied both sides of another debut disc, for Danny Davis on Parlophone. Perhaps unfortunately, an old Elvis Presley song, 'Love Me', was an inappropriate choice for the A-side; and the flip, 'You're My Only Girl', was similarly run-of-the-mill. Disc and Davis soon faded into oblivion, despite some good reviews.

EMI, ever keen to keep the momentum going, hedged their bets on Barry's third Columbia single by combining an overtly commercial offering with another example of JB's jazz-tinged film work. Although 'Blueberry Hill' was the official A side, its reverse, 'Never Let Go', received at least as much air play. The former, taken at a similar pace to Fats Domino's famous version, was dominated by the guitar of Vic Flick, backed by a small string section playing in a mainly pizzicato style, plus percussion from Dougie Wright. On 'Never Let Go', Flick's guitar again took the lead in a theme written by Barry for the film of the same name, although it was heard on screen only via a café juke box. The single managed to nudge into the Top Fifty, but what would have been considered a major achievement in 1957 proved a disappointment in 1960, particularly as yearly polls in the music press put the JB7 as second in popularity only to the Shadows.

On August 14th the much delayed recording of Adam Faith's debut album, Adam, finally got under way. Faith and the JB7 travelled to London from Blackpool overnight and put in a six-hour session that Sunday. The same formula was repeated the following Sunday, a reminder of how albums of that time were very far removed from the 'concepts' of later years, with groups locked together in retreat for months on end. The record business John Barry knew at that time was very much that – hard business, and extremely hard work. While making the record, Faith revealed a desire to do a TV and West End play as well as becoming an LP artist. At the same time, John Barry announced his intention of toning down the pizzicato effect on Faith's next single, released on September 9th and combining 'How About That' with 'With Open Arms'. Apparently manager Eve Taylor jokingly suggested to Johnny Worth that he should write a song called 'How About That, Then?' in recognition of one of her most over-used catchphrases. He duly obliged, more as a joke than anything else, but did not tell anyone until he had finished it. The end product, shortened to 'How About That', became another huge hit for the team. Commenting on the arrangement, Barry said: 'I've used strings and rhythm as before for the main side, but kept the pizzicato down to a minimum.' In truth, the difference was not all that apparent, although the short B side, a gentle, pretty Burt Bacharach/Hal David composition, featured the distinctive sound of a tuba.

From the start of the JB7's Columbia career, EMI had managed to stagger their single release dates to ensure that they did not clash with Adam Faith's – but September 9th saw new records from both artists. The release from the Seven came in the shape of 'Walk Don't Run', a number composed by American jazz guitarist Johnny Smith which had been a huge hit in the States for the Ventures. Barry saw the opportunity to boost the Seven with his own arrangement of it, quite different in style from the American group's. In a British chart hot on instrumentals – in early September, the Shadows' 'Apache' and Duane Eddy's 'Because They're Young' were at one and two – both the JB7 and the Ventures reached the Top Ten, while another version by Rhet Stoller missed out. Barry's B-side saw him again revamping an old vocal, this time the Hank Snow country standard 'I'm Movin' On'. He used an identical arrangement to the one on 'Hit And Miss', and the Seven were again 'Plus Four'. The band often included the number in their live appearances – especially on tour, when moving on was the name of the game.

Christmas, 1960 was fast approaching – and in keeping with the tradition of the day, Faith went into rehearsal for pantomime, where he was signed to play the bosun's mate in *Dick Whittington* at Wimbledon. It fitted in very well with Eve Taylor's wish to turn him into a family entertainer, a trend not welcomed by fans who had first taken to him for his mean, moody, blue jeans and leather jacket image. The panto opened on Christmas Eve, and it was there that he began talking about his wish to widen the scope of film roles offered him. After playing two rebellious characters, he was afraid of becoming typecast.

With the pantomime role in mind, his management team decided to issue a novelty Christmas song with the added advantage of being suitable for the show. The session took place at Abbey Road on October 30th, and for once Johnny Worth composed neither side. The A side, 'Lonely Pup', was written by Scottish bandleader Archie Alexander, as Freddy Poser of Mills Music explained: 'Archie brought it in to me and wanted a decision on the spot. I liked it, so I took a chance and accepted it, with Adam in mind. When I took it round and showed it to him, Eve Taylor and John Barry, they all flipped for it at once.' Jack Lewis wrote the B-side, 'Greenfinger', a jokey song about a poor boy who bought his girl a cheap ring. The record again made the top ten, but not for long, and Barry's arrangement for 'Lonely Pup' was criticised by the Scandinavian duo Nina and Frederik on *Juke Box Jury*. Faith replied that the aristocratic Danes were out of touch with the current music scene, though it has to be said their Christmas novelty song of that year, 'Little Donkey', was a bigger and certainly better remembered hit than his 'Lonely Pup'. In school playgrounds at that time there was much rivalry between followers of Adam and Cliff, and fans of the latter were much happier with his Christmas hit 'I Love You' than were Adam's with that soppy pup.

The album Adam was released on November 4th to much acclaim – as much for the inventiveness of musical director John Barry's arrangements as for Faith's performance. The breadth of material ranged from standards as diverse as 'Summertime', 'Hit The Road To Dreamland' and 'Singin' In The Rain' to such contemporary

songs as Doc Pomus and Mort Shuman's 'I'm A Man', Johnny Worth's 'Fare Thee Well My Pretty Maid', and Howard Guyton's 'Wonderful Time'.

After successfully covering the Ventures' 'Walk Don't Run', Barry must have thought about doing the same with their follow-up 'Perfidia', yet another instrumental version of an old song. In the event, the Ventures had a free run and climbed to number four in the UK charts, while Barry countered with 'Black Stockings'/'Get Lost Jack Frost', both self-penned. Released in time for the Christmas market, it sold well enough, reaching number 27. The intricate guitar work of Vic Flick was again dominant, particularly in 'Jack Frost'. This seasonal B-side, although credited to John Barry, bore a strong resemblance to 'When The Saints Go Marching In', a number played by the Seven on many a live date.

Barry also found time to write a track for Parlophone's compilation album, *Saturday Club*, based on the hugely popular and influential BBC Saturday morning radio show, on which the Seven appeared regularly. In fact the sound of clear, ringing guitars remains most fans' abiding memory of the programme. Barry wrote 'Saturday's Child', a number which bore a certain resemblance to 'Walk Don't Run'.

After Christmas, Barry finally achieved some success as arranger and accompanist to an act other than Adam Faith – in the rather unlikely form of pop pianist Russ Conway, who was normally associated with Geoff Love or Tony Osborne. It was the Conway version of the film theme 'Pepe', and although it was covered by many others, in particular Duane Eddy, who reached number two, Barry's distinctive backing helped to raise it above the rest and it climbed to number 19 in the UK charts. The B-side was 'Matador From Trinidad'.

January 1961 saw Faith bouncing back after the lacklustre critical response to his Christmas record with a double A sided Johnny Worth disc much more in line with his earlier songs. 'Who Am I?' and 'This Is It' both climbed into the Top Ten, bringing the Faith/Barry/Worth team back to the heart of the British scene once more.

An early singing protégé of John Barry was Johnny De Little. He was born Brian King at Penrhiwceiber, in Glamorgan in Wales, and was all set to join his father down the coal mine until he was considered too short. After the regulatory two years in the army – during which he grew to nearly six feet! – he started singing at the Chase Hotel in York while working at the Armstrong Patent Shock Absorbers Company. When he decided he would like to branch out a little he went to see Barry's father, who got him an audition with JB at the Rialto. De Little was worried throughout the audition: 'John just sat there, staring at the floor, registering no emotion whatsoever.'

He need not have worried. Barry persuaded Norman Newell to sign him to a Columbia recording contract, and not surprisingly supervised both sides of his debut disc, recorded on January 20th, 1961. The titles were 'Not Guilty', written by Barry's friend Trevor Peacock, and 'They', written jointly by Barry and the well known American lyricist Bob Russell. The record was generally well received and got a lot of air-play, especially on Radio Luxembourg, but it did not quite make the charts. Don Nicholls, writing in *Disc*, certainly rated both song and singer: 'Johnny

Trevor Peacock, Bob Russell, Johnny De Little & John Barry at Abbey Road Studios in 1961.

John Barry & Norman Newell at a Johnny De Little recording session.

has a voice that will be with us for a long while. He sweeps through this quick lilter expertly, and gets a colourful Barry backing. It could make a Top Twenty debut for this boy. "They" is a slower song which De Little sings in deeper, more thoughtful vein. Not quite so successful, but it illustrates the fact that there is a lot of potential to be tapped in this performer.' De Little, perhaps wisely, decided to hang on to the shock absorbers job until he was certain of a successful showbiz career.

Back in the early sixties, singles were released far more regularly than they are today – so within two months of releasing 'Black Stockings', the JB7 were busy promoting their next 45, an interpretation of Elmer Bernstein's 'Magnificent Seven', probably with a view to recording a ready-made signature tune for the band. Given the huge success of the film, this ought to have been a heaven-sent chart opportunity, but an uncharacteristically lacklustre arrangement and performance produced only moderate sales. It is true that competition from the American Al Caiola split the sales, but it was noticeable that their rival's record grabbed the higher chart placing – 34 against 48, despite the Seven's bonus of an appearance on the new ABC TV show *Thank Your Lucky Stars*, which was networked throughout the UK on May 5th. The main problem was that Bernstein's masterful original arrangement was written for full orchestra. As a result, the band's version was bound to sound thin in comparison; the full John Barry Orchestra would have been a more appropriate proposition. The B-side, 'Skid Row', turned out to be much more typical Seven material – a classic 'Stringbeat' arrangement written by Barry. The record was his sixth successive Top Fifty hit.

Barry was quickly involved in another four records by other artists, beginning with 'Big Wheel', a Johnny Worth number written especially for Gerry Dorsey. Known these days as Engelbert Humperdinck, Dorsey had already made three unsuccessful singles but had not released anything for 18 months. When asked why, he put it down to a lack of suitable material, and of 'Big Wheel' he said: 'It was written by Johnny at my request. At first I didn't like it very much, but then we got together on it and he wrote in another chorus. Then John Barry did a wonderful arrangement and the whole thing sounded great. Eighteen months away from the studios is a long time, but I think it's been worth it. My voice has matured, I feel a lot more confident and I'm very pleased with the new disc.' The backing of the John Barry Orchestra certainly added greatly to the attraction of the up-tempo topside – but like Barry, back in early 1961 Johnny Worth was not having much success outside his involvement with Faith, and this promising venture joined the ranks of the also-rans. It was to be another six years, and in a pop era far removed from the pre-Beatles 1961, before Dorsey finally made it with a new name and a song written by the ex-Barry pianist Les Reed.

Denis Lotis, with his roots deep in dance band music through his years with Ted Heath, had long been seen as one of the classiest pop singers around, and a couple of years after he had worked with Barry on *Drumbeat*, the two got together on record for the first time with 'Where You Are' and 'Love's A Secret Game'. Though the disc meant nothing in terms of the UK charts, it was played constantly on radio, particularly on EMI's Radio Luxembourg shows, hosted by easy-listening presenters David Jacobs and David Gell, and it must have generated a lot of royalty payments. That kind of singing was not what the record-buying public wanted at the time, however, with the occasional exception of offerings from the likes of Matt Monro and Nat King Cole.

Diz Disley and the Downbeats' 'Django's Castle' was another commercial disappointment, despite Barry's involvement. It was a modern version of a Django Rheinhardt composition, with the Barry-directed accompaniment sounding rather overdone and out of place on this occasion. Indeed, Disc said as much, and preferred the B-side, which was without assistance from Barry.

The release on April 22nd, 1961 of Adam Faith's next single, 'Easy Going Me' coupled with 'Wonderin'', saw him renew his acquaintance with Lionel Bart, who wrote the A side. All the characteristic ingredients were there, but some reviews were lukewarm, and the record reached only Number 12. Some of the music press criticised the arrangement, and suggested that Faith's sound was becoming too predictable and formalised. The disc stayed in the charts for ten weeks, but there was a growing feeling that the steam was going out of what has since proved to be just the first phase of Adam's long, long career. The A-side was simple almost to the point of being banal, the B-side wholly unmemorable. Those who had come half to expect double A-sides from the Faith camp were just one sector of his following who were disappointed.

The failure of the next Barry single, 'The Menace', came as a considerable blow. Coupled with 'Rodeo', this was arguably the JB7's most complete recording to date, creating the kind of atmosphere and tension you would find in the theme to a thriller. It was yet another Barry original and showed off the full range and strength of the John Barry Orchestra; the almost always admiring *Record Mirror* liked the guitar work, reverb and pizzicato backing, while the *Melody Maker* noted that 'Rodeo' was a fine update of the 1958 recording and just like a Western film theme. Not for Tin Pan Alley, then, but a disc on which both sides evoked stirring film music. It was the clearest indication yet of the way in which John Barry's career would develop.

John Barry studying the score circa 1961.

CHAPTER 7

$\mathcal{S}$TRINGBEAT

Barry was now hard at work on his second Columbia album. He had commissioned tracks from other composers, one of whom was Jerry Lordan – writer of 'Apache', a mammoth hit for the Shadows. He supplied 'Starfire', which was also chosen as the group's new single. Unlike 'Apache', the record featured clavioline alongside Vic Flick's guitar work, an instrument played on the session by Ted Taylor of the Ted Taylor Four. According to Dougie Wright, Barry often used Taylor to augment the sound of the Seven in the studio, along with fellow TT4 member Bob Rodgers on guitar. TWW, the ITV station then serving South Wales and the West Country, chose 'Starfire' as the theme to their Kent Walton-hosted pop programme, *Discs a Go-Go*, but even with a weekly airing in that part of the world and a massive advertising campaign nationwide, the record failed to chart. As the B side Barry chose the Seven's recording of the theme from the new Terry Thomas comedy film *A Matter Of Who*, in which Barry and his band made a brief appearance.

Within a few days of putting out 'Starfire', EMI released a new single by a hitherto unknown act calling itself Michael Angelo and his Orchestra. It was no coincidence that it sounded exactly like the JB7 plus four, because in reality it was the John Barry Orchestra recording under a pseudonym, an apparent attempt by JB to cash in on his popularity in Italy, where he had rejected an offer of £250,000 from a businessman which would have tied up both him and the Seven for four years. For Michael Angelo's debut, Barry picked Nino Rota's theme from a new Visconti film, 'Rocco And His Brothers'. The flip side, 'Spinneree', was a Barry number named after a café he frequented in Cumberland. Whether or not this release harmed the chances of 'Starfire' is hard to tell; but as neither record was a hit, it did not work.

Adam Faith's new single, released on July 14th, was clearly a response to the criticism of his previous release, for what was noticeable on 'Don't You Know It' was the complete absence of pizzicato strings. Suddenly, here was an Adam Faith 45 without the archetypal Faith sound. Experimentation was the buzzword on this release, an arrangement dominated by Ted Taylor on clavioline. In truth, the song was simply a product of the standard pop form of the day, in typical 'Runaway' style. It was now clear that Faith could not please everyone, and some reviewers this time round accused him of being too gimmicky. The flip-side, 'My Last Wish', was the first time

Barry and Johnny Worth combined to write a song. In the end, the record made exactly the same progress in the charts as its predecessor – a money-maker from an artist who was still big but no longer red hot.

In September, Barry made his final stage appearance with the Seven. He was finding touring more and more difficult to manage, bearing in mind his writing and his recently acquired duties with Topline, an artists' agency formed with fellow musician Geoff Love. He installed Vic Flick as on-stage leader of the JB7 and replaced himself on trumpet with Bobby Carr.

Above: John Barry's last stage appearance with the JB7, September 1961.

Above right: Vic Flick fronting the JB7 in 1961. Bobby Carr has replaced John Barry on trumpet.

Nineteen-year-old Anita Harris made her recording debut for Parlophone in October, 1961. She had started in show business some three years earlier, first as an ice skater and then as a cabaret artist who sang and danced. This took her from appearing on Belgian TV to a show in Las Vegas, but back on the cabaret circuit in Britain she was heard by an EMI executive at the Hyde Park Hotel. A recording contract soon followed, and she was aided considerably by having both sides of her first record written by top composers, with accompaniment by John Barry. Apart from this, she was extremely attractive – her long legs and trim figure kept her in work as a panto principal boy well into middle age – and her voice was deep and natural sounding. Given a lot of hype from EMI, the sky should have been the limit – but it was the Gerry Dorsey story all over again, and Anita would have to wait another six years for her first major hit record, 'Just Loving You'. This early failure must have been bitterly disappointing for her, especially since the main side, 'I Haven't Got You', was written by Lionel Bart, who rarely failed at that time. The flip side, by Jerry ('Apache') Lordan, was 'Mr One And Only', another excellent track, but a cover version by Cleo Laine attracted more attention.

In November, Barry decided to return to his rock 'n' roll roots by releasing an out-and-out rocker, 'Watch Your Step', as the A-side of the Seven's next single. It had been a recent hit in America for its composer, the rhythm and blues singer Bobby Parker, and it was a track the Seven had adapted into their stage act. The record was built around the usual solid Vic Flick guitar solo, together with more excellent clavioline work from Ted Taylor. As a way of acknowledging the latest dance craze, Barry named the B-side 'Twist It', and guitar and clavioline once again dominated proceedings. Not for the first time, Barry misjudged the market, and the record sold very few copies; all this despite his having recently returned from a trip to America where he had discovered new recording techniques far in advance of anything to be heard in the UK.

Barry told *The Record Mirror* that he was determined to incorporate everything he had learned into the production of this new release: 'I spent two days in Los Angeles discussing and watching recording techniques with Duane Eddy's recording manager, Lee Hazlewood, and some of what I saw and heard rubbed off.' Doubtless he also benefited from meeting Phil Spector. The principal technique he learned was that

John Barry at home with his record collection in 1959.

of recording individual instruments and artists on separate tapes, so engineers could balance and produce the finished record after the performers had departed. Although these skills did nothing to enhance the chart prospects of 'Watch Your Step', Barry was able to put them to good use when it came to producing his new *Stringbeat* album. This was released in time for Christmas 1961, and record buyers were able to hear the characteristic Barry sound in stereo for the first time. His decision to hand over the on-stage leadership of the Seven to Vic Flick so that he could concentrate more on writing and arranging had paid rich dividends. Here there were 15 tracks of breathtaking originality and excitement, five of them self-compositions. The others were a combination of reinterpretations and fresh material from contemporary writers, among them members of the Seven. The orchestra consisted of the Seven plus a 12-string section and the now inevitable Ted Taylor's clavioline. It is worth analysing each track, since this was a landmark in Barry's career.

The opener harked back to his *Drumbeat* days of backing Adam Faith, with Barry paying tribute to the Dick Jacobs arrangement of the Buddy Holly hit 'It Doesn't Matter Anymore'. On 'Sweet Talk', Barry updated one of his earliest compositions, 'Snap 'n' Whistle', in a much improved and fuller form. Clavioline featured strongly throughout, and in particular on a reworking of Pat Boone's minor hit of the summer, 'Moody River'.

'There's Life in the Old Boy Yet' was the tongue-in-cheek title given to another updating of an earlier recording, 'For Pete's Sake'; it was later used by the BBC to introduce their Saturday afternoon sports programme on the old Light Programme. 'A Handful of Songs', originally a hit in Britain for Tommy Steele, was one of Barry's special favourites, and he managed to breathe new life into it, with Vic Flick's guitar particularly prominent.

The first completely new Barry composition, 'Like Waltz', was also the most experimental, an intriguing bar blues concoction in waltz time, juxtaposing guitar and strings with startling originality. The next track, 'Rodeo', had of course already surfaced in its re-recorded form as the reverse side of 'The Menace' single. To close side one, Barry turned to his pianist Les Reed for the first recorded composition in what became a very distinguished career. Like Barry, Reed had recently become a father for the first time, so he named 'Donna's Theme' after his little daughter.

Side two opened with the Jerry Lordan number 'Starfire', the curiously unsuccessful single; and this was immediately followed by 'Baubles, Bangles And Beads', a song taken from the show *Kismet*, famously based on the themes of Borodin. On the surface this might have seemed a surprising choice, but in fact it fitted well into the ambitious scope and range of the album. Vic Flick's guitar pyrotechnics were a huge influence throughout, and it came as no surprise to find that Barry also asked him to write a number. Vic's début track was the excellent 'Zapata', characterised by a then innovative 'fade-intro' which gradually introduced the listener to the familiar Flick guitar sound.

In contrast to the songs he wrote for Adam Faith, Johnny Worth composed an instrumental number, 'Rum Dee Dum Dee Dah', which proved a bright and breezy romp on which Barry used high picked strings with clavioline and guitar. JB then gave Ben E King's 'Spanish Harlem' the full 'Stringbeat' treatment, with Vic Flick demonstrating his versatility by playing both classical and electric guitars. Tony Osborne was a much-admired English writer and arranger behind many a hit record. In fact it was he who wrote and performed the original theme for *Juke Box Jury*, under the pseudonym of Ozzie Warlock and the Wizards, before it was ousted by the Seven's 'Hit And Miss'. He contributed to the album the Latin influenced 'Man From Madrid', so in keeping that it sounds as if it might have been written with this LP in mind.

Barry showcased his most ornate arrangement on the album's final track, 'The Challenge' – arguably its standout cut, and one whose orchestral colouring again hinted at the direction in which Barry was heading. It was evocative mood music at its very best, a soundtrack to an epic that had yet to be made, a magnificent ending to a marvellous album. And how did it succeed in terms of hard cash? On release, *Stringbeat* attracted wonderful reviews throughout the music press. True, it did not sell in large enough quantities to register in the album charts, but it was still a steady seller, prompting a reissue in 1983 and another on CD in 1990.

Mrs Mills, Danny Williams, Helen Shapiro, John Barry & Nipper.

CHAPTER 8

ABBEY ROAD

Adam Faith's third film was the comedy *What A Whopper*. The title song was not considered strong enough for single release, so instead he chose another song from the film, 'The Time Has Come', by Johnny Worth. It was an attractive, wistful number, generally seen as one of his best for a long time, and it reached number four in the charts. In doing so, it fared a great deal better than the movie, which opened on September 28th at the Rialto – in London, not JB's father's place in York! – to a terrible pasting from the press. In reaching number 11 in November, 'The Time Has Come' ended a six weeks' absence from the charts – Faith's longest gap since 'What Do You Want?' That statistic is a timely reminder of the pressure on the top artists of that time to turn themselves into hit factories, churning out the numbers. No wonder so many careers were comparatively short – and not every song they recorded was a world-beater.

The *New Musical Express* responded to criticism from Faith fans that it had treated him unfairly compared with Cliff and Elvis by printing a track-by-track review of his next album – *Adam Faith* – and praising it to the skies. The 14-track LP included three songs composed by the writer and actor Trevor Peacock, who like Johnny Worth had first encountered Faith on the set of *Drumbeat* when he acted as compere. John Barry was again responsible for arrangements and accompaniments.

Just after Christmas Parlophone unveiled the début offering from dancer and choreographer Peter Gordeno. 'You're Following Me' was an early example of Burt Bacharach's *oeuvre*. John Barry supplied the accompaniment for this and its flip-side, 'I Got Eyes'. Gordeno was thought to be very promising, and the disc even made the lower regions of some charts. Barry continued to move from one débutant to another. Soon after Gordeno, he was overseeing former office boy Robert Farrant's first recording. The story goes that while working at Apollo, Lionel Bart's music company, he was heard by Bart when impersonating various star singers of the day. On the strength of it, he was re-named Bobby Shafto and Lionel wrote two gimmick-laden songs for him and arranged for the John Barry Orchestra to back him. The result was at least one pleasant enough number – the A-side, 'Over And Over'. The B side, 'I Want My Bed', was rather embarrassing, though, and there was nothing any kind of Barry arrangement could do to help. Another failure maybe, but with another budding Faith or Cliff Richard always waiting in the wings, there was always a chance of striking gold. Opportunity knocked all over again in March, but this time with Tony Rocco, a singer/songwriter thought to be a promising prospect.

The 21-year old Rocco originated from North Borneo, where his father was Deputy Postmaster-General, but he moved to Britain with his family in 1957. He took a five-year course in electrical engineering, but half way through chose to take a couple of years off to see if he could make it in show business. By chance he was overheard rehearsing by a record executive and successfully auditioned for EMI. John Barry's company, Topline Artists, asked him to sign, so it was not surprising that Barry backed him on both sides of his first release for Parlophone. 'Stalemate' and 'Keep A Walkin'' were both excellent and deserved to succeed, with Rocco promoting them vigorously at personal appearances around the country. Alas, his talent and enthusiasm were not enough to break the record, and after one more non-Barry backed release, he returned to the safer waters of electrical engineering.

The arrival of 1962 coincided with a distinct change of approach for Adam Faith, with the release on January 20th of the ballad 'Lonesome'. The flip-side, a raucous vocal version of the recent JB7 instrumental 'Watch Your Step', was more in character – but in 'Lonesome', Faith took an artistic gamble in promoting a slower number as the A side. Most reviewers welcomed the change of mood and could not see the disc failing at all; a few wondered how Faith's following would react. In the event the record peaked at Number 12 and spent nine weeks in the charts, so the gamble could be said to have paid off. Certainly Faith was reported to be happy with the change.

On February 12th he recorded the Johnny Worth song 'You Can Do It If You Try', but this was never released in any form at the time – probably because of the impending release of Peter Gordeno's version, using a very similar Barry arrangement. In March, Faith undertook an 11-day nature cure at a Surrey rest home. He had not stopped touring and recording for eight months, and was exhausted. Tiring though these tours may have been, Vic Flick fondly recalls days when the Seven were backing Faith on the road. In particular, he recalls many occasions when drummer Dougie Wright, who bore a passing resemblance to the star, teased Faith's patiently waiting female following to the point of ecstatic frenzy whenever he momentarily appeared at a dressing room window.

On another occasion, Flick remembers an incident when Faith and the band, armed with water pistols, hid behind the stage curtains and soaked comedian Dave Allen in the middle of his act. Dougie Wright was not so amused when the prank was turned on him, while he was in the middle of a frenetic drum solo. Flick later reckoned that these high spirits were a way of fighting travel fatigue. Some years later The Who, with rather more drastic solutions to letting off steam, were to develop the water treatment by driving cars into hotel swimming pools.

At the Surrey retreat, Faith absorbed the script for his next film project, *Mix Me A Person*, which was due to start production immediately after his short recuperation. He also revealed that he was writing a comedy script with his agent, Colin

Berlin. Recording, however, always took priority, and on March 29th he embarked on further sessions with the John Barry Orchestra, some destined for the proposed movie. His new single, 'As You Like It', coupled with the tongue-in-cheek 'Face To Face', was released on April 28th, and climbed to a creditable number five. It was Adam's 13 consecutive hit – one more than his rival Cliff Richard had managed at this stage.

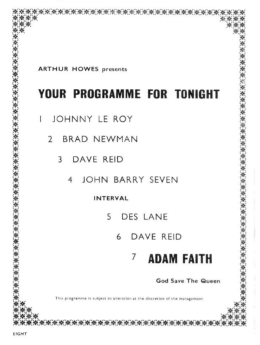

The jazz musician Dave Brubeck made a surprise British chart entry with his colleague Paul Desmond's 'Take Five'. Always on the lookout for new and successful ideas, Barry wrote and recorded 'Cutty Sark' using the same time signature and a striking staccato brass arrangement to highlight its rhythmic possibilities. The British record-buying public was partially won over, since the disc entered the top forty, peaking at number 35. It also proved just how successful Barry had become in writing distinctive arrangements, for no sooner had he appeared conducting a small orchestra miming to the record on *Thank Your Lucky Stars* than the track was adopted as the signature tune for a current affairs programme, *Dateline London*. Strangely, the flip-side, 'Lost Patrol', a much covered Maxwell composition, was used as a signature tune by the BBC TV regional news programme, *Look North*, as well as for an Australia TV series, *The Four Corners*. It even made the top ten there, as 'The Four Corners Theme'.

Once again, EMI issued a single by the Michael Angelo Orchestra within days of the official Barry release. This time Barry coupled another Maxwell composition, 'Tears', with Richard Addinsell's theme from the film *The Roman Spring Of Mrs Stone*. The record was covered by others, with Johnny Gregory even issuing an identical single, but neither version proved commercially successful. In contrast,

The John Barry Seven: the classic line-up from 1959–62.

Barry's next 45 has proved to be one of the most enduring instrumentals ever written, 'The James Bond Theme'. In the meantime, there were no fewer than ten accompaniments to be handled as Barry's studio work schedule grew heavier and heavier – among them two more from Peter Gordeno and two oddities from Billy Cotton and Kathie Kay.

During his long association with Adam Faith, Johnny Worth had continued to make his own solo records for labels such as Oriole and Embassy, without much success. He was now with Columbia, and teamed up with John Barry to release 'You Know What I Mean' and 'All These Things'. The former was a novelty number sung in a heavy cockney accent, the kind of thing that would probably have suited Tommy Steele or Mike Sarne. The flip side was the better of the two, having already been covered by Adam Faith on his recent album. Vic Flick is especially to the fore on this side, but it seemed that Johnny was still better off concentrating on writing for others.

Peter Gordeno tried his luck again with a cover of the US hit 'Uptown', coupled with 'The Makings Of A Man', both recorded at Abbey Road on May 19th. This disc, arguably one of Barry's strongest arrangements, failed to attract much attention, as did the teaming of Billy Cotton and Kathie Kay with two songs from the Lionel Bart musical *Blitz*. The pair were familiar from radio and television, in particular the long-running *Billy Cotton Band Show*, but the popularity of the veteran bandleader and his singers did not wash with the youngsters who accounted for most of the singles market. 'Opposites' and 'If The Young Ones Can Be Happy' were fine in the structure of the musical, but simply not strong enough to mean anything away from the show. *Blitz,* in any case, was no *Oliver!* in terms of catchy tunes or rave notices, and a planned Barry album of instrumental versions of its songs was quietly dropped.

More disappointments: Liverpool-born Darren Young had already been on the pop scene for some time, but coming from the Larry Parnes stable, where all the boys were Wilde or Eager, he was originally known as Johnny Gentle. He was very popular on the Parnes nationwide package tours, but had so far not met with any recording success. A change of name and label was expected to do the trick, and he talked over the former with new manager Norman Newell; his final choice was based on his admiration for the American Country singer Faron Young. His Parlophone début was 'My Tears Will Turn To Laughter' and 'I've Just Fallen For Someone', the latter a self-penned number already recorded on EP and album by Adam Faith. They were

John Barry and some of the Seven on the set of *Tin Pan Alley* in 1961.

Peter Gordeno recording 'Uptown' at Abbey Road Studios in 1962.

Adam Faith, Vera Lynn, John Barry and Lionel Bart.

pleasant enough numbers vaguely reminiscent of the style of Lance Fortune of a couple of years previously, but not strong enough to make an impression. It was noticeable that if Barry worked with a new artist without any sign of success, he rarely repeated the experience; Darren Young was no exception.

Van Doren was a young, classically trained pianist who decided to take his chances in the world of pop. Barry was involved only in the topside of his new HMV single, 'The Coffee Grinder', and despite some very good reviews, the disc soon faded into the ether. TV favourite Russ Conway was still very much the king of the keyboards in the UK, so the chances of a young pretender were limited without the kind of constant exposure which Conway enjoyed.

CHAPTER 9

FAREWELL ADAM, FAREWELL EMI

The most unexpected music industry story that broke during the autumn of 1962 was the decision for Barry and Faith to sever musical links – explained as a purely amicable arrangement designed to enable both to develop alternative projects. JB told *The Record Mirror's* Peter Jones: 'In the early days, Johnny Worth, Adam and I were concentrating on one thing, Adam's records. We were after bread. We were all starting in the business and we were all ambitious. But towards one end only. We were all in the same boat, but eventually you reach a climax in all that channelled activity. I'd say it is impossible for three people to stick together permanently in this way. You are bound to develop into different adult channels. We wanted financial gains. When you've got those, you can relax and choose your work. It's a matter of sitting back and considering precisely what you want to do in your career. Do you want to be tied by the boundaries of pop music? Do you want to include all kinds of music? Or all art forms? As an artist, a musician, you can learn something from all forms – from literature, films and comedy. So no, it wasn't a surprise I left. But you might say it was a surprise I stayed so long.'

The pop world is traditionally quiet during the summer months, so it was not until September that the next single involving John Barry was released. This was yet another Peter Gordeno disc, 'The Boys Kept Hanging Around' and 'Down by the Riverside'. Geoff Love handled the arrangements for the first, so Barry was relegated to the flip-side, an update of the traditional song. Gordeno made an equally good job of both, but he was left still looking for his first hit record.

Meanwhile, newcomer Mark Tracy was rewarded with a rare opportunity to début with a Barry composed song. 'Caravan Of Lonely Men', with lyrics by Pretlow, was coupled with 'Never Ending', written by Michael Carr and Norman Newell. That was quite a pedigree for a first record and EMI must have placed a lot of faith in it – but in an unpredictable business it failed completely.

Marion Ryan, a seasoned singer, was among the highest paid performers on television in 1962, but her only hit had come years before, early in 1958, with a cover of 'Love Me Forever'. On her new one, 'No Love But Your Love' she teamed with John

Barry and his orchestra for a strong sounding ballad; despite good TV and radio exposure, it failed to reinstate her chart pedigree.

The final accompaniment of this period for Barry took the form of a new Kathie Kay 45, this time joined by Billy Cotton and the Rita Williams Singers for just one side, 'Someone Nice Like You'. It was again from a show – *Stop The World, I Want To Get Off* – written by Tony Newley and Leslie Bricusse, and a much bigger success than *Blitz*. It was officially the B-side, but Kathie managed to give it several plugs on TV, without succeeding in pushing it into the charts. Although was this quite often the case, it is nevertheless erroneous to suggest that a lack of chart placing necessarily constituted failure during the early sixties, bearing in mind this was the era in which the singles market dominated the popular music scene. Sales were considerably higher than they are in the nineteen nineties. Some 45s recouped their investment on the strength of their sales, only to find that they were not sufficient enough to put them in the charts. Regional variations also played its part. What's more, certain releases, such as 'Hit & Miss', remained on catalogue for a number of years. In peaking at no. 8, this barely represented its cumulative sales over the decade.

Barry's next project, 'The James Bond Theme', resulted in a successful single for EMI – but the story behind it belongs firmly in the film section of this book. In the meantime, JB's EMI years continued with another chapter in the career of Johnny De Little. Everyone associated with him was disappointed with the failure of his first release, 'Not Guilty' – not least John Barry, who considered him an outstanding prospect. For their second try Barry picked out a couple of standards, 'Lover' and 'You Made Me Love You', and designed and arranged them especially to show off the range of De Little's voice. This time the music press fell over themselves in praise, with one critic even making it his record of the year. Both sides of the disc received plenty of exposure, with De Little belting it out on *Thank Your Lucky Stars*, but its chart failure was a sign that the average teenager found it old hat. It was another huge disappointment for Barry, who would continue to champion De Little's cause.

Two years previously, Nina and Frederik had panned the John Barry arrangement for Adam Faith's novelty Christmas song 'Lonely Pup'. Frederik had mused: 'I don't see how anyone can do anything with an arrangement like this. I consider it in very bad musical taste.' Life moves on, however, and their Christmas record of 1962 was 'White Christmas' and 'Silent Night' – both arranged and accompanied by John Barry! In fact he recorded two other Christmas songs with the Danish duo, 'Away in a Manger' and 'Santa Claus is Coming to Town', and all four were issued on the EP *Christmas At Home with Nina and Frederik*. Both records picked up their fair share of Christmas sales without making a dent in the charts, but Columbia obviously liked the idea of Nina and Frederik with Barry, because shortly afterwards they issued another single, 'There Once Was A Time of Man' backed by the much-recorded 'Inch Worm'.

'The James Bond Theme' was still in the charts when Barry's penultimate official

Nina and Frederik after recording 'Silent Night' at Abbey Road Studios in 1962.

Columbia disc was issued, the main theme to the film comedy, *The Amorous Prawn*, full details of which are again contained within the film section. The main title number, 'The Lolly Theme', was coupled on the single with 'March Of The Mandarins', an obvious attempt at experimentation using quite different musical textures.

In January, 1963, the Seven made a surprise appearance in the film *The Cool Mikado* [see film section]. Then came what Barry has often described as the biggest break in his career, when in the same week that he started work on *Dr No* he was offered work on *The L-Shaped Room*. This was the first of several movies made with the director Bryan Forbes, and is discussed in the Forbes section of the book.

By now, Barry's EMI career was being overshadowed by increasing film commitments, and his involvement in small movies starring Adam Faith and Tommy Steele is examined in later chapters. The Seven's final Columbia release of this period was in March, 1963, when Barry was talking to Jeffrey Kruger of Ember Records about a possible move to that label. The A side was the theme from the popular ITV series *The Human Jungle*, starring Herbert Lom, which was composed by Bernard Ebbinghouse. Barry's arrangement was magnificent both in its TV format and as a highly evocative single. It should have done well in the charts, but despite much radio play, together with its weekly TV airing, it did not even make the Top Fifty. The B-side was another experiment, 'Onwards Christian Spacemen', later adapted for use in Barry's TV score for *Sophia Loren in Rome*.

American Dick Kallman was spotted by Norman Newell when he was appearing in a musical in New York. Newell was so excited by what he saw that he immediately signed him to EMI, and Kallman came to London to make an album for HMV. In those days of a singles-dominated music industry, it was very unusual for a new artist to be commissioned for an album without any 45s chart success, and this gives some indication of how highly this young man was regarded. Curiously, Newell used four musical directors on the album, among them John Barry, who was responsible for the arrangement and accompaniment of five of the 12 titles – 'Deed I Do', 'My Romance', 'Mam'selle', 'The Glory of Love' and 'Say it Isn't So'.

Despite their early enthusiasm for the singer, EMI spent very little on publicity for the album, with *Disc* the only music paper to print a review. It remarked on 'some beautiful pop songs sung by a remarkably pleasant light tenor voice, with splendid arrangements and accompaniments.' The B-side of Kallman's second single in the UK, in February, 1963, was a track from this LP, the Barry-accompanied 'Say It Isn't So'. It was finely sung with immaculate backing that displayed a touch of Nelson Riddle, but the pop world cared as little then as it does today for remarkably pleasant light tenor voices. Both the single and album sold sparsely and, once again, are extremely difficult to find today.

Peter Gordeno returned one last time with Barry on the Johnny Worth number 'You Can Do It If You Try', a single on which Barry was once more relegated to the B-side. *The New Record Mirror* admired the dramatic opening, but thought the lyrics repetitive. Again Gordeno was shown to have a good voice, but neither this nor the main side was strong enough to establish him as a chart singer. As with several other Barry-accompanied artists, the critics rated him more highly than did the public.

John Barry and the Seven had worked on stage with Marty Wilde many times in the late fifties. Now Wilde had signed with Columbia he was able to enjoy the benefit of a Barry arrangement and accompaniment on record for the first time. On hearing the news, Marty said: 'I've no idea what kind of a kick I shall go on. I leave that to Norman Newell, just as I leave the sort of backing to John Barry.' Newell was asked if Wilde might record an oldie like 'I Believe', a favourite in his stage act. 'I'm not too keen on reviving songs for singles,' he replied. 'I know I've done it with Shirley Bassey, but that's because it's so hard to find good new songs. Just the same, if Marty has an oldie in mind, I'll seriously consider it. If it's "I Believe" – if John Barry can come up with an arrangement as brilliant as the one he did for Johnny De Little's "Lover", we might be on to something.' Barry commented: 'I'm raring to go with this disc. I've known Marty since I backed him on tour more than three years ago. He's one of the best singers we have in his field. Marty has an exciting voice – and I'll try and give it an exciting backing.'

Wilde had recorded for Philips for years, scoring many hits, but after a gradual decline in his fortunes his management felt a move to Columbia might kick-start

John Barry, Lionel Bart and Tommy Steele.

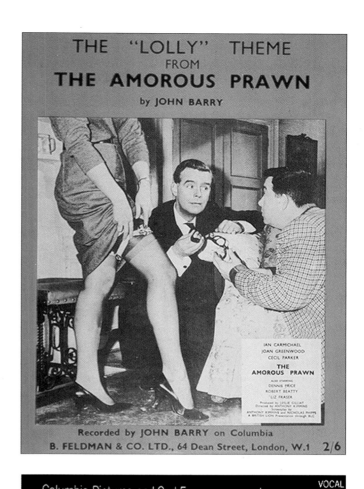

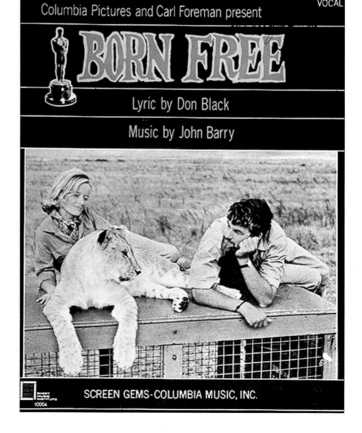

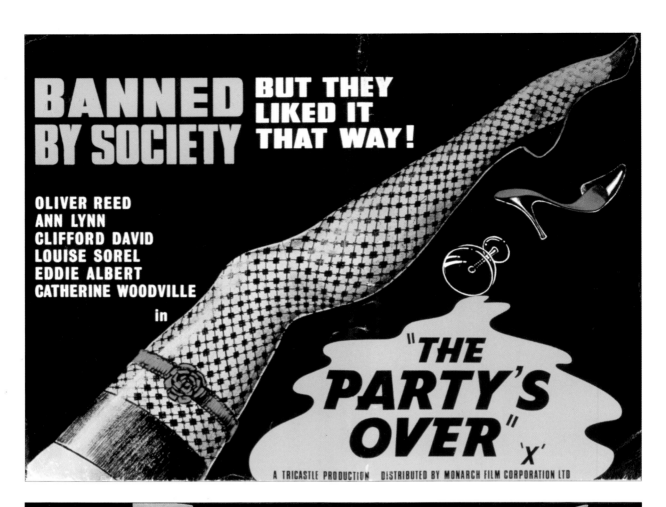

(PAX) PRESENTS A **MICHAEL BALCON** PRODUCTION

LEO McKERN
JANET MUNRO

A JOLLY BAD FELLOW

CO-STARRING
MAXINE AUDLEY

DENNIS PRICE

MILES MALLESON

DUNCAN MACRAE

THEY ALL DIED LAUGHING

EXECUTIVE PRODUCER STEVEN PALLOS
DIRECTED BY DON CHAFFEY PRODUCED BY DONALD TAYLOR
SCREENPLAY BY ROBERT HAMER & DONALD TAYLOR · MUSIC BY JOHN BARRY SOLO JAZZ ORGAN BY ALAN HAVEN
A BRITISH LION-PAX RELEASE through B L C

CAMPAIGN BOOK

BLC FILMS LTD BROADWICK HOUSE BROADWICK ST LONDON W1 TEL GER 8676

The John Barry Seven on the set of *Drumbeat* (Dezo Hoffman/Rex Features)

Eve Taylor and Adam Faith pictured in 1961.

Don Black and John Barry prior to the recording of *Alice's Adventures In Wonderland*.

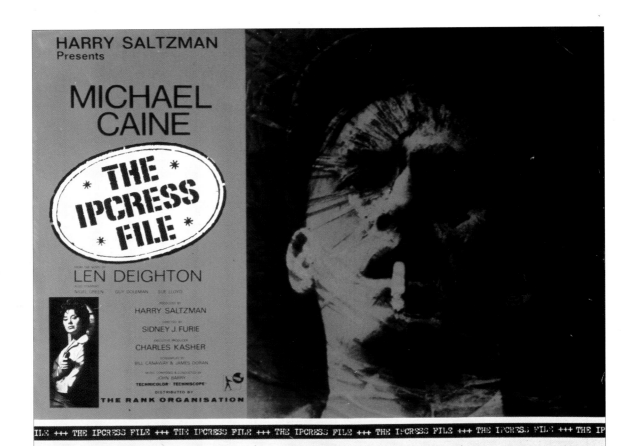

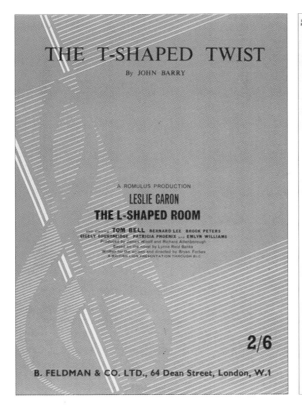

John Barry at the piano at home in 1960 (Pictorial Press).

John Barry at home in 1960 (Pictorial Press).

John Barry at the London Première of *Thunderball* (David Waterman, Camera Press)

his career. For his début, they chose the Doc Pomus standard 'Lonely Avenue', similar in style to 'Heartbreak Hotel', with Wilde even joining in the backing on harmonica. He part-wrote the flip, 'Brand New Love', but this was fairly undistinguished. The topside got a lot of favourable reaction without pushing Marty back into the best sellers, and the two old friends would doubtless have worked together again had Barry not left EMI shortly afterwards. As it worked out, this was the only Wilde/Barry record.

The Academy Award-winning title song from the Jack Lemmon film *The Days Of Wine And Roses* was an ideal number for Johnny De Little to make a further stab at the UK charts; but backed with 'Ride On', featuring some intricate Barry orchestral arrangements, it unhappily went the way of all his previous efforts. Like Peter Gordeno, De Little was continuing to show off his singing ability without recording anything remotely in the current chart vogue.

Barry was now coming to the end of his long association with EMI, and with the Beatles on the crest of their first wave, his accompaniment of 'Well, You Started It', coupled with 'Nevertheless' – a speculative offering by brothers Don, David And Dean – sounded dated. It was well sung by the trio, but it is hard to imagine why HMV bothered, given the musical climate of the time.

Barry was also involved in arranging many of the songs in the Tommy Steele film *It's All Happening*. Rather by accident than design, Barry's career at EMI was filmed for posterity, as a result of his cameo appearance in the film, which was designed as a celluloid promotional showcase for some of EMI's current roster of acts. Singles by Johnny De Little, Steele and Marion Ryan with accompaniment by JB were issued on Columbia. That label had one more try to find the charts with a Barry-backed Nina and Frederik single; 'Puff The Magic Dragon' was released in time for Christmas, 1963, coupled with 'The Worm Song', which was accompanied by Tony Osborne. Recorded at Abbey Road before Barry's move to Ember, 'Puff' was included in the John Barry BBC TV show *Around Seven*, which also showcased Vic Flick, Johnny Scott, Annie Ross and Chad and Jeremy. 'Puff', with innocent words but alleged drug undertones, was already closely identified with Peter, Paul and Mary, a hip, folksy New York trio whose image could not have been farther removed from Nina and Frederik. The genteel Danes achieved some success with the song, but it was strictly limited, and Barry did not work with them on record again.

Meanwhile, group changes were in the air again. Of the regular band of the past few years, Dougie Wright and Les Reed had departed during 1962, the former in search of more regular work and the latter wisely seeking a career in writing and producing. Dickie Harwood replaced Dougie for a short while, followed by Ray Cooper, while Brian Hazelby (known as Rachmaninoff!), came in for Les Reed, followed by Kenny Sammon. With Barry concentrating on his own future, the band was not finding the same amount of work, particularly now it was no longer associated with Adam Faith. Since 'The James Bond Theme' they had not achieved any chart success, and other members started to look to where the grass might be greener.

Vic Flick had been with the Seven since late 1958 and had led the band on stage for the past two years, but increasing demands on his time as a session player forced him finally to quit. Although Flick gave three months' notice, Barry was unable to find a suitable replacement and he was forced to disband the group temporarily. Vic's last performance as a member of the Seven was at Torquay in August, 1963, after which he spent years around the London recording studios as a much sought freelance session musician, accompanying a roll call of the top names in the business.

CHAPTER 10

EMBER RECORDS

That unexpected announcement that Barry had signed an exclusive contract with Ember Records coincided with Vic Flick's farewell to the JB7, and it was plain that life for the band would never be the same again. Ember was an independent label set up in 1958 by the promoter and impresario Jeffrey Kruger, owner of the London jazz club The Flamingo. His coup in capturing John Barry as 'associate producer and creative A & R man' was aimed at cranking up his company in order to compete in a market then dominated by EMI and Decca. The move surprised many – on the inside of the business, as well as fans, to whom the name meant little – so it is well to trace the development of Ember up to the point of JB's arrival in 1963. Until then, Ember had been considered a good catalogue specialist label that showed little or no inclination to compete with the 'majors' of pop. For a start, they did not possess the huge resources necessary to sustain a concerted and successful challenge. That said, their place in the market was assured, on a modest scale. They had been set up by Kruger as a means of showcasing the best in modern British jazz, and at first they specialised in promoting artists who played at his Flamingo Club in Wardour Street, Soho. The Flamingo had a reputation for introducing the cream of black music to Britain, and was innovative enough to book styles from rhythm and blues to ska. Jimi Hendrix made one of his first British appearances there.

Kruger's enthusiasm was compounded by Decca's fading interest in the jazz scene. From at first licensing material from other labels, Ember started issuing their own recordings from 1960 onwards. They were the first British label to release licensed James Brown tracks from America; they expanded their catalogue by introducing the French singer Charles Aznavour; and they were also responsible for introducing a variety of American Country styles to the UK record-buying public. It was fun, but among many in the know, Ember's diversity was soon seen as a major weakness; in the eyes of the public, such an eclectic approach created a blurred and confusing image, with no clear identity.

Taking on John Barry was aimed at rectifying this state of affairs. JB's attraction to this specially created job stemmed from a desire for complete artistic control and musical freedom – a role he could never have entertained at EMI. There, his function was more circumscribed, and held in check by the inertia that is almost

Barry at the controls.

John Barry directs the orchestra in 1962.

John Barry directs the orchestra during the recording of BBC 2's 'Impromptu' programme in 1964.

inevitable with corporate monoliths. Barry knew Kruger, casually, from his early days with Adam Faith and through their mutual friendship with Rex Berry, the publicist, who was now a public relations man at Ember. Kruger would control the financial side of the business, while Barry was offered complete sway over the creative input in an exclusive arrangement designed to lead to part ownership of the company. In other words, Barry was given a virtual *carte blanche* to initiate any project he desired, with total control over the choice of studio, artist, musicians and repertoire. It seemed no less than an opportunity to set up his own record label.

He would be the musical equivalent of an actor/manager. No wonder, after the endless frustrations at EMI, Barry jumped at the chance. For the British record industry at that time, the arrangement was a ground-breaking development. It was the first time a British company had brought in an independent 'overlord' to run the creative side. Barry could hardly refuse. What is more, he had nothing to lose, because the Seven were still a viable touring band, with a little fine-tuning, and he was emerging in his own right as a much sought-after composer.

Under the terms of his new contract, Barry could record film projects for any company prepared to finance their release. This explains the perplexing myriad of labels on which Barry's name appeared during this period, as the discography in this book shows. Before he had even set foot in a recording studio, he set about changing Ember's image by commissioning the animator Richard Williams, later of *Pink Panther* and *Roger Rabbit* fame, to design a new logo for the label – a distinctive, bright orange and yellow motif which reflected the 'swinging' era far more evocatively than the drab black labels EMI had recently introduced. Jeffrey Kruger later recalled that the design of the logo cost more than the previous two years recordings!

Style was clearly the order of the day to establish Ember as a competitive 'quality' label. The unprecedented use of picture sleeves for most singles – an innovative feature adopted by the label from day one – was in perfect harmony with the fresh approach, and was kept for subsequent releases – in particular, Barry's own! Clearly, Ember were challenging many conventions, ranging from internal organisation to packaging. The philosophy extended to a concerted attack on the hitherto impenetrable American market, until then a graveyard for British exports, and Kruger succeeded in persuading World Artists to release records by Barry's protégés Chad Stuart and Jeremy Clyde. With Barry-produced material, they enjoyed considerable success there a good year before the Beatles took America by storm.

Early problems of lack of air time, and later patchy distribution of the label to the major record stores, were probably the major setback to the career of Chad Stuart and Jeremy Clyde, at least in the UK. They were arguably Barry's most successful signing to the Ember label, but other than a minor chart success with their first single, 'Yesterday's Gone', they achieved only limited success in their home country. Indeed, according to Kruger, Barry grew so frustrated and disappointed with his failure to 'get them away' that he gave up producing them after their first two recordings; he was replaced by Shel Talmy, who later found fame producing The Kinks and The Who, among other leading sixties groups.

Chad and Jeremy, as they eventually became known, first met at the Central School of Speech and Drama in London. Their common love of rock music led them to form a trio known as the Jerks, with another acting friend playing bass guitar, before they eventually settled down as a duo playing folk music in Tina's, a coffee house in London's West End.

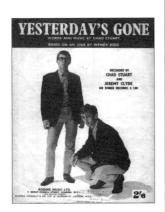

Around this time Clyde completed his drama course and left to try to make his way as an actor, while Stuart decided the stage was not for him, opting for steady employment as an arranger/copyist with a music publisher. It was during this time that he wrote and arranged 'Yesterday's Gone', a good beat number that could have been a very big hit indeed at the hands of Herman's Hermits, perhaps, or Peter and Gordon. As it was, he was unable to attract any record company interest until fortune grinned broadly when the duo was spotted by Ember representatives during a session at Tina's, and was recommended to Barry. Their first Barry-produced single, that same 'Yesterday's Gone' backed by 'Lemon Tree', was a creditable debut chart success in the UK, reaching number 37; but there was no such luck for the follow-up, 'Like I Love You Today' and 'Early In The Morning', and it was at this stage that Barry made his excuses and allowed Shel Talmy to take over production duties.

To be fair to Barry, he was being bombarded with film score offers following his early success with the James Bond series, and he may simply have decided that he could no longer devote enough time to break a new act. In the event, Shel Talmy also failed to achieve any measure of success in Britain for the pairing – but as we have noted, they struck up a profitable rapport with America, once the persevering Jeffrey Kruger was able to sign them to World Artists Music.

During 1965 and '66 and the remainder of the decade, Ember made fresh attempts to exploit the duo's American success, not only with a succession of single releases but with a number of repackaged albums. In truth, there was only sufficient material for two *bona fide* Chad and Jeremy LPs, but various compilations – *Greatest Hits*, *Best Of* and even a *John Barry Meets Chad and Jeremy* – were an indication of how desperately hard Ember tried to persuade the UK of the duo's undoubted talent. Unfortunately, the British public appeared to be entirely satisfied with the steady stream of beat groups that continued to pour out of Liverpool, Manchester, Birmingham and other major cities, and ignored all Ember's entreaties.

Chad and Jeremy eventually followed John Barry in signing for CBS Records in America, though they had no further connection with him as a recording duo as they enjoyed further album success with the company. Clyde reacquainted himself with Barry on the rather short-lived stage musical *Passion Flower Hotel*, appearing on the original cast album and releasing a solo single of the best song in the show, 'I Love My Love'. Since then he has concentrated on a successful acting career, both on stage and in films and television. Stuart, on the other hand, has continued to pursue musical activities. He scored the film *Three In An Attic*, and has become a respected record producer based in California.

Barry's first project for Ember was the satirical LP *Fool Britannia*, with Peter

John Barry at home in the early sixties.

John Barry pictured at home in 1963.

Sellers, Leslie Bricusse, Anthony Newley and Joan Collins. The album was recorded in New York on August 6th, 1963 at the RCA Victor studios, before an invited audience. Probably because it mocked the British establishment, and in particular a Macmillan-led Conservative government by then in its last, post-Profumo throes, major British record companies refused to release it in the UK. John Barry soon got wind of it, and rush-released the offending item on Ember. Engineer Eric Tomlinson recalls him supervising the editing of the original American tapes at CTS Studios in Bayswater, and Kruger believes it was literally done overnight.

Johnny De Little, Frankie Vaughan, Steve Cassidy and Jack Prendergast backstage at The Rialto, York in 1963.

Perhaps surprisingly, Ember's biggest single record success during Barry's régime resulted from his next production. The highly controversial 'Christine' was an obvious attempt to cash in on the summer story of 1963, the scandal that linked the Tory War Minister John Profumo with the call-girl Christine Keeler. The song, sung by Miss X (a pseudonym for Lionel Blair's sister Joyce), predictably won an instant ban by the BBC; but it was also blacklisted by the usually less politically sensitive Radio Luxembourg, and not for the first time, notoriety attracted curiosity and respectable sales returns. The record climbed to number 37 in the British charts, a decent achievement in view of its lack of air-play. A front-page story in *Melody Maker,* under the intriguing banner headline '29 words, 2 giggles and 1 sigh' clearly assisted its cause. In fact the headline said almost all that was necessary about this satirical novelty number co-written by Leslie Bricusse, According to Kruger, it sold well around Soho mostly by word-of-mouth recommendation, an effective antidote to any air play ban.

Two other artists Barry introduced to Ember did meet with the Kruger seal of

John Barry with Chad Stuart and Jeremy Clyde at Olympic Sound Studios, London, August 1963.

John Barry portrait circa 1964.

approval. These were the York-born singer Norman Fowler and the then Coronation Street star Philip Lowrie. Fowler's first tentative steps into the music business could be traced as far back as 1960, when as a 14-year-old choirboy he doubled up as leader of the Gambling Men, a York band who played anything from rock to skiffle. As a son of York, John Barry heard and saw them performing at a charity function, and after his move from EMI to Ember he thought Fowler would be just right for a song he had recently been offered – 'Ecstasy', written by Buddy Kaye, Marty Wilde and Mike Pratt. Fowler duly signed a three-year contract with Ember and recorded it, together with the flip side 'I'm A Worryin'', at a two-hour session at Olympic Studios, with Keith Grant engineering. He believes he was given his stage name Steve Cassidy immediately after the session. 'I'm A Worryin'', was composed by organist Alan Haven, who rehearsed Cassidy on the morning of the session in his local garage studio before joining the rest of the session musicians for the recording. Cassidy recalls that Big Jim Sullivan was on lead

John Barry, Annie Ross, Jeffrey Kruger and David Jacobs at Ember Records re-launch party in August 1963.

guitar, and the general atmosphere was one of great enthusiasm, anticipating considerable success for the record.

According to Kruger, Barry saw Cassidy as a second Adam Faith, but it was not to be, as Ember were unable to generate the publicity to turn good vibes into solid sales. A live appearance on an early edition of *Ready Steady Go* with Barry and Chad and Jeremy was arranged in a bid to promote Ember's relaunch, but Cassidy did not get to perform. In fact he says the only time he heard his record played was on Ember's own Radio Luxembourg show! With a three-year contract signed and sealed, other records would surely have followed, but he decided to leave the label once Barry departed for CBS early in 1965. He went into teaching, while continuing his music career part-time, and he was good enough to appear on TV's *New Faces*, as well as working on his summer holidays on gigs in Belgium, France, Italy and Spain. He is now head teacher at a York primary school, and has recently recorded and produced two albums of his own songs. Despite his successful 'day job', singing was and always will be his first love.

On the other hand, little is known about the Lowrie session, save the large number of 'takes' needed to reach the final versions of 'I Might Have Known' ('Before And After'). Lowrie was an enormously popular TV star in his role of the sexy Elsie Tanner's feckless son Denis, but he was clearly not used to singing. The song was written by Coronation Street scriptwriter Barry Cawtheray, and clearly custom-built to cash in on the artist's television appeal. Sadly, Philip's ability as a singer failed to match his acting skills, as the master tapes amply illustrate; producer Barry can often be heard patiently coaxing his protégé to greater efforts. The record achieved very little air-play, and thus negligible sales, despite an extensive music paper advertising campaign. Ember soon had to face the fact that with the emergence of the Beatles, their best hope of publicity and air play was indeed with their own sponsored Luxembourg show; what a pity that it went out only in the early hours of the morning!

Barry could certainly be loyal. His EMI records with Billy Cotton and Kathie Kay had been flops, but in 1963 he recruited them for an album for Ember. Alan Breeze, another of Cotton's veteran singers, was added to the proceedings and the trio was billed as the Billy Cotton Lot on an album entitled *Saturday Night Sing-A-Long*. This was a collection of various medleys containing 28 tunes in total, all standards and favourites of Cotton fans. The same degree of expertise went into this album as on another by Annie Ross, with John Barry the producer, Eric Tomlinson sound engineer and arrangements credited to Pete Moore and Jackie Brown. Lush settings, pleasant vocals and a strong performance by the orchestra made this an excellent album, but again it was not a good seller. It was reissued in 1972 under the title *Let's All Join In* – and this change was not the only notable difference. The album jacket was revamped and the tracks were presented in stereo-enhanced mono, an attempt to give old recordings some modern verve.

Major chart success in the UK was to elude Ember under Barry. Why this was so is difficult to explain, although it is clear that Barry's perception of the market did not always mirror reality. Barry and Kruger soon found themselves diametrically opposed in their approach to achieving the delicate balance between creating a quality prod-

John Barry and Bob Graham at Ember Records re-launch party in August 1963.

uct and commercial viability. Barry, ever the perfectionist, wanted to establish Ember's credentials by using the best studios in London (CTS), together with the finest engineers, such as Eric Tomlinson; he was also always eager to make use of any state-of-the-art studio technology. As a result, his productions were always immaculate, and all would have been well if this emphasis on quality had generated large enough sales to warrant it. Kruger, clearly adopting a profit and loss perspective, saw Ember's investment evaporate in a market that he did not necessarily believe existed at that time.

Those albums by Annie Ross and Billy Cotton simply did not justify their costs, though the business of balancing aesthetic considerations with financial ones will always be difficult. Kruger admits that up to that point Ember had failed to get it right and that various reissues of Barry's material were attempts to recoup losses. Nevertheless, to this day, he is keen to acknowledge Barry's artistic pedigree and talent, insisting that he anticipated a market that was not to emerge for a number of years. There was nothing wrong with his basic tenets; they were just years ahead of their time. Full details of Barry's productions during his two years at Ember can be found in the discography – and in the case of the soundtracks from *Zulu* and *Four In The Morning*, in the film section. Barry and Kruger parted amicably in a final twist that again took the British music business by surprise – the first contractual transfer of a British recording artist to a major American label. What may nowadays seem mundane and commonplace raised eyebrows in 1965; it also led to Barry becoming the only British artist to record for Columbia Records (CBS in the UK) at that time.

Kruger sold Barry's contract to Marty Erlechman, who at the time managed Barbra Streisand, and as part of the deal assumed a similar role on Barry's behalf; it was out of this that the Columbia deal was finalised. It was now becoming clear that Barry was being offered far too many projects for him to keep a tight rein on his Ember commitments. Above that, he was embarking on Hollywood film projects, emerging as a name in his own right. For some years his priorities had firmly been in film scoring, and he was creating a niche for himself in a *genre* that was always his ultimate goal. Once John Barry, film composer, had arrived, he intended to stay. 'Most people don't start out wanting to be film composers,' he later mused. 'I actually did.'

The John Barry Seven travelled with him to Ember, as records released in their name between 1963 and 1964 testify, but these tended to feature session musicians. The first release, 'Kinky' and 'Fancy Dance', featured the alto sax of Johnny Scott on both sides. 'Kinky' was in fact a Scott composition, while 'Fancy Dance' was a Barry original later adapted as the theme for BBC TV's *The Newcomers*. Both sides won substantial air-play, but Ember's patchy distribution at that time contributed to its relative failure. The follow-up, 'From Russia With Love' and '007', with its Bond picture sleeve, fared much better and peaked at number 39. Had it not been for three other vocal versions, it might well have made the Top Ten.

'Elizabeth' and 'The London Theme' were both based on tunes from the TV documentary *Elizabeth Taylor in London* made by CBS TV and screened on the BBC in

Britain. Although the melodies were similar to the titles included on the sound-track album by the Johnny Spence orchestra, both Barry versions featured piano solos. [Further details of this score can be found in the television section.] Unlike 'Elizabeth', the last of the Ember singles, 'Zulu Stamp' and 'Monkey Feathers', was packaged in an attractive picture sleeve. Both tracks were beat versions of traditional Zulu themes taken from the film. Ember also issued an EP coupling both of these sides with two Bond titles – and later, the complete soundtrack album of *Zulu*.

The John Barry Seven around 1965. From the back: Dave Green, Terry Childs, Ernie Cox, Stan Haldane, Ron Menicos, Mike O'Neil, Alan Bown.

CHAPTER 11

THE NEW JOHN BARRY SEVEN

By October, 1963, Barry had been able to put together a new band, helped by the acclaimed session drummer Bobby Graham. Graham had taken over the leadership at Barry's request and he recalled that JB was determined to resurrect the Seven to cash in on the lucrative bookings they were still attracting at universities and colleges. Graham had a good pedigree in the pop world. He was a member of Joe Brown's Bruvvers and Mary Wilde's Wilde Cats before moving into regular session work. He recalls how difficult it was to get to see Barry, even at this early stage of his career; all appointments had to be negotiated through his redoubtable secretary, Miss Ackers. When the two did get to meet, they would spend hours listening to Stan Kenton records, for both were huge fans. Graham, in fact, had one of the biggest collections of Kenton's music in the world. At this point, the band consisted of Graham (drums), Dave Richmond (bass guitar), Ron Edgeworth (keyboards), Ray Russell (lead guitar), Terry Childs (baritone sax), Bob Downes (tenor sax) and Alan Bown (trumpet).

Dave Richmond came from a jazz background, and until shortly before joining the band he had played exclusively on double bass. It was during a short stint with the Mann-Hugg Blues Band that he injured his hand; he switched to bass guitar, and stayed with the band when it became Manfred Mann, playing on their first hit '5-4-3-2-1' before being encouraged to join the JB7 by Bob Downes. He especially remembers the band promoting its single 'Zulu Stamp' at gigs, though he confirms that only Bob Graham played on the recording. During his fairly brief stay he never met John Barry, though once he chose to concentrate on sessions he worked with him regularly on James Bond film score recordings.

Ray Russell got his job after reading in *Melody Maker* that Vic Flick was about to leave in order to concentrate on sessions. He took the day off work to go to an audition as his replacement planned for a huge cinema in Archway, North London. He arrived early to check out the opposition, but miraculously, no other guitarists arrived. For some reason the band could not get into the auditorium, so rather than waste the morning, Bob Downes volunteered to crawl into the pay kiosk in the foyer and plug Ray's amp into a socket. So it was that shoppers and passers-by were treated to the sound of Ray's Burns Vibra-Sonic blasting through his Burns Orbit III amp in the lobby of their local cinema. A lot of music parts were spread out, and Ray, still only 16 years old, seemed to sail through them without a problem. The guys were so impressed by his apparent reading ability that they asked him to join them there and then, and he was a full member of the band when, four months later, they had to learn some new material. This was the moment of truth: he could not read a word of music. A week before his audition, Ray had bought every record John Barry had made, and played the tunes over and over on his Dansette record player until he knew every note. He had to own up, but bass player Dave Richmond kindly helped him learn all about 'the dots'. The reformed JB7 made its début at the Locarno Ballroom, Coventry, and according to the publicity blurb, featured three of its personnel as a vocal trio.

After only a few months, Ray Styles was recruited to replace Dave Richmond on bass guitar and Tony Ashton came in for Ron Edgeworth on piano and vocals. Bob Graham has fond memories of Tony Ashton. During one gig the band was playing its usual James Bond medley, which culminated in an energetic drum solo from Graham during which the other guys left the stage. He was putting everything into it when he gradually became aware of laughter from the audience, rather than the customary sustained applause. He redoubled his efforts, but to no avail. No wonder. When he glanced behind him, there was Tony Ashton cycling around the stage with a broom balanced on his nose!

After only a year, Graham, like Flick and Richmond before him, decided to concentrate on ever-increasing session work – he played on all the Dave Clark Five records, for instance, a mind-boggling claim to fame. Alan Bown then took over as leader of the JB7, with only Terry Childs remaining with him from the Graham-led band. Bown had joined the original line-up in '62, following the death of Bobby Carr. He had a jazz background and was a member of the London South Jazz Orchestra that was gigging at the Richmond Jazz Festival when he was spotted by Len Black, a member of John Barry's agency. Bown was keen to book the new band into a studio and the result was the single '24 Hours Ago', the first JB7 vocal since Barry's efforts seven years previously. It featured new vocalist Mike O'Neil, who doubled on keyboards, and apart from Bown and Childs, the line-up was Dave Green (tenor-sax), Stan Haldane (bass guitar), Ernie Cox (drums) and Ron Menicos (lead guitar). Green and Cox were both ex-members of the Flintstones.

'24 Hours Ago' leaned a lot towards the style of Georgie Fame with its gritty R 'n' B feel – a deliberate ploy, according to Alan Bown. The band reverted to the instrumental format on the flip-side; the sax-dominated 'Seven Faces' was an attempt by writers Bown and Keith Mansfield to capture and yet update the Barry sound. Unfortunately, the disc was given only minimal publicity by EMI, and failed to make any impact. This was the very last single made by the Seven, but they continued to tour extensively until early 1966. They included a fair number of vocals in the act, including cover versions of records by Curtis Mayfield and The Impressions. According to Bown, Barry still took a keen interest and would often be watching

The re-formed John Barry Seven in late 1963. From the left: Ray Styles, Tony Ashton, Ray Russell, Bob Graham, Terry Childs, Bob Downes, Alan Bown. The club-owner is in the foreground.

from the sidelines at concerts. He particularly remembers an occasion when they were accompanying Marty Wilde, who had persuaded them to indulge in a few dance step routines in the style of the Shadows with Cliff Richard. The early Seven had done much the same thing, but now Barry was furious, and during the interval he made them and Marty aware, in no uncertain terms, that it must never happen again.

Bown recalls that when the JB7 was in Hamburg in around 1965, it had just played a date with Brenda Lee. They approached her manager, who was a little reluctant to hand over their promised bonuses, and when they persisted he pulled a gun on them.

On another occasion, back in the UK but still supporting Brenda, they were in a motorway café when she was recognised by some of the customers. A lorry driver approached her for an autograph, only to be sent rudely away by the manager. Shortly afterwards, the manager went to the washroom, to be followed by the driver and several of his friends. He wore dark glasses for the rest of the tour.

The John Barry Seven circa 1964.
Top row from left: Ray Styles,
Ray Russell, Terry Childs,
second row from left: Bob Downes,
Tony Ashton, Alan Bown.
Lying on floor: Bob Graham.

The John Barry Seven circa 1963. Top row from left: Ray Russell, Dave Richmond, Bob Graham, Ron Edgeworth, Terry Childs. Bottom row from left, Bob Downes and Alan Bown.

The John Barry Seven in '65 on the
Brenda Lee tour.

There was one more change to the line-up when Mike O'Neil was replaced on keyboards/vocals by Jeff Bannister, who became a close friend of Bown. Bown was disappointed when Barry gave him three months' notice that he intended to disband the group for good, as bookings were still very solid at venues such as winter gardens, hotels, universities and colleges. He is convinced they would still be performing up to the present day and making a good living had the Seven continued. As it was, he quickly formed the Alan Bown Set, which included Stan Haldane, Jeff Bannister and Dave Green from the remains of the group. Although they were able to take over many of the JB7's regular bookings, the money was not the same.

Alan Bown leads the last line-up of
the JB7 in 1966. From the left: Ernie
Cox (drums), Jeff Bannister
(keyboards/vocals), Dave Green
(tenor-sax), Alan Bown (trumpet),
Ron Menicos (lead guitar), Stan
Haldane (bass guitar), Terry Childs
(alto-sax).

CHAPTER 12

INDEPENDENT PRODUCTIONS AND FILM SCORES

Barry's agreement with Ember allowed him to make film sound track recordings for other labels, and this coincided with the start of his long relationship with the James Bond films. United Artists released both the films and the music, and, although Barry had no connection with the *Dr No* soundtrack album, apart from the main theme, he was responsible for the albums for *From Russia With Love* and *Goldfinger*. The latter also spawned a UA single and EP released in Barry's name, while there was an EP from the former, alongside the Ember single.

His deal with Ember also let him form his own record production company. Among discs he produced in this period were releases by Alan Haven, the Countdowns and A Band Of Angels, Mike d'Abo's first group. All were issued on the United Artists label, with limited success. Barry's relationship with d'Abo's group grew out of a chance encounter at a London concert. A Band Of Angels had been formed by five friends at Harrow School in 1960, and d'Abo recalls they were all 15 or 16 at the time; he himself was born in 1944. The original members of the band were d'Abo on piano/vocals, James Rugge-Price, drums, David Wilkinson, bass, Johnny Baker, lead guitar and Johnny Gaydon, rhythm guitar/vocals. Up to that time the only modern music heard in the school came from jazz groups, and A Band Of Angels was the first school group to play in the speech room before the occasional film shows there. They did mainly covers of current hits by such as the Shadows, Duane Eddy and Cliff Richard; d'Abo vividly remembers singing 'The Young Ones'. The band became very popular, mainly by word of mouth among their fellow scholars, and played several dates on the London débutante circuit. This was usually for £10 or £15 a time, though on one memorable night they got £25. Mike d'Abo was by this time also playing vibes.

Leaving Harrow, d'Abo and Johnny Baker went to Cambridge University to study theology and maths respectively. At the time d'Abo had thoughts of entering the Church, but soon changed his mind, switching to economics, but after failing his first year exams he was sent down. He soon found work with a subsidiary of Boosey and Hawkes – Rudell Carte of Denman Street, Soho, who specialised in musical

Below: A Band of Angels.

instruments. While Baker continued at Cambridge, Rugge and Wilkinson were working for the London underwriters Lloyds, so it was not hard for the band to continue to play the deb. circuit and clubs in the evenings and at weekends. They were such a hit that you were a social outcast if you didn't hire them for your private party or ball; it was simply the thing to do, darling. Among this round of exclusive engagements was the annual 'Shake' at Kensington Town Hall. This was the social event of the year, and d'Abo believes they played it three times.

Their first recording contract came about in 1964, when John Barry, very much the man-about-town, turned up at the Town Hall with his friends Michael Caine, Terence Stamp and David Warner. He liked what he heard, and asked the band if they would be interested in recording for him for a company he was thinking of setting up independently of Ember. Barry had in fact already been given the go-ahead for this project by Jeffrey Kruger, and A Band Of Angels was his first signing. He already knew Noel Rogers of United Artists Music, and the band's first recordings were for this company. Mike d'Abo well remembers the sessions for this first single, which consisted of 'Me' coupled with 'Not True As Yet', both composed by the new song-writing partnership of d'Abo and Baker. They took place at the old Olympic Studios in London, with d'Abo the only band member to touch an instrument on the session, playing piano and duetting with Johnny Gaydon on vocals. Barry explained to the band that he knew he could get the sound he wanted with certain session players, who included the former JB7 leader Bobby Graham on drums and Big Jim Sullivan on lead guitar. The idea was for d'Abo to supply the secondary vocals, but in the end Barry turned his voice up and Gaydon's down, thus effectively reversing their roles.

The band then turned professional after an offer from their new manager John Coast, who also managed Nina and Frederik and Marlene Deitrich. Only Rugge was not interested in going professional, and as a result he was replaced on drums by Andy Petrie. Coast occupied an office in Knightsbridge, above which was housed United Artists music publishers and in particular Noel Rogers, the British head of the company. Together with publicist Rex Berry and John Coast, Barry set about creating an image for the band, playing on their up-market background and their name. They were dressed in natty mohair suits, for instance, and photographed by the up-and-coming Gered Mankowitz. They were playing regularly at the London night spots Brads and the Ad-Lib, the latter being just about the hottest spot in town. One time d'Abo spotted the Beatles and their wives and girlfriends in the audience, and the band quickly switched to playing Fab Four hits. They were later asked to join the Beatles for a drink, during which time d'Abo did his best to chat up Jane Asher. This was an act of some audacity, since at the time she was famous not for advertising biscuits but as the luckiest girl in the whole, wide world, the widely predicted future Mrs Paul McCartney.

The Angels made a film with several other stars of the day, *Just For You*, as well as appearing on all the big TV pop shows. Mike d'Abo remembers an appearance on *Thank Your Lucky Stars*, when it became clear that some of the other groups looked down on them because of their privileged background; thinking they could not be taken seriously musically because they did not have to perform for a living. 'All the other groups were spending money on new homes for their parents, but our parents were already well off and didn't need our money,' d'Abo recalls. It was at that point that he became even more determined to succeed, because for him the music was the most important thing. The band made two or three discs under its UA contract, and d'Abo believes that Barry was involved in the first two. He regularly phoned d'Abo, using him as the group contact, even though he was not the leader, and began to lose a little interest only when his film career took off. Mike recalls Barry being very 'cool' and laid-back, always surrounded by beautiful women. At this point JB had divorced his first wife and had yet to meet Jane Birkin, whose brother was coincidentally at Harrow with d'Abo. As for the Angels, the UA contract did not produce much record success, and in 1965 they acquired a new manager and signed for Decca, effectively ending their relationship with Barry.

Barry was now heavily involved in writing music for films. Despite this, from the mid-sixties to the early seventies he signed recording contracts with CBS and Polydor to make both singles and compilation albums, details of which can be found later in this book. For now, however, we concentrate on film soundtracks – starting with the mysterious world of 007.

CHAPTER 13

JAMES BOND

Noel Rogers, head of the publishing arm of United Artists Music in London, telephoned Barry one evening to ask him to work on the arrangement of the main title theme for the film Dr No, then about to finish production. According to Barry, after accepting the job he was given only a few days to arrange and record the main theme with his Seven plus an orchestra.

In an interview with film music writer Royal S. Brown, Barry said the call from Noel Rogers came on a Friday evening. Rogers explained that the producers weren't entirely happy with the arrangement of Monty Norman's original theme, so would he call and meet with the two of them at United Artists in the morning to discuss how he could become involved? Rogers stressed that the situation was urgent, with the theme needed by the following Wednesday. Barry knew very little about the James Bond scenario but was keen to further his experience in the world of films. The following morning, after he heard what Norman had written, he told Rogers the only way he felt he could help was if he was given a free hand to make whatever changes he considered necessary. He wanted the theme to be more in keeping with the type of material he was then recording. Barry went on to say that he had worked on the tune during a weekend, without seeing even a rough-cut of the film, using the style of Henry Mancini's 'Peter Gunn' and Nelson Riddle's 'Untouchables'. Also somewhere in there was a reference to one of his own compositions, 'Bees Knees', which had a similar plucked guitar intro. Barry explained that the orchestra for the recording consisted of five saxes, nine brass, solo guitar, a rhythm section and no strings. He agreed a fee of just £200 for his work on the theme, plus the rights to make a single of it for Columbia. Barry's version of events was confirmed by the film's director, Terence Young, who added that Norman originally wanted to use 'Underneath The Mango Tree' as the theme for the whole series.

Monty Norman has only rarely publicly volunteered his side of the story, but in a letter to the authors in 1989, his version differs crucially from Barry's: 'I had written the music and lyrics of a theatre musical called Belle, and one of the main backers of the show was Cubby Broccoli. He called me to his office to meet his partner Harry Saltzman, and they offered me the score of their new film called Dr No. I didn't know too much about the subject at the time, but it sounded intriguing – and there was also a trip to Jamaica thrown in! In Jamaica I wrote all the local atmosphere music, such as "Underneath The Mango Tree", "Three Blind Mice Calypso", "Jamaican Jump Up" and other sections of the movie that could be written "wild" [without the final timings]. Back in London, I wrote the remainder of the score. There was a suggestion that "Underneath The Mango Tree" should be over the titles, but everyone agreed there didn't appear to be much mileage beyond *Dr No* for that particular song. At the same time, I rejected my first stab at a James Bond theme [the number is still in the film called "Dr No's Fantasy"]. I then suggested to Cubby and Harry that I go into the studio and record a number I had just finished writing, to see if they liked it. It was a number that I felt had the right character reference and atmosphere for James Bond. Incidentally, as so often happens with composers, I had written the main melodic theme two years earlier in a different context, for an aborted project. It became "The James Bond Theme". I approached John Burgess, the record producer, who loved the piece, and he suggested John Barry for the orchestration. I worked with John Barry on what I wanted: a rhythmic sustained sound for the opening four-bar figure; low octave guitar for my main melodic theme; big band for the hard-riding middle section, etc. The two Johns did brilliantly! Barry, a superb arrangement, and Burgess an equally superb recording. John Barry's recording became an enormous hit, and even though there have been many excellent recordings since, it's still, to my mind, the definitive "sound" for the number.'

While no one, above all the authors of this book, can dispute Monty Norman's writing input, it is worth recounting a few other recollections of the period. Vic Flick, the lead guitarist on the original session, believes that producer Broccoli had liked the first few bars of the Norman theme, but was not too enamoured of its development, which explains why it was handed over to Barry for 'rearranging'. 'The original theme was scored an octave higher. It was written as a first-line E in the treble clef [2nd fret, fourth string],' says Vic. 'I suggested to John that it would have a more ominous feel if I played it down the octave, starting on the sixth string. We tried it, and it turned out to be very effective.'

This account tends to be confirmed by the memories of Peter Hunt, the editor on the film. He discussed with film music writer Alexander Gleason how Barry came on the scene, and their subsequent work together: 'Terence [Young] had directed the film as best he could, but they'd had dreadful weather in Jamaica, they couldn't shoot all the things they wanted and the rushes came back in a terrible state. I thought "Well, I'm an experienced editor, now, and I think I know what I'm doing," so I got to work on it. Thank goodness for Terence. He gave me a lot of encouragement and if I felt I wanted to do something outrageous in the editing he was the first to say "great terrific – do some more like that". So we got things into shape.

'Monty Norman was a great friend of Harry Saltzman, and Harry wanted him for the music. He'd never done a film score before, he was a songwriter, really, and a very good one. So Monty and his wife flew out to Jamaica and he recorded masses of Caribbean music – rhythms, drums, anything he could come across. Anyway, finally the film is finished, and by the grace of God we've got the whole thing hanging together. It's starting to cause a bit of a stir even in the cynical cutting rooms. Everyone who's seen it loves it, and the producers really think they've got a hit on their hands. So we come to the music, we go through all the musical requirements with Monty Norman, we give him all the timings and cues and so on, and we think we can manage about two sessions with an orchestra to record it in – we're quite short of money by this points, remember – a morning and afternoon, and maybe we could manage an extra hour or so if absolutely necessary, just to finish everything off.

'So we start the first session and the music comes up – there's just myself, a couple of assistants and the mixer there. Well, it just doesn't seem to fit the pictures, somehow. Anyway, Terence arrives a little late and says: "How's it going, boys?" "Well," I say, "I think we'd better have a little talk. I really don't think it's working." So we play a couple of the cues back and then Monty does another session, and then Terence says: "Oh lor, it's mining disaster music!" I've never forgotten that! Anyway, we had to complete the session, but Terence goes away to consult with the producers, and the decision is made to scrap the second session and put a brake on the whole thing. The score was very good in its own right, but just not quite appropriate for the film as we saw it. So anyway, we are now presented with the problem of what to do next. Do we use what we have, readjust it in some way?

'Terence says to me that he thinks we've got to bring someone else in on this, and starts talking about William Walton and Arthur Bliss. He always thought big! So it's off to see Saltzman and Broccoli, and I drive up with my young assistant Ben, and I'm wondering who on earth we can get to buck up this music. They're obviously going to want us to come up with a few names, and I'm not sure I know anyone who can fill in at a moment's notice. Anyway, I remember young Ben telling me he's seen a film or documentary with John Barry and his Seven, and he'd said he thought Barry was a great musician. I'd heard some of his music myself so when we were finally in the office and everyone was talking away and names were being thrown around – not available, too expensive, not right for this kind of movie – I finally threw into the pot "What about this John Barry?" "Yeah, good idea," says Saltzman. He picks up the phone and barks "Francine, get John Barry on the phone." Well, it must have gone through agents and contacts and so forth, but in a matter of days we had John Barry on *Dr No* – as simple as that.

'John Barry was relatively new to film scoring, and I really had to take him by the hand and show him the ropes, but he took to it all quite quickly. Now, Monty Norman had done a James Bond theme of sorts, but John didn't like it very much, and I said "Well, you know, it's not a bad tune, really," and we had a long discussion about it. You must remember we had long discussions about everything, because John was still very new to the game. Anyway, he finally said "Well, I'll use it, but I'd like it to be something else, with a new arrangement, a guitar, different accompaniment and so forth." So I said fine, let's go ahead, because we didn't have much time by now. We set up another session and completely redid the score, and it worked like a dream. From then on we've been great friends, and he's gone on to do marvellous things and we always enjoy working together. We worked on all the early Bond films, and in all modesty I think the finest score he ever did was for my film *On Her Majesty's Secret Service* – a great, great score.'

Nowadays, when questioned about the theme, Barry's standard reply is: if he had not written it, why was he later asked to write all the others? It seems a reasonable point. What is certain is that the finished article remains a classic. John Burgess remembered producing the Columbia single – indeed, he was producing all Barry's output at that time. It was recorded at Abbey Road, and he recalls how fastidious Barry was in arranging the orchestra before the recording, giving special attention to the trumpets and trombones to get the sound he wanted. Vic Flick recalls using an f-hole Clifford Essex acoustic guitar with a DeArmond pick-up. He also used his faithful Fender Vibrolux amplifier: 'The guitar was played with a plectrum for that very hard, clacky tone, and fairly near the bridge, but not so near that the tone of the string died. I hit it very hard for an urgent, almost over-played sound.'

Barry's single was issued to coincide with the release of the film, and was a huge success in the UK. Depending on which chart is used, it peaked at either nine or 13 and spent nearly three months there. He wasn't exactly thrilled when after paying to see the film, he found the theme had not only been used over the titles but in various places throughout the movie. That said, Rogers was able to assure him that his contribution had been appreciated, and would be borne in mind by the producers when it came to further films in the series. So it proved when it came to *From Russia With Love*.

The John Barry Seven and Orchestra single was issued only in mono, primarily because in 1962 stereo was still relatively new and confined mainly to albums. Barry coupled 'The James Bond Theme' with 'The Blacksmith Blues', on which he reverted to his policy of reviving big sellers from yesteryear. Stereo versions of both were made, however, and can be found on EMI's *John Barry – The EMI Years Volume 3*.

Broccoli and Saltzman were obviously impressed by Barry's work on *Dr No*, and after his disappointment at the lack of credit he received for it, they made sure he was involved right from the start of *From Russia With Love*. He recalls meeting Lotte Lenya, Ian Fleming and Robert Shaw at Pinewood, and then being flown out to Istanbul with Broccoli, Saltzman, Sean Connery and director Terence Young. In a conversation with John Williams, editor of *Music From The Movies*, Terence Young looked back to those early days of the series: 'John Barry came into our lives when we were making *Dr No*. We had someone else doing the music and although the score was all right, we didn't have anything exciting for the title music. I think it was someone at Chappell who said you must listen to him. He had a little band called the John Barry Seven, and he came in and wrote this Bond theme.

'Then, I don't know why, they were awfully wary about him. They thought he was too young and inexperienced in film music, and I had a little bit to do with his finally doing *From Russia With Love*. Somebody wanted Lionel Bart to do the music. Lionel came into my life a few years earlier when I chose a song of his for a film I was making, *Serious Charge*. The song was called 'Living Doll', and of course it is still around today. I said that if John Barry was inexperienced, then so was Lionel, and I think we owe it to John to give him a chance. Harry Saltzman, I think, was keen on Lionel Bart, and I must say I was, too. I liked him very much, but I couldn't see why they were doing John down because of his inexperience. If they had taken someone like Williamson, who was one of the classical composers, it would have made more sense. Cubby Broccoli was on my side and in the end it was two to one. I think Cubby was the decider we should go with John. In the meantime, I think Harry had committed himself to Lionel Bart, and that's why Lionel wrote 'From Russia With Love', which was a charming song.

'I was running the film in French for some students recently and my God, the music is awfully good. In fact there are a couple of scenes in it where he's pinched the music for the rest of the Bond series. There's a big action scene, when there's a shoot-out at a gypsy camp, and I've heard that played in other Bond films, because it's very exciting. It's the best Bond film. Dilys Powell said that when she talked to her fellow film critics about the Bond films, that's the one they remembered. She analysed it by saying it was the best story he ever wrote, the only book by Ian Fleming you could read without thinking you were reading down a little bit. It's a very well written book, very exciting characters, and she said the film was so well cast. Apart from Sean Connery, who was then getting into the skin of Bond, there was Pedro Armendariz, Robert Shaw and of course Daniela Bianchi, who was extremely attractive. Anyway, it worked, and that was the main thing. John Barry is a marvellous guy. I admire him enormously.'

As Young indicated, to a certain extent the producers played safe by securing the services of the noted songwriter Lionel Bart to compose the main title theme, but the original music was the first of many Bond scores written by John Barry. The producers were not convinced about the suitability of a vocal version of the title theme to be played over the opening credits, so Barry again found himself with a main theme he hadn't written, but which he needed to rearrange to fit in with the opening titles and credits sequence. Still without a Bond theme of his own, Barry decided to introduce us to '007' as an alternative action theme, possibly not wishing forever to use 'The James Bond Theme' in view of Norman's writing credit. He was apparently very fond of '007', and as Young pointed out, he used it again in several later Bond films.

The soundtrack album contained most of the important music from the film and included a splendid track entitled 'The Golden Horn', which was not used in the movie. Matt Monro was chosen to sing the theme, and this was first heard briefly a few minutes into the film, as background radio music. It is heard again, though, in almost complete form, as the end credits roll. The highlights of the album included 'Girl Trouble', 'Leila Dances', '007' and 'Gypsy Camp'. Many of these were illuminated by excellent guitar work from Vic Flick, now a prized session player after leaving the John Barry Seven.

Goldfinger is without doubt Barry's favourite of all the Bond scores, and he has often said how he believes he caught the mood of the action. It contained the most internationally successful title song to date, sung by Shirley Bassey. It reached only number 21 during a nine-week stay on the UK best seller lists but scored heavily elsewhere, including number one in Japan in June, 1965. Interestingly, Bassey's single featured a slightly different vocal from that on the soundtrack album. Subtle differences can easily be detected in her phrasing of the words and also on the play-out, where she holds the note on 'gold' far longer on the single than on the album track. Bassey has surprisingly claimed to loath performing 'Goldfinger' in concert.

Having finally been given the responsibility of writing the theme song, Barry invited Tony Newley and Leslie Bricusse to compose the lyrics. Bricusse and Newley had known Barry for some time, though they had not worked together professionally. Barry had been a frequent visitor to Bricusse's restaurant, The Pickwick Club, along with his friends Michael Caine and Terence Stamp, and the group of them used to have lunch there most Fridays. In his recent biography, Caine revealed that while temporarily lodging in Barry's flat, he was kept awake one night by JB composing at the piano. In the morning, Barry played him the finished piece, which turned out to be the theme for *Goldfinger*!

Barry said 'Goldfinger' was the craziest song ever: 'I went to Tony Newley to ask him to write the lyric. He said what the hell could he do with it? I said it was "Mack The Knife" – a song about a villain. Tony was able to go with that, and the end result worked just perfectly.' In fact Newley and co-writer Leslie Bricusse at first dumbfounded Barry after he played them the opening bars of 'Goldfinger' by jokingly singing the next line as 'Wider than a mile' – the second line of Henry Mancini's 'Moon River'. Happily, there were never any plagiarism writs from Hank!

Although sales of the soundtrack album were steady in the UK, they were sensational in America. There, 'Goldfinger' succeeded in knocking the Beatles' 'A Hard Day's Night' from the top of the album charts, winning Barry his first gold disc for over a million dollars in sales. It sold two millions' worth in six months, was number one for sixteen consecutive weeks and stayed high in the US charts for 70 weeks. The score also won a Grammy nomination. The US album contained less music than the UK release, omitting 'Golden Girl', 'Death of Tilley', 'The Laser Beam' and 'Pussy Galore's Flying Circus'. Unlike the UK release, however, it did include the instrumental version of the main theme, which had been released as a single both in Britain and America. The CD reissue disappointingly stuck to the American format, but completists were able to pick up the missing tracks by buying the double CD *The Best Of James Bond 30th Anniversary*.

For *Thunderball*, the fourth film in the Bond series, the

John Barry with his gold disc for *Goldfinger*, in 1965.

producers realised from the outset that *Goldfinger* would be a difficult act to follow. They had already started introducing more and more gimmicks into the movies, and for this outing they felt it a good idea to do away with the usual title song. *Thunderball* was thought to be a lyrical banana skin, in any case. Instead, they decided to use the name by which Bond had become known in Italy and Japan – 'Mr Kiss Kiss Bang Bang'. Accordingly, Barry based the entire score around this title song, which had lyrics written solely by Leslie Bricusse, Tony Newley being in America at the time. The Bond team had even chosen the singer, Dionne Warwick, who produced her own arrangement after Shirley Bassey's original version had failed to impress. Barry takes up the story: 'Dionne's was a marvellous song and she did a great arrangement for it. It was a really strange song. I had about 12 cowbells on it with different rhythms, along with a large orchestra, and thought it a very original piece. Then, at the last minute, they got cold feet and decided to have a song called 'Thunderball'.' The official reason given for the change of mind was that a song with the title 'Mr Kiss Kiss Bang Bang' could have been too overtly sexy for American tastes. Another reason might have been a threat from Bassey to sue following her replacement by Warwick. Obviously if the song was not used at all, there could be no case to answer.

Whatever the reason, it led to Barry's long partnership with lyricist Don Black, as by the time the decision to change the song had been taken, Bricusse had also gone to work in America. Don Black was born in Hackney, London in 1938, the youngest of five children. His father worked as a tailor, and although the family was by no means affluent, he enjoyed a happy and stable childhood. This was a music loving family: 'In one room my mother might be singing "Besame Mucho", while in another, father would be singing a Paul Robeson song. Meanwhile, my sister might be playing "Legend Of The Glass Mountain" on the piano, and my brother would be listening to a Sarah Vaughan record.' Words, too, had fascinated him from an early age, and he recalls constantly asking the meaning of every one new to him.

The cinema was another love. An early memory was of a family visit to *The Al Jolson Story*. It created such an impact on the impressionable youngster that he was to return to see the movie more than 30 times. After leaving school, his first job was at the London Palladium, where he took on the 'bread and butter' tasks expected of a raw recruit, from polishing brass to ushering customers to their seats. Unhappily, it was noted that he spent too much time watching the shows, and he was asked to leave. Showbiz had clearly taken a hold, however, and after a stint on the *New Musical Express*, first as an office boy and eventually as a show reviewer, he went on to an ambitious yet very short-lived career as a stand-up comedian. 'Comedy', Don would later admit, 'was in my blood – if not always in my act.' Wisely, he moved on and found a niche in the publishing world of Tin Pan Alley. He worked as a song plugger for established names such as David Toff and Joe 'Mr Piano' Henderson, and it was his Denmark Street location that brought about his first meeting with John Barry, some of whose early compositions were published by Mills Music and Campbell Connelly. A closer relationship developed when he moved to Harold

Shampan's Filmusic, the company responsible for plugging some of Barry's first movie themes. By this time Black was already writing his first lyrics, one of which, 'Heart of Stone', was recorded by Al Saxon and was often included by Cliff Richard in his stage shows around 1959.

Black also encountered Matt Monro, a session singer not long out of driving buses, who had performing aspirations of his own. In fact Monro not only sang many of the songs plugged by Black, but encouraged him to develop his own lyric writing skills. One early example, 'April Fool', written with Al Saxon, was later recorded by Monro. Black's first lyrical success turned out to be 'Walk Away', originally the Austrian entry for the 1964 Eurovision Song Contest. Monro admired the melody but needed it in English. 'You're always on about words – have a go, son,' Monro urged. The rest, as they say, is history. A lifelong friendship developed which was firmly cemented when Black became Monro's manager and ended only with the singer's untimely death in 1985. After this early success, perhaps it is no wonder that John Barry encouraged Black to try writing for films.

When director Terence Young heard 'Thunderball' for the first time, he said it sounded more like 'Thunderfinger'. Barry's laughing reply was to the effect that 'I gave them what they wanted'. It was obviously far too late for him to alter the main thrust of his score, and as a result, 'Mr Kiss Kiss' can be heard throughout the film and to a large extent on the soundtrack album. Tom Jones was chosen to sing the title song, and gave a bravura performance at the recording session. According to Don Black, he put so much into his vocal that he collapsed after holding the final note for the last few vital seconds. Strangely, a different arrangement of 'Mr Kiss Kiss Bang Bang' turned up in instrumental form on mono copies of American issues of the album. All other releases carry a more traditional arrangement with a full orchestra. Buyers of *The Best Of James Bond 30th Anniversary* double CD can hear both Shirley Bassey's and Dionne Warwick's original vocal versions of 'Mr Kiss Kiss Bang Bang', but not the instrumental, which remains unreleased on CD.

You Only Live Twice, Sean Connery's last outing as Bond for the time being, marked a fairly radical change of direction for John Barry's music score. By now he was an accepted member of the Bond team and expected to conjure up something different for each new film while retaining the familiar sound he had established. This film gave him a welcome opportunity to do just that, by exploiting through music a plot that ranged from Bond's venture into space to his 'marriage'. After limited success with Tom Jones's resounding 'Thunderball' vocal, Barry chose a much gentler, romantic melody on which to base the theme song. He teamed up again with lyricist Leslie Bricusse to produce a beautiful number which was sung over the opening credits by Nancy Sinatra. Years later, the appearance on the *30th Anniversary* double CD of a completely different song entitled 'You Only Live Twice – Demo' raised a few questions. The vocal is by an unnamed female session singer, with Barry and Bricusse credited as writers. Leslie Bricusse confirmed that this was their first attempt at the title song, which they eventually discarded, but he could not recall the name of the singer.

For
Robin and Marian

Love is the greatest adventure of all.

COLUMBIA PICTURES and RASTAR PICTURES present

SEAN CONNERY **AUDREY HEPBURN** **ROBERT SHAW**

"ROBIN AND MARIAN"

A RICHARD LESTER FILM

NICOL WILLIAMSON

DENHOLM ELLIOTT   RONNIE BARKER
KENNETH HAIGH   IAN HOLM

and **RICHARD HARRIS** as Richard the Lionheart

A RAY STARK-RICHARD SHEPHERD Production • Music by JOHN BARRY • Executive Producer RICHARD SHEPHERD
Written by JAMES GOLDMAN • Produced by DENIS O'DELL
Directed by RICHARD LESTER

It's a hot summer.
Ned Racine is waiting for
something special to happen.

And when it does…

He won't be ready
for the consequences.

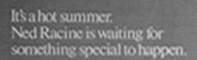

*As the temperature rises,
the suspense begins.*

"BODY HEAT" WILLIAM HURT   KATHLEEN TURNER
and RICHARD CRENNA Written and Directed by LAWRENCE KASDAN
Produced by FRED T. GALLO PANAVISION® TECHNICOLOR®

R A LADD COMPANY RELEASE

He's a Cowboy...She's a woman
He's the best at what he does.
So is she!

LEE MARVIN
in
"MONTE WALSH"
co-starring
JEANNE MOREAU
JACK PALANCE

Produced by HAL LANDERS and BOBBY ROBERTS
Screenplay by LUKAS HELLER and DAVID Z. GOODMAN
Based upon the novel by JACK SCHAEFER   Music by JOHN BARRY
"THE GOOD TIMES ARE COMIN'" Sung by MAMA CASS
Directed by WILLIAM A. FRAKER   PANAVISION® and
TECHNICOLOR®   A Landers-Roberts Production
A 20th CENTURY-FOX Release
A CINEMA CENTER FILMS Presentation

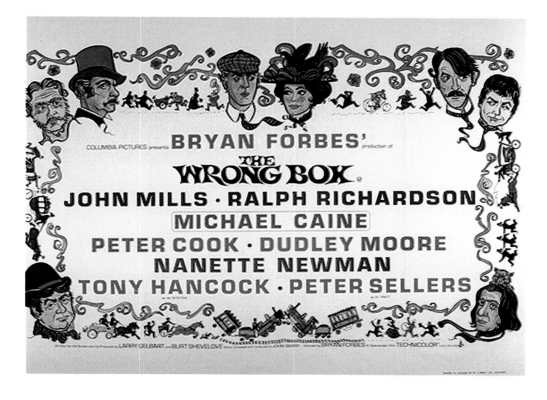

COLUMBIA PICTURES presents   BRYAN FORBES' production of
THE WRONG BOX
JOHN MILLS · RALPH RICHARDSON
MICHAEL CAINE
PETER COOK · DUDLEY MOORE
NANETTE NEWMAN
TONY HANCOCK · PETER SELLERS

...he played the most
dangerous game in Europe...
and he played it alone.

QUILLER

THE RANK ORGANISATION Presents

GEORGE SEGAL · ALEC GUINNESS · MAX VON SYDOW · SENTA BERGER

IVAN FOXWELL'S PRODUCTION
THE QUILLER MEMORANDUM

GUEST STARS
GEORGE SANDERS · ROBERT HELPMANN

Produced by IVAN FOXWELL · Screenplay by HAROLD PINTER · Music by JOHN BARRY · Directed by MICHAEL ANDERSON   COLOUR   PANAVISION

A JOURNEY THAT BEGINS WHERE EVERYTHING ENDS

THE BLACK HOLE

THE BLACK HOLE starring MAXIMILIAN SCHELL, ANTHONY PERKINS, ROBERT FORSTER, JOSEPH BOTTOMS and YVETTE MIMIEUX and ERNEST BORGNINE.
Music composed and conducted by JOHN BARRY, Production Designed by PETER ELLENSHAW, Director of Photography FRANK PHILLIPS, A.S.C.
Story by JEB ROSEBROOK and BOB BARBASH & RICHARD LANDAU Screenplay by JEB ROSEBROOK and GERRY DAY Produced by RON MILLER
Directed by GARY NELSON. A Walt Disney Production. Technicolor.

Graham Rye, the president and driving force behind the James Bond 007 International Fan Club, is not a man to be defeated by any Bond mystery, however, and after a few plays of the song he was convinced that the singer was Julie Rogers, best known in the UK for her hit 'The Wedding'. He was able to track down her manager and husband Michael Black – Don's elder brother – who immediately confirmed that Julie was indeed the uncredited singer. On learning the news, Julie was quick to point out that her recording was not intended for demo purposes only. On the contrary, she was chosen to sing the new Bond title theme on the strength of 'The Wedding'. As she points out: 'Successful TV and recording artists do not record demos!' Her song was recorded at CTS studios, Bayswater with Barry conducting a 60-piece orchestra. Julie believes that only late pressure from the producers resulted in Sinatra taking over.

Not that Sinatra was at first even second choice. Harry Saltzman brought in a musical advisor, over Barry's head, and he suggested Aretha Franklin. Barry felt her style wasn't suitable, and in the end the two producers decided on using Frank's girl, who had just topped the charts with 'These Boots Are Made For Walkin''. Asked about it later, she said: 'That was a scary experience. John, whose music I just treasure, wrote the song with Leslie Bricusse, who is an old friend of mine. Cubby Broccoli had known my mother and father for years – he'd been there when I was born. The London Philharmonic played on the session. Real pressure.' Pressure indeed. According to the composers, nerves got to Sinatra so badly that numerous takes were needed before a definitive recording was in the bag.

As usual, the score was recorded at the Bayswater studios of CTS, where Sid Margo acted as fixer for the sessions. The London Philharmonic, in reality, were session musicians brought together by Margo on this and many other occasions to record a Barry score. Margo had worked with Barry on his first film score, *Beat Girl*, and fixed (or hired) musicians for him nearly every time he worked in England right up until his retirement, shortly after the recording of *A View To A Kill*. Once he knew the size and structure of the orchestra needed by Barry, Margo would try to engage his regulars for film music sessions. These were tried and trusted musicians who were well used to working under pressure, and most had worked for Barry on many previous occasions.

The original soundtrack album provided its own curio in the form of differing final tracks for the British and American markets. While the British album contained 'Twice Is The Only Way To Live', an instrumental play-out of the main theme, the American release contained 'You Only Live Twice – End Title' (vocal by Nancy Sinatra), which is precisely what cinema audiences heard during the closing moments of the film. All later European reissues corrected the final track title to bring it in line with the American album, but the record itself still included the instrumental. More recently, EMI have issued the album on CD in America only, and on this occasion the credits and the music coincide to include the Sinatra vocal.

Although John Barry has often described *Goldfinger* as his favourite Bond music score, many Bond fans consider Barry's scoring reached its creative zenith with *On Her Majesty's Secret Service*. Certainly, the director, Peter Hunt, who had worked on all five previous Bond films, is on record as choosing this as his personal favourite. With Sean Connery temporarily missing from the title role, newcomer George Lazenby (fresh from the Frys chocolate commercial) stepped a trifle uneasily into his shoes. There is little doubt that had Connery remained, this movie would have ranked alongside *From Russia With Love* and *Goldfinger* as the definitive James Bond. Despite his absence, it remains the favourite of many a Bond fan, and John Barry's score is one of the outstanding features.

For the first time since *From Russia With Love*, an instrumental was used to accompany the opening titles – probably resolving the problem of fitting suitable lyrics around the rather cumbersome film title. Although Barry's most recent Bond theme collaborator, Leslie Bricusse, was convinced of his ability to write a suitable lyric, the decision to opt for an instrumental proved inspirational. The end result featured prominent use of fuzz-box infused guitar pyrotechnics and synthesizer, which acted as a complete contrast to Nancy Sinatra's romantic ballad from the previous Bond.

The film's screenplay was based on Fleming's story of Bond's romantic entanglement and eventual marriage to Tracy. To complement the courtship scenes Barry wrote a beautifully haunting melody with the working title 'We Have All The Time In The World', directly lifted from one of Fleming's own lines in the book. This combination of music and title provided Hal David with the skeletal framework around which a lyric could be constructed. Although he had only just left hospital after a long illness, Louis Armstrong was considered the ideal superstar to sing the finished song – at John Barry's suggestion: 'There was a line in the script, almost the last line, "We have all the time in the world", as his wife gets killed, which was also in Fleming's original novel, and I liked that as a title very much. Now I'd always liked Walter Houston singing "September Song" in the film *September Affair*, where as an older character he sang about his life in a kind of reflective vein. So I suggested to Cubby Broccoli and Harry Saltzman that Louis Armstrong would be ideal to sing our song in this fashion. Tragically, it was to be his last recording before his death. He was the sweetest man alive, but having been laid up for over a year, he had no energy left. He couldn't even play his trumpet, and still he summoned the energy to sing our song. At the end of the recording session in New York City he came up to me and said "Thank you for this job".'

Talking about the song recently, George Lazenby confessed to wanting Blood Sweat and Tears to perform it but with hindsight recognised that Armstrong was the right choice. The song was a huge hit in Italy, thanks, according to Barry, to a DJ based in Rome, who played it virtually non-stop for an entire evening. That sent it hurtling to Number One, where it remained for nine months. Barry recalls: 'Italy was the only country where we had any success with the song. It was a very heavy song, so we couldn't use it as the title track. It was buried inside the film, and that probably hurt its chances of success. The song was written for a very emotional moment. I'd pictured Sean Connery in the role of Bond when Hal and I first wrote the lyrics. If it had been Sean who married Diana Rigg and then lost her to Blofeld, then the song would have been beautiful and highly appropriate. Having Sean Connery and Diana Rigg together in the last scene would have really created a bombshell of a moment. With all due respect to the inexperience of George Lazenby, he couldn't have created a boiled egg in that last scene!'

A trifle harsh, perhaps, but those words suggest that Barry might well have written the song before he had even seen a rough cut. Since the film must have taken at least six months to complete, and Lazenby was sure to have been confirmed in the title role before shooting began, Barry's comments seem to indicate that he wrote the song when the producers were still hopeful of persuading Connery to continue. Alternatively, it could simply mean that on viewing the completed film, Barry was unable to function with Lazenby in mind as Bond, so instead imagined he was still working with Connery. If indeed the song was written well in advance of Barry viewing the final print, this might have been the only time he worked in this way on a Bond film.

Barry met Lazenby at the recording studios, and the actor did not endear himself to him when, obviously trying to be helpful, he really did suggest Blood Sweat and Tears for 'We Have All The Time In The World'. Barry told NME's Gavin Martin: 'He stood at the back and listened to the score for one of his scenes. He said to me "It fits!" I thought, "What do you think I do for a living? Christ, we've got a real brain going here, obviously." He said it as though it was the greatest compliment I could ever have hoped for.' There was clearly little chemistry between the two.

The lack of success for Armstrong's song outside Italy was remedied in England almost exactly 25 years later, when it was used for a television commercial for Guinness. Public demand saw EMI issue it as a single, coupled with Barry's 'OHMSS – Main Title', and it climbed to number three in the charts.

As with all his previous Bond scores, the music was recorded at CTS Studios, Bayswater – with the notable exception of Louis Armstrong's vocal. Armstrong was obviously far too weak to endure the long trip from America, and that is why Barry found himself using the A & R Studios in New York. This track was produced by Phil Ramone, who became responsible for the production of the entire album – an innovation in itself – since Barry had handled all the production chores in the past. Although the soundtrack album contained a large proportion of the music from the film, there were still many excellent cues that were not included. Bond's raid on Gumbold's office in Berne immediately springs to mind, together with the skating sequence towards the end of the film. More obvious omissions was the cue used to accompany Bond's romances with Ruby and Nancy, where flute-led melodic lines dominated. This was too good to waste, and was resurrected to appear on a subsequent Barry compilation album, Ready When You Are JB, rejigged and retitled 'Who Will Buy My Yesterdays?'

Another single was issued, 'Do You Know How Christmas Trees Are Grown?', sung by Nina, backed by 'The More Things Change'. Lyrics for both songs were also written by Hal David, but the latter did not appear in the film. 'Christmas Trees' was used as source music on two occasions – when Bond arrives in Switzerland and at the ice-rink.

Actor Charles Gray met an early death in *You Only Live Twice* in the guise of Dikko Henderson, Bond's initial contact in Japan, but he was reincarnated in the form of Ernst Stavro Blofeld for *Diamonds Are Forever*; the seventh film of the series. Sean Connery was persuaded back for a final appearance as James Bond after United Artists agreed to pay him the then record fee of a million dollars and promised to back two of his own future film projects. John Barry needed no such encouragement to work on his seventh Bond score, although afterwards he was reportedly furious with co-producer Harry Saltzman's low opinion of his theme song, performed by Shirley Bassey in her inimitable style.

The track was recorded at a special midnight session at CTS. According to Don Black, Saltzman thought the lines 'Hold one up and then caress it, touch it, stroke it and undress it' were 'dirty'. Barry, after questioning his competence to make such a critical analysis of the song, virtually threw him out of his Cadogan Square apartment. His anger with Saltzman even influenced his decision not to score *Live And Let Die*, the next film in the series; fortunately, others did not share the producer's reaction, since the song ended up winning an *Ivor Novello Award* for Barry and Black. As usual, Barry produced some moments of memorable music for the film score, particularly for the action scenes, but very few of these found their way on to the soundtrack album, a lot of which sounded more like Las Vegas mood music.

After missing Roger Moore's début as Bond the previous year, Barry, having honoured his commitment to the musical *Billy* – another reason he was not able to score *Live And Let Die* – was once again able to lend his considerable talents to an 007 film. In fact, after turning down many other film scoring opportunities because of *Billy*, he was now faced with a particularly heavy schedule, and perhaps found it hard to devote sufficient time to *The Man With The Golden Gun*. Apparently he wrote the complete score in just three weeks, and according to Don Black, he hated the title song they wrote together. Vocalist Lulu was not at her best at the recording session, either, with a sore throat, and the resultant single sold very poorly, one of the few Bond theme vocals to miss the charts completely. Barry's soundtrack was a reasonable reflection of the film action, and also included an excellent jazz-style version of the main theme, which didn't appear in the film. However, he seemed to be giving out signals that he was getting a little bored with James Bond. In the event, he was to take a break of five years before scoring *Moonraker*.

Barry's musical influence was badly missed on the 1977 Bond film *The Spy Who Loved Me*. His absence from this movie could be explained by his now permanent residence in America, and the tax problems that would have resulted from his setting foot again in Britain. His replacement, Marvin Hamlisch, wrote an excellent theme song, 'Nobody Does It Better', but the rest of his score did not match the requirements of a 1970s Bond film. It was rather surprising when it received an Oscar nomination – something not yet achieved by any of John Barry's Bond scores!

Thunderball supper party 29th December 1965.

Cubby Broccoli looks on from the control room as Barry conducts the orchestra for the recording of *You Only Live Twice* at CTS Studios, Bayswater, London.

Above: Nancy Sinatra with John Barry.

Right: John Barry and Hal David with Louis Armstrong in 1969.

Fortunately, with *Moonraker* shot partially in France, Barry was able to return and record the music at the Davout Studios in Paris. He brought Danny Wallin over with him to act as his supervising sound engineer, and also back for her third Bond title theme song was Shirley Bassey. For this number, Barry was reunited with Hal David, with whom he had worked on *On Her Majesty's Secret Service*, most notably on that beautiful ballad 'We Have All The Time In The World'. 'Moonraker' is another excellent, haunting song, performed by Bassey in her most sensual fashion, and it was a major surprise when the single failed to register in the charts. A much faster, almost disco-style, Bassey rendition of the song accompanied the end credits, and both versions formed the aforementioned single. With the label credits mistakenly reversed, there was doubtless considerable confusion caused to radio presenters.

The film's plot gave Barry another opportunity to experiment with space music, and he did not disappoint. Particularly memorable were 'Space Laser Battle' and 'Flight Into Space', the latter thankfully given a decent airing on the album, the track lasting in excess of six minutes. On this occasion Barry, unusually for a Bond score, uses a chorus, but this only adds to the effectiveness of the cue. Absent from the album is the version of 'The James Bond Theme' used to accompany 007's pre-credits free-fall drop from an aeroplane, which perfectly suited the action and showed how well the original arrangement has held up. Barry's 'Moonraker' melody crops up in instrumental mode in 'Miss Goodhead Meets Bond', where it acts as a

Above and left: Barry conducts the studio orchestra for the recording of *You Only Live Twice*.

Above and below: Barry conducts the studio orchestra for the recording of *You Only Live Twice.*

John Barry with recording engineer John Richards at the *You Only Live Twice* recording sessions at CTS Studios.

John Barry jokes with director Lewis Gilbert at the *You Only Live Twice* recording sessions.

John Barry gives notes to trumper players Greg Bowen, Leon Calvert and Ray Davies, at the *You Only Live Twice* recording sessions at CTS Studios.

John Barry with John Glen at the Royal Première of *A View To A Kill*.

John Barry at the Royal Première of *A View To A Kill*.

Laurie and John Barry with another guest at the Royal première of *A View To A Kill*.

love theme, and again in 'Bond Arrives In Rio' and 'Boat Chase', though the latter in part is scored with '007'. 'Bond Lured to Pyramid' is a typically wistful Barry theme, giving an appropriate air of intrigue to its scene, while 'Bond Smells a Rat' oozes with tension and menace.

The absence from the album of much of the action music one would associate with a Bond film is disappointing, as is the fact that it lasts only 31 minutes, but again the record gave proof of Barry's unique ability to capture the style and flavour of a Bond score. *Moonraker* was not a classic among Bond films, though Michael Lonsdale as Hugo Drax was a satisfyingly evil enemy, and delivered the classic line to Chang, his assistant: 'Look after Mr Bond. See that some harm comes to him.' Frank Sinatra, it is rumoured, was originally approached to sing the theme song, then known as 'Think Of Me', with lyrics by Paul Williams, but turned it down. It was then recorded by Johnny Mathis, but eventually dropped from the film.

It was on John Barry's recommendation that Bill Conti got the job of stepping into his conductor's shoes for *For Your Eyes Only* in 1981, when JB was unavailable. In 1983, however, he made the decision to return to England, where he not only chose to settle an outstanding tax bill, but bought a property to use as a London base, returning to Cadogan Square, where he had owned two flats in the sixties.

John Glen had started his long run as Bond director with *For Your Eyes Only*, but *Octopussy* was the first time he and Barry had worked together as director and composer. As he later told the film music writer John Williams, however, he had known Barry from many years previously: 'In the fifties, when I was a national serviceman stationed on the east coast of England, playing at the local town hall was the John Barry Seven. Later our paths were to cross again. As a film editor I was associated with John on several movies. I remember *On Her Majesty's Secret Service* particularly well, as this was my introduction to the "big time". John wrote a particularly memorable score for the ski chase sequence, using a Moog synthesizer, at that time a novel instrument. He was always searching for that unique sound, sometimes new and sometimes from an ethnic source. Of course, the search for the broken guitar that gave the Bond theme in *Dr No* such a great quality is legendary in Bond circles. Never to be repeated, as Vic Flick apparently threw it away. What else would a great guitarist do with a cracked guitar? John was lost to the Bond films for a number of years, and I was fortunate that he was able to return for three of the films I directed: *Octopussy*, *A View to A Kill* and *The Living Daylights*. As a director, what can one say

The Barrys at the Royal Première of *The Living Daylights*, 29th June 1987.

to John Barry about the music for a Bond film? His contribution to the success of the series has been enormous. His needs were always very simple. A piano, a Moviola and not very much time. Six weeks was about as long as he got. Bond films always had a pressing release date, and then there was always the title song.'

Most Bond theme songs match the title of the films, but this is not always possible. Such was the case in 1977, when although the words 'The Spy Who Loved Me' were cleverly incorporated in it, the theme song was actually 'Nobody Does It Better'. 'Octopussy' was considered entirely unsuitable for a song title when Barry and his new lyricist Tim Rice began work on the theme, and Barry had some unusual though shrewd advice for Rice. He told him that whatever he wrote, at least one of the film executives was sure to dislike it. The way to proceed was for him to write half a dozen songs, in which case the chances were that they would all like at least one of them. This is how it worked out, and 'All Time High' got the nod. For the singer, it was perhaps surprising that Rita Coolidge turned out to be flavour of the moment, since it had been more than five years since her last chart success in England with 'Words'. Not only that, only a few months before the recording took place, Cubby Broccoli had suggested publicly that Laura Branigan would be the chosen vocalist. However, the producers were convinced they had a standard on their hands, however, and wanted someone of the class and easy-listening style of Coolidge to perform it. They were right. The single reached only Number 75 in the UK charts, but it has since gone on to become an evergreen.

The music for 'A *View To A Kill*', Roger Moore's last outing as 007, was recorded as usual at CTS Studios in Wembley. Recording took place in March and April, 1985, although Duran Duran had already taped their vocals separately in America with the backing of their own instruments. When Barry arrived at CTS for the first session, his prime purpose was to add the backing of the full orchestra. The session lasted all day, with Barry first recording the orchestra conventionally before sections were isolated. At the beginning of April the main sessions took place, later recalled by cellist Andrea Hess, who had previously worked with Barry on *The Golden Seal* at Olympic Sound Studios in London: "Each day's sessions normally started with the fixer, Sid Margo, outlining the day's work. But sessions do suffer from a certain lack of communication at times, and although we all had a pile of music in front of us, it was never absolutely clear whether this was for just that day's work or for the complete film. This session in particular suffered from other communication problems between Barry, engineer Dick Lewzey and certain sections of the orchestra, due to technical problems. John Barry didn't make a grand entrance each day, it was more a question of looking up and seeing him on the podium. On the first day, Sid Margo simply finished his directions and said, almost as an aside, "Oh, this is John Barry", and we started almost at once.

'As it was April Fool's Day, a few us couldn't resist playing a joke on one of the more intense members of the orchestra, a regular with the Royal Philharmonic. During a break we switched the next part of the score and substituted a very complex technical piece I and others "composed" on the spot. When he returned he quickly became alarmed at what he saw, and called over Sid Margo. Sid, who was not in on the joke, couldn't make out what was going on, and he called for John Barry's assistance. He, of course, realised at once that it was a prank, and thoroughly enjoyed the joke. Not so the recipient, who was furious.'

John Taylor of Duran Duran, a keen Bond/Barry fan, had originally suggested to Cubby Broccoli that the group would be ideal to write and sing the theme song for *A View To A Kill*. When they got the job, their initial reaction was one of fear, but of course it was too late to back down and Barry was apparently keen to work with them. Lead singer Simon Le Bon recalls: 'He didn't really come up with any of the basic musical ideas. He heard what we came up with and he put them into an order. And that's why it happened so quickly, because he was able to separate the good ideas from the bad ones, and he arranged them. He has a great way of working brilliant chord arrangements. He was working with us as virtually a sixth member of the group – not really getting on our backs at all. He gets half a writing credit but all he really did was make sure he was able to use what we wrote later on in the film, to add orchestration and so on. He just wanted to make sure that what we did didn't make him wince.' Barry was amused by John Taylor's knowledge of his work: 'He knows more about stuff I've done than I know myself. He'd pick out a scene from an old movie, and I mean old, and talk about it like I'm supposed to remember it as if it were yesterday!'

The Duran Duran single was a huge success worldwide, but especially in Britain and America, where it reached number two and number one respectively. Following the departure of CTS's resident engineer John Richards to work in America, 'A View To A Kill' was the first time Dick Lewzey had been entirely responsible for mixing. It was also he who recommended the orchestrator Nicholas Raine to Barry, and the two have worked together many times since.

For the next film in the series, *The Living Daylights*, Barry unusually wrote a separate theme for the end titles sequence: 'I thought it would be lovely at the end of the movie, instead of going back to the main title song, to have a love ballad which is the theme that is used throughout the four or five love scenes in the picture.' It was sung by Chrissie Hynde of the Pretenders, who also wrote the words. Another Barry/Hynde song was included in the body of the film, and both were recorded with synthesised backing at Paradise Studios in Chiswick. Before the recordings, Hynde had demonstrated both songs to John Barry one evening at her London flat, while he sat on the floor, sustaining himself with a bottle of rum.

Barry had started work on *The Living Daylights* in May 1987, and the score was recorded digitally on a 24-track machine in a single week, again at CTS in Wembley. Both Barry and Lewzey were impressed with this format, with Barry recalling that he had recorded the very first digital film soundtrack, Disney's *The Black Hole*: 'I love it – it's just that much better than analogue, everything major I've done has been on to digital.' Most of the score used synthesised rhythm tracks, and Barry explained: 'I wanted to put in these tracks, as they really cut through. We've used them on about eight pieces and when we got them mixed in with the orchestra it sounded really terrific, with a lot of energy and impact – a slight fresh-ness and a more up-to-date sound.' Barry wrote some 57 minutes of music for this film in just four weeks. Band tracks were laid down at Maison Rouge Studios in south London, and the orchestral overlays were done at CTS. The tapes were finally remixed at the Power Station in New York.

John Barry was reportedly not too happy working with a-ha, who were selected to sing the main theme song, comparing the experience to 'playing ping-pong with four balls'. He was even less pleased with their attitude after the completion of the theme song, when they refused to have anything further to do with the film. There was undoubtedly a certain amount of creative friction – 'The old meeting the new,' said a-ha. Ray Still, who had been involved with the Duran Duran project and was then director of the US label Warner Brothers, recommended them to Michael G Wilson. Pal Waaktaar, leader of the group, liked the idea of working with Barry, but afterwards described it as 'a strange experience', and admitted that 'the song was not really a favourite in its current form.'

CHAPTER 14

THE BRYAN FORBES FILM SCORES

There is not a great deal of original music in *The L-Shaped Room*, as most of the score is music composed by Brahms and adapted, arranged and conducted by Muir Mathieson. Barry's role was to write some jazz sequences for party scenes, which he recorded with a small group. There was a press report in August, 1962 intimating that he had written three trad themes for the film which were to be played by Bob Wallis and his Storeyville Jazzmen, but the film credits do not confirm this. In fact the jazz music that can be heard in the movie cannot be described as trad at all. Director Bryan Forbes recalls: 'I was first introduced to John Barry on a sound stage at Shepperton Studios during the making of the film. I needed two very short pieces of contemporary music to fit a scene set in a night club. He listened to me between takes, said very little, seemed very shy and departed without ceremony. Two days later he returned with something that delighted and amazed me. It was a humble beginning to a relationship that I now value enormously.'

Seance On A Wet Afternoon was Barry's second film for Forbes. It starred Kim Stanley, who persuades her husband (Richard Attenborough) to kidnap a child so that she can become famous by revealing its whereabouts – an odd story line with superb performances by the two leading actors and Nanette Newman, Forbes's wife. Bryan Forbes told Barry he wanted a really unusual score, and he got it. The main theme is sombre, opening with piano and harp, extended by the use of flute, which aptly encapsulates a scene of rain dripping on the pavement outside the house. Most of the score is built around this theme which recurs, slightly differently, at the end. A faster version of the theme was recorded on a now much sought-after single for United Artists. The main theme was recorded by the John Barry Orchestra in the mid-sixties for CBS records and released on a compilation album. No soundtrack album materialised because of the small amount of music in the film, so fans must relish these two tracks. Barry played the theme with the Royal Philharmonic Orchestra in a 1973 concert with Muir Mathieson, sadly unrecorded.

Barry's first Hollywood score was *King Rat* in 1965. A lengthy prisoner-of-war story set in Singapore's Changi gaol during World War II, it starred George Segal, Tom Courtenay, John Mills, James Fox and a collection of marvellous British char-

Right: Bryan Forbes pictured on the set of *Séance On A Wet Afternoon* in 1964.

acter actors aptly cast by Forbes. Barry tried to change radically the way music should be conceived in the context of a war film, and he used traditional military music only sparingly. His one concession to the regimental rhythm, 'The King Rat March', was appropriately used as the prisoner-of-war camp came into view. The rest of the score was dominated by a theme entitled 'Just As You Were', while the most shocking moment in the film showed a scene where inmates were invited to eat a dog. His use of percussion was to emphasise how in such extreme circumstances, eating a dog could be considered a luxury.

The Wrong Box, adapted from the novel by the American writer Larry Gelbart, tells of the rivalry between the final two participants in a tontine – a kind of Victorian lottery in which all the spoils went to the last survivor of a group. There were tontine houses, for instance, whereby ownership of the whole row went to the one who survived the rest. Although distinguished by an excellent cast, the film was not successful. John Mills, Ralph Richardson, Michael Caine, Nanette Newman, Peter Cook, Dudley Moore, Peter Sellers and Tony Hancock starred, backed by numerous guest appearances by British character actors. Wilfred Lawson gave a remarkable performance as the butler in one of his last screen roles. The film also provided some excellent title montages in pastel colours, accompanied by Barry's

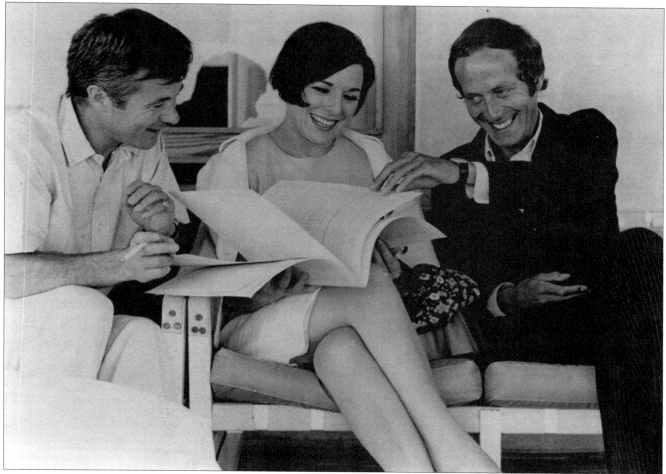

Bryan Forbes, Renata Terrago and John Barry discussing the 'Romance For Guitar and Orchestra' from *Deadfall*.

harpsichord dominated music. His score was a Mancini-style Valentine in the manner of 'The Sweetheart Tree' from *The Great Race*. Mainstream Records released an album in America – while Fontana, having planned a British issue, cancelled it at the last moment. It means the US pressing has become one of the rarest soundtracks ever issued. A planned CD reissue by Sony, who bought the entire Mainstream catalogue, was cancelled in the early nineties.

During 1967, Barry again collaborated with Bryan Forbes by scoring *The Whisperers*, a poignant and moving study of old age. There is little music in the film, but what there is is enchanting, written at a deliberately slow tempo to capture the cumbersome gait of an elderly lady, brilliantly portrayed by Dame Edith Evans. Dame Edith was nominated for an Academy award for her superb performance, and she was ably supported by Eric Portman and Ronald Fraser, as her errant husband and son. Another Forbes regular, Gerald Sim, played the National Assistance officer. The long out of print United Artists soundtrack album was re-issued on CD by Rykodisc in 1998.

Deadfall, the last of Barry's series of Bryan Forbes films, starred Eric Portman and Michael Caine, supported by Nanette Newman. The score was distinguished by

Barry's decision to write a fully orchestrated concerto to accompany the main robbery sequence, in which the camera cleverly switches between the scene of the crime and the concert attended by the victim of it. Barry, in a rare screen appearance, conducts the orchestra – actually the London Philharmonic – featuring guitar soloist Renata Terrago performing the specially written 'Romance For Guitar And Orchestra'. The guitar part was arranged by Vic Flick, who flew out to Majorca to join Barry at his remote villa, where much of his music was written. In fact Barry spent eight weeks in Majorca writing the concerto, before rehearsing back in London with Terrago and the London Philharmonic Orchestra. Apart from this extended piece, the score featured the theme 'My Love Has Two Faces', co-written with Jack Lawrence and sung by Shirley Bassey over the opening credits. A soundtrack album was issued by Twentieth Century Fox, while Bassey released the song as the B-side of her single 'To Give'. The instrumental version of the theme was recorded again in 1970 for release on the CBS album *Ready When You Are JB*. The album was reissued on CD in 1997 by Lukas Kendall's Retrograde label, and included two bonus tracks – an instrumental and vocal demo of 'My Love Has Two Faces'.

CHAPTER 15

SWINGING SIXTIES

In 1960 Barry's music for *Beat Girl* towered above the rest of the production – first class music for a second-rate movie! In an interview in *Disc* he commented: 'The film score is not all rock. I'd call it more of a jazz score. I've always wanted to get into the film business, and was happy when this offer came along. We've also cut an LP from the film, on which I use a 20-piece orchestra. It's all very much on a jazz key.' In other early articles he revealed how he came to be offered the score: 'This is the sort of work I've always wanted to do. Producer George Willoughby has asked me to tackle the job, which requires three songs and a complete underscore. There is also a main title theme – "Beat Girl". This film writing realises a deep ambition. In the early days of my career with the Seven I was always on the lookout for my break into movies. Well, the day came when I drove Adam Faith to the studios for the screen test which led him to landing his lead role in *Beat Girl*. They asked me to write the music and I jumped at the opportunity double fast.' By the time the much delayed film received its British release on October 28th, 1960, at the London Pavilion, Faith was a major star with three or four top ten hits behind him, and it was sold partially on his name. The LP – which was the first soundtrack to be released from a British film – sold very heavily, reaching the Top Ten and winning almost unanimous critical acclaim. The film contains alternative arrangements to those tracks that appeared on the album; in fact, 'The Beat Girl Song' sung by Faith does not appear in the final print at all! There are some excellent action cues both in the film and on the album; four of them strong enough to stand up eight years later as source music in their own right during a party scene in *Deadfall* – 'Lindon Home Rock', 'The Sharks', 'Time Out' and 'Beat Girl – Main Title'. In a much later interview Barry commented that the film was 'a pop-orientated kind of youth movie of that period. It was a pretty horrendous kind of movie of the time – like a really poor man's James Dean...'

A single by Faith taken from the soundtrack, 'Made You', made the Top Ten despite a ban on airplay from the BBC, who considered it obscene and instead played the flip side, 'When Johnny Comes Marching Home'. That song played over the titles of another Faith film, *Never Let Go*, which, although his second film, was premièred before *Beat Girl*. This time Faith was able to return a favour to Barry, who had got him the job on the TV show *Drumbeat*, by suggesting him as

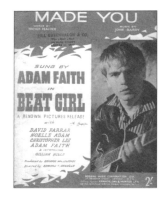

musical director. It was, as Barry later acknowledged, his first decent shot at scoring a dramatic film.

Originally entitled *Moment Of Truth*, Barry's second film, *Never Let Go*, starred Peter Sellers in a rare villainous role, along with Richard Todd. The only music from Adam Faith was 'When Johnny Comes Marching Home', so there was no scope for a soundtrack LP. The Faith song was written by Barry, who based it on an old traditional American song, with lyrics by Lionel Bart, who was credited under the pseudonym John Maitland. The JB7 released an instrumental version of the main title theme as a single in July 1960, which was heard in the film via a café jukebox, with its familiar pizzicato intro and medium-paced guitar line. A few months later, Barry recorded and released 'Beat For Beatniks' coupled with 'Big Fella', both of which were based on themes from the background score. In an interview in June, 1960, Barry said he drove out to Beaconsfield each day, to see rushes of the previous day's shooting with the director and producer. Although he did not write any music until filming was complete, he used these previews to give him an idea of the atmosphere and the kind of music likely to be needed. He also mentioned an arranged meeting with Lionel Bart, with whom he was collaborating on the title song, although when the single was released, Barry was given sole credit. The film opened at the Odeon, Leicester Square in June, 1960. Adam Faith won much better notices for this performance than for *Beat Girl*, and Barry again attracted attention in the film world for his score, which was just right for the overall mood of the film. The Kenton influence was never more to the fore.

Despite these good reviews, Faith's advisers had great difficulty in finding him another suitable film, and eventually they unwisely chose the comedy *What A Whopper*. Again, John Barry was the choice for the background score, but during production he dropped out to be replaced by Laurie Johnson. He did, however, arrange the title song, together with the hit from the film, 'The Time Has Come', both sung by Faith. The movie opened at the Rialto in London at the end of September, 1961 to terrible reviews.

Barry's final involvement in a film associated with Adam Faith was with 1962's thriller, *Mix Me A Person*, in which Adam spent a great deal of time behind bars. He did get to sing a couple of songs, however: the title and a version of 'La Bamba', both arranged by Barry. JB took on all the musical arrangements for the film, while Johnny Worth composed the music and Muir Mathieson acted as musical adviser. The title song was released as a single by Faith, but by then he had split with Barry, so John Keating provided the accompaniment.

An adaptation of the successful stage farce, *The Amorous Prawn* had a plot based on life at an army general's official Highland residence after his wife has taken in American paying guests – right under the nose of the nearby military establishment. This gave Barry a wonderful opportunity to write martial music in a style suited to the comic nature of the film, which was quite successful. The highly infectious main title theme, 'The Lolly Theme', was released as a single. It is probably best remembered now for innovatively using a cash register till as part of the

rhythm section, pre-dating Pink Floyd's 'Money' from *Dark Side Of The Moon* by eleven years. The version played over the titles was arranged differently to the single, Barry basing a good deal of his score on it.

The *Cool Mikado* was one of Michael Winner's first directorial jobs, and he engaged the JB7 to appear in it, masquerading as an American group. Their only number, 'Tit Willow Twist', credited Barry as composer, but it need hardly be said that in reality it was an arrangement of Gilbert and Sullivan's song. The 60-minute film did not fare well, but the album proved extremely collectable, often selling in the 1990s for upwards of £50. 'Tit Willow Twist' is notable for an excellent guitar solo from Vic Flick.

1963 saw a vast increase in Barry's film activities. With four complete movies and a television documentary under his belt, he was clearly moving towards fulfilling his life long ambition. The first of the films was *It's All Happening,* a vehicle for Tommy Steele backed by a supporting cast of many of EMI's leading artists of the time. John Barry played himself, handling a recording session with a nervous Johnny De Little and the American newcomer Dick Kallman. He also arranged several other songs from the film, which were all included on the soundtrack album that followed. Quite a few singles were also released, and one curio was from Tommy Steele, 'The Dream Maker', which originally had 'Maximum Plus', a duet with Marion Ryan, as its flip side. Its release was quickly cancelled after a row with Steele, who had threatened to leave Columbia, for whom he had only just signed. The disc was hastily re-pressed, with the B-side featuring another Steele number from the film, 'Egg and Chips'. All three were arranged and accompanied by Barry.

John Barry on the set of *It's All Happening* in 1963.

The *Party's Over* was a controversial film which Barry has only rarely since discussed; neither has he included music from it on any of his many compilation albums. It starred Oliver Reed and Eddie Albert, and was later disowned by its backers, Top Rank. The director was Guy Hamilton, later to work with Barry on a much larger scale with the Bond films, and he well remembers the controversy: 'The story line was that of a nascent beat generation in the UK who were rejecting establishment values and replacing them with … what? A very moral tale shot completely on location in Chelsea with a talented young cast. The censor, John Trevelyan, took one look and decided to use his muscle to remove anti-establishment references. This I refused to do. We had a good old ding-dong about it in the columns of *The Sunday Times*. The film was half financed by the Rank Organisation, and Jack Hawkins, Jules Buck and myself owned the other half via the National Film Corporation. We refused to back down and thanks to the gutlessness of the Rank Organisation, the film was never released.'

Some reference books claim the movie was released – nearly two years later, after which it quickly sank without trace. On discovering in 1994 that EMI had put out his theme, Barry recalled his work on the film: 'Let me say straight away that *The Party's Over* was a very low budget black-and-white film, They said they were going to buy the rights to the song to be able to include it in the film, and I told them they wouldn't be able to afford it – the cost would exceed their total budget for the movie. This proved to be the case, so I wrote a song called "Time Waits For No Man" for Annie Ross. There was nothing called "The Party's Over", so I don't know what this theme is they have.' Unfortunately, the film's problems meant a score release of any kind was out of the question at that time, but EMI did indeed include what appears to be the end title theme on their *John Barry – The EMI Years Volume 3* compilation.

Arguably, Barry's most prestigious work by 1964 was heard in *Zulu*, the film that also launched his friend Michael Caine to stardom. Starring co-producer Stanley Baker and featuring excellent supporting performances from Caine, Jack Hawkins, James Booth, Nigel Green and Glyn Edwards, this epic film told the true story of a British Army company's heroic stand against thousands of Zulu warriors at Rorke's Drift, South Africa in 1879.

Although Barry's score for *Zulu* was not one of his longest – there was just 36 minutes of music in the film – he successfully captured the savage, wearying battle which unfolded on the big screen. The soundtrack album, released by Ember Records, devoted just one side to Barry's original score, which was disappointingly recorded in mono. Side two contained a selection of 'Zulu Stamps', some of which were based on traditional dances performed by the modern day Zulus.

In 1964 Barry scored the British Lion picture *A Jolly Bad Fellow*, which was released in America as *They All Died Laughing* – a title that well reflected this black comedy about a chemistry don who tries a new poison on his enemies. Barry's score was dominated by organ work from Alan Haven, and a single, 'A Jolly Bad Fellow', was recorded by him on United Artists, with JB arranging and producing. The

Far left: Jack Hawkins and John Barry at the *Zulu* première party.

Left: Stanley Baker John Barry at the *Zulu* première party.

Haven single was unsuccessful as far as the charts were concerned, but it served as a very good memento of the film, and is now extremely hard to find.

Man In The Middle was another film directed by Guy Hamilton, who was rapidly cementing a strong working relationship with Barry. The main theme, 'Man In The Middle (No More)', was written by Lionel Bart, but it was Barry who arranged and conducted the incidental music, including three of his own jazz compositions – 'Chicken Delhi Cold', 'Kate's Blues' and 'Barney's Blues'. A soundtrack album appeared both in the UK and in the States, and Stateside also released a single of 'Man In The Middle (No More)' and 'Barney's Blues' in the UK. The star of the film was Robert Mitchum, with support from Trevor Howard and Keenan Wynn. The story, set in Word War II India, tells of an American lieutenant, accused of murder, struggling between his conscience, sense of justice and his loyalty towards a cause involving the world's powers.

The score for *Mister Moses* was recorded for director Ronald Neame while Barry was in Italy. It featured some tormenting jungle-sounding music to accompany scenes set in Africa. A quack doctor, played by Robert Mitchum, is the only person able to persuade an African tribe to move before their land is flooded. Having done so, he leads them to their destination. Afterwards, Barry admitted that in try-ing to respect the wishes of both the director and producer, he compromised the final outcome. As a result, he considered the end product unsatisfactory. No music was recorded for commercial release.

Four In The Morning was a low budget picture made by West One Productions, featuring Judi Dench in one of her first screen appearances. Director Anthony Simmons asked Barry for the score on the understanding that the budget had already been spent, leaving money only for a small orchestra and nothing for Barry himself. Although it was hardly an offer he couldn't refuse, JB thought enough of the movie and the director to go ahead anyway, using only nine musicians and completing the recording in just three sessions. He said later that with a better budget more musicians would have helped on certain sequences. The score was performed on four cellos and percussion with a soft and romantic mood setting the scene between the two young lovers, with occasionally a sense of fierceness to

accompany moments of erupting tension. The main theme dominated the film and the album included many variations on it, almost to the extent of repetition. That said, Barry's gut reaction to the film was sound. It won four awards in 1965, including one at the prestigious Cannes Festival. In 1966, Ember recorded and released a soundtrack album that included various dialogue excerpts; and in 1992, Play It Again reissued the score on CD, this time cutting the dialogue in favour of music from Barry's *Elizabeth Taylor In London* TV special. Barry was not particularly happy with this, telling the authors that although he thought the music was entirely appropriate for the film, he did not feel it was suitable for a record.

Be My Guest was a low-budget Rank film for director Lance Comfort for which Barry wrote only one song, 'Gotta Getaway Now', sung by Joyce Blair. Lyrics were by actor Michael Pratt, and all the incidental film music was composed and conducted by Malcolm Lockyer. This was rather a dull film with a most unlikely story about youngsters breaking into the pop world, though it was enlivened by plenty of guest artists, including Jerry Lee Lewis, the Zephyrs and the Nashville Teens. Bearing in mind that for Barry 1965 was an extremely busy year, it seems quite likely that he agreed to be involved merely as a favour to Joyce Blair, who of course had been the mystery voice on 1963's Christine Keeler spoof. The song was not recorded commercially.

The Ipcress File, on which Barry again teamed up with producer Harry Saltzman, is a prime example of his diversity. It also reunited him with editor Peter Hunt, set designer Ken Adam and Michael Caine – fresh from *Zulu* fame and now an established star, as well as being an old mate. Barry claimed that despite his experience of working on the Bond films, it had not proved difficult working on another, utterly different, English spy film. 'With Bond I concentrated on the action and adventure, whereas with *Ipcress* I built the score around the hero or anti-hero Harry Palmer,' he recalled. Palmer was after all the complete antithesis of Bond – neither flamboyant nor glamorous. He was essentially a loner suited to a profession which valued sobriety. Barry used the forlorn sounding Hungarian instrument the cimbalom to anchor the mood. 'I felt it caught the whole feeling of the action,' he later told film critic Barry Norman. The cimbalom is like an open piano – you hit it with sticks.' The main theme, 'A Man Alone', dominated the film and in particular, the soundtrack album. It was used four or five times in varying forms on the album.

With some justification, Barry considers *The Knack*, his first film for director Richard Lester, among his finest scores. Adapted for the big screen by Bristol-based Charles Wood from an original play by Anne Jelicoe, the movie, one of the first of its kind to set out to explore the sixties youth culture, starred Ray Brooks, Michael Crawford, Donal Donnelly and Rita Tushingham. Jane Birkin, Jacqueline Bisset and Charlotte Rampling all made their film debuts in *The Knack*, which took the much-coveted *Palm d'Or* at the 1965 film festival. For the two JBs (Barry & Birkin) this film was a prelude to an even more significant event later in the year, when they were married at Kensington Registry Office.

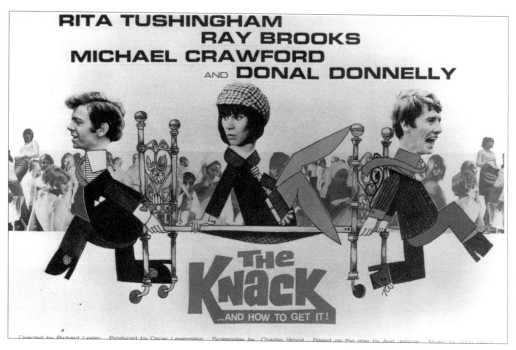

Ray Brooks and John Barry at the première of *The Knack* at The London Pavilion, on 2nd June 1965.

Musically speaking, *The Knack* was the perfect vehicle for Alan Haven to display his idiosyncratic yet virtuoso organ style. Scored in three-four time for organ, cellos and a girl choir, the soundtrack succeeded in sounding contemporary without being derivative. Lester was reported to have commented to Barry: 'Look, you've done everything I wouldn't have done – but it works.' As for JB, he reflected: 'What it needed was a protest, youth answering back. Well, I could have used guitars, but that was a bit corny. Instead I used girls' voices humming a melody against the dialogue. It was very effective.'

A concoction of supper-club jazz, pastiche beat music and mock blues came together for one of John Barry's most exciting scores of the sixties – Sam Speigel's *The Chase*. The score was based on American negro spiritual themes and gospel songs, but although critically well received, the film was only moderately successful. That did not prevent a soundtrack album from being issued, containing most of the music from the movie, modified in places. A different version of the theme included on this album appeared on the American compact disc *The Film Music of John Barry* in 1988.

Dutchman (1967), a 'short', running for 56 minutes, represented the start of a lasting relationship with director Anthony Harvey. He had originally intended not to use any music whatsoever in the film, but changed his mind once he realised the sound effects did not work as well as he had initially envisaged. Having run out of money, he called on Barry to bale him out of his difficulty. Barry duly obliged, by supplying one gripping theme, which was to occur on three separate occasions during the film – at the beginning, in the interlude and at the end. It had been Barry's intention to score the film this way, using a menacingly chilling piece to lift the movie almost like 'a musical sound effect'. Barry said: 'Dramatically, one could get more stridency and horror through the music, which was the effect we were looking for.' A version of his theme was recorded on CBS in the mid-sixties.

The *Quiller Memorandum* was a spy thriller directed by Michael Anderson, starring George Segal with Alec Guinness. Following his success in scoring the Bond films and Len Deighton's *Ipcress File*, Barry was again faced with tackling a spy story in a different way. He later discussed his idea of writing a childlike, almost nursery rhyme melody in the mid-nineteenth-century European tradition: 'It was a kind of simple waltz melody which went against the picture.' Barry's score used many different instruments, including a version of the main theme, 'Wednesday's Child', played on a barrel organ. Lyrics for this gentle, romantic ballad were by Mack David, and sung in the body of the film by Matt Monro. The soundtrack album, which spawned a single release of the main title, also contained an instrumental version of 'Downtown', composed by Tony Hatch. Like the Monro song,

George Martin, Matt Monro, John Barry, Ivan Foxwell and Mack David at the recording of 'Wednesday's Child'.

'Downtown' was used as source music in the film. The album was reissued on compact disc in America on the Varese Sarabande label.

Petulia was Richard Lester's second collaboration with Barry following their success with *The Knack*. George C Scott, Julie Christie and Richard Chamberlain were among the stars of a somewhat flashy movie set in San Francisco, with photography by Nicholas Roeg, and their efforts met with a mixed reaction. The plot has Petulia meeting Archie at a fashionable San Francisco ball, and although she has only recently been married, she decides she wants this cynical, divorced doctor. The soundtrack album was released by Warner Brothers in America, Japan and Germany – but not in the UK, because of the poor box office response to the film. According to Barry, 'the interpretation was cold and icy, but worked in a strange way.'

Joseph Losey's *Boom!* starred Richard Burton and Elizabeth Taylor. Barry was recommended by Richard Lester after Losey disliked an earlier score. Because he was already committed to starting work on *Secret Ceremony*, another picture with Elizabeth Taylor, Losey needed someone who could write to the tightest of deadlines. Barry, then a friend of Lester, had a reputation for working under severe pressure and proved himself again with this assignment. He completed the entire score, including the recording, in three weeks of first seeing the picture. According to Barry, the scenario was 'like a nightmare', and despite his efforts, the movie, shot on location in Sardinia, was not well received. Despite this, Universal released Barry's score on LP and it has since become one of the most sought-after soundtrack albums, by the late 1990s fetching more than £200 for an original copy. An orchestral version of the main theme was recorded in 1974 for the *Play It Again* album, and was later included on Polydor's Barry compilation CD.

The Appointment (1969) was an American production by Martin Poll, directed by Sidney Lumet. No original soundtrack album was issued, although a recording of the main theme, coupled with an incidental piece called 'Café', was released as a single by MGM in France, where the film had been better received than in America or the UK. A different arrangement of the main theme appeared on CBS's *Ready When You Are, JB* album, and later the double album, *The Film Music Of John Barry*.

In the early sixties, Barry had worked on music for TV commercials directed by John Schlesinger. Now, in 1969, the two joined forces for an incomparably mightier venture, the hugely significant movie *Midnight Cowboy*. It will forever be remembered for a song recorded by Harry Nilsson two years earlier and written by Fred Neil – the haunting 'Everybody's Talkin''. Schlesinger, who according to Barry has a 'specific knowledge of music', found it while shooting the film and laid it into the final print, to accompany Joe Buck's journey to New York. For Barry: 'It worked so incredibly well. It had a marvellous kind of movement. Jon Voight kicks the swing door open, and he's off as that guitar comes in. It's integrated into the score.' Although other pop songs were also chosen, all the original cues written for the film were Barry's. For all the merits of 'Everybody's Talkin'', arguably the most mov-

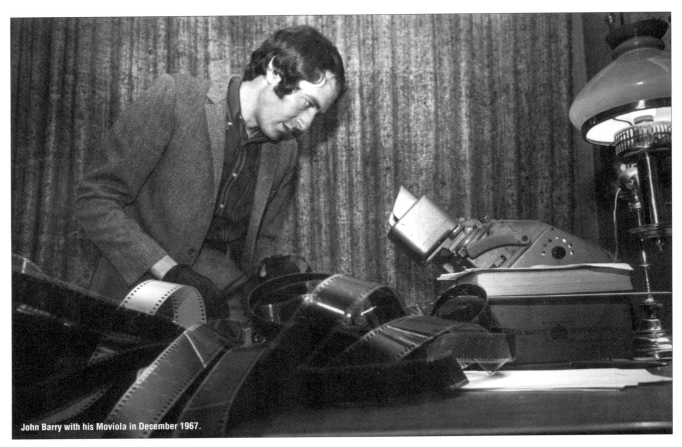

John Barry with his Moviola in December 1967.

John Barry at the piano in December 1967.

ing musical moment comes at the end of the film when Rizzo (Dustin Hoffman) dies on the pair's escape coach journey to Florida. Barry told fellow composer David Arnold: 'You drive down New York City's bad streets, seeing these guys walking around. The scene keeps turning over and over, there's no hope. That's what life is like there, not going any place, a terrific sadness. That's where it came from. I wrote the whole thing in an apartment on 72nd Street in 20 minutes.' Interestingly, this theme was the subject of much air-play many years after the movie's release, when in 1980 the BBC Radio disc jockey Noel Edmonds influenced a single release which dented the UK Top Fifty. The soundtrack also includes a cue called 'Florida Fantasy', which was later used by BBC Television to introduce highlights of both rugby and cricket. Many years later, as if to prove its versatility, it introduced their nature series *Wildtrack*.

A studio portrait of John Barry in 1970.

CHAPTER 16

*E*ARLY SEVENTIES

In the seventies, John Barry adopted a lower public profile. In deciding not to court publicity, he simply allowed his music to act as his mouthpiece – inconspicuous to the general public, maybe, but omnipresent in the moviegoer's ear. By this time he had established himself as a much sought-after film composer, and was in the most privileged of positions – able to pick and choose the projects that most interested him. As a result, the seventies proved to be a truly eclectic period – a time in which he accepted a whole range of diverse assignments for film, TV and theatre.

Monte Walsh was Barry's first Western, scored for producer Walter Coblenz. With direction by William A Fraker, it starred Lee Marvin and Jack Palance as two ageing cowboys facing up to their twilight years. Hal David supplied the lyrics to the title song, 'The Good Times Are Comin'', which was sung by Mama Cass and released as a single on EMI's Probe label, using Barry's arrangement and accompaniment. By 1970 the traditional Western was dying, and Fraker aimed to kill it off altogether with a true-to-life depiction of the emergence of modern ways in an Old West band of ruffians. Monte Walsh is the elderly cowpoke beset by change. The land is being bought up and fenced in by never-seen business interests back East, and Monte (Marvin) and his kind are out of work and out of place. Some marry and settle down, like Monte's buddy Chet (Palance). Others turn outlaw, like the ones who gun down poor Chet. It is with this in mind that Monte takes to the trail, gun in hand, for one last mission – good, old-fashioned revenge. Beautifully filmed with reverence for the wonders of untamed nature, *Monte Walsh* is an adult tale of social and physical survival that captures a time, place and breed of men on their way to becoming history.

Filmed entirely in the Australian bush, *Walkabout* links Nicholas Roeg's colourful photography with an understated and atmospheric Barry score. It is a movie of magical images, exotic locations and innocent surprise: a journey of mystery for a small boy, his adolescent sister and an Aborigine, all discovering in their own way if there is a place for the innocent in a cruel world. John Barry's music transcended all *genres* with a melody of rapturous contours and sublime melancholy. To many Barry aficionados this rates as one of his finest works, and its lack of official release in soundtrack form was a great disappointment. Demand was partially met by a poor quality mono reproduction on bootleg in 1978, but this Poo Record release was scant consolation. It was later reissued by GSF in the eighties using Poo's original artwork, although the rear sleeve preferred photos to Japanese notes. There is no title song in the film, although lyrics were later added to the theme by Don Black and recorded on CBS by Tony Bennett, without the assistance of John Barry.

The Last Valley was a historical drama set in the seventeenth century against the backdrop of the European Thirty Years War. It teamed Omar Sharif with Michael Caine under the direction of James Clavell, who also wrote and produced. Normal protocol decrees a strict alphabetical billing in circumstances where at least two principal players vie for equal recognition 'above the title'. However, on this occasion, Sharif suggested that whoever was being paid the greater fee should take precedence, no doubt assuming it would be him. After at first agreeing, Caine, on discovering Sharif's fee, insisted on his own being increased so that he could top him in more ways than one. In spite of its disappointing box office *The Last Valley* remains one of Caine's favourite films. His portrayal of a German officer won him the best actor award for 1970 from *Films and Filming*. Barry used a full symphony orchestra and choir, the Accademia Monteverdiana, to authentically capture the setting.

'Fixer' Sid Margo with John Barry discussing the score for *The Last Valley*.

Murphy's War marked a début collaboration with Ken Thorne, who composed and conducted additional music for this Peter Yates film. Barry was responsible for the musical themes and supervision. The movie centres around the life of a British merchant seaman, played by Peter O'Toole, who survives a torpedo attack and pledges to bomb the offending U-boat with a custom-built plane. Although no music from the film has been commercially released, Ken Thorne issued a promotional CD in 1996 which contained virtually everything written by Barry and him. Barry's professional relationship with Thorne was to continue with *They Might Be Giants* in 1971.

An odd story, *They Might Be Giants* tells of the exploits of a lawyer (George C Scott) who, on believing he is Sherlock Holmes, decides to locate Moriarty. This was the second and final film on which Barry collaborated with Thorne, the former as composer and musical supervisor, the latter as arranger, orchestrator and conductor. An album of music from the film again failed to appear. One can only attribute this to poor public response to the movie and to the unobtrusiveness of its music. The end theme, however, was recorded on a bootleg album released in the eighties, *Missing… Great Movie Themes Volume I*, which unfortunately is in mono, and of poor quality.

Produced by Hal B Wallis and directed by Carol Reed, *Follow Me* starred Topol and Mia Farrow and was known in America as *Public Eye*, the title of Peter Schaffer's one-act play on which it was based. The plot revolves around an eccentric private eye whose assignment in following an accountant's wife eventually draws the two of them together. The surveillance is all performed against a backdrop of an attractive Barry melody on which a Don Black lyric is added when it accompanies the credits. This song, 'Follow, Follow', was sung by an uncredited Thelma Keating. Most of the music can be heard on the original soundtrack album which was released only in Japan, along with a single. In Britain, Barry re-recorded the theme and released it in 1972 as the flip side of 'The Adventurer' single.

Alice's Adventures In Wonderland was an ambitious musical version of the classic Lewis Carroll story. Barry worked closely with lyricist Don Black, while former King Brothers member Denis King acted as a personal instructor for Fiona Fullerton, a 15-year-old newcomer playing Alice. As soon as her role was confirmed, a meeting was arranged with Barry in his London apartment, on the Albert Embankment opposite the Tate Gallery. Michael Crawford, Don Black and Denis King were all present as Barry played them piano tapes of the songs. Fiona Fullerton later recalled this scene with great fondness, revealing that, at that time, she 'had a huge crush on JB'. Barry wrote most of the music in Majorca, where he was joined by Don Black. For the recording, he used the Royal Philharmonic Orchestra – with some 80 musicians – for the first time. Not a great success in the UK, the film proved popular in America and in Australia, director William Sterling's home country.

While some of the music on the album was not in the film, the disc is still a good representation of the score, with instrumentals such as 'The Royal Procession', 'The Croquet Game' and 'The Lobster Quadrille'. There are also both instrumental and vocal versions of 'Curiouser And Curiouser', 'I've Never Been This Far Before' and 'The Me I Never Knew', with vocals by Fullerton. Matt Monro later recorded 'The Me I Never Knew' and 'Curiouser And Curiouser' for a Columbia single produced by George Martin, with accompaniment by Colin Keyes. The following year, Scott Walker also recorded 'The Me I Never Knew', and released it as a single with 'This Way Mary' from *Mary Queen Of Scots*. *Alice* was the first score on which Richard

John Barry greets the Queen at the Royal Première of *Alice's Adventures In Wonderland* at the Odeon, Marble Arch, London on 4th December 1972.

Lewzey, an engineer at CTS studios in London, worked with Barry, as assistant to John Richards.

Two film versions of *A Doll's House*, Ibsen's powerful play about a wife trapped in domesticity, appeared in 1973. Joseph Losey's version starred Jane Fonda, but Patrick Garland's faithful adaptation of his own Broadway production was thought the stronger of the two. It included a marvellous cast, among whom were Claire Bloom, Anthony Hopkins, Ralph Richardson, Denholm Elliott and Dame Edith Evans; it also benefited from a sparse, apt John Barry score. In fact there was very little music; one theme which was used to good effect on three separate occasions – as main and end title and once in the body of the plot. A soundtrack album was clearly not feasible, but there was no denying the merit and beauty of this melancholy Barry melody. Indeed, it was too good to forget, and JB recorded a version during the *Play It Again* sessions in 1974, releasing it finally in 1977 as part of Polydor's *Very Best Of John Barry* compilation.

Charles Jarrott directed a first production by veteran Hollywood actor Gregory Peck in *The Dove*, co-starring Joseph Bottoms and a young Deborah Raffin in a tale of the perils of yachtsman Robin Lee Graham's five-year voyage around the world. 'Postcard views flick by to the strains of a saccharine score,' according to a review in *Films And Filming*. The vocal version of the main title theme, 'Sail The Summer Wind', was sung by Lyn Paul, complete with lyrics from Barry's regular partner Don Black. An album did not materialise in Britain, but Paul's record company Polydor considered the tune commercial enough to re-record, with Barry, then contracted to them, at the producer's desk. The aim was to release a single for the British pop market, and the result was a completely different arrangement. An instrumental version, again different in all respects, was recorded in the *Play It Again* sessions in the same year.

Omar Sharif and Julie Andrews were inspired casting in *The Tamarind Seed*, a Blake Edwards film set in Barbados and London. It includes a wonderful song, 'Play It Again', sung by Wilma Reading, which was released as a single. Though not arranged by Barry, the recording was very faithful to the version heard on screen. No album has so far been released, though there were rumours that a bootleg went out in Italy. Barry's instrumental theme was re-recorded in 1974 for the title track of the album *Play It Again*, but with a slightly different arrangement.

The Day Of The Locust, the second of John Schlesinger's films with John Barry as composer, starred Karen Black, Donald Sutherland and Burgess Meredith. Based on Nathaniel West's story set in 1930s Hollywood during the Depression, it concerns a sketch artist, who, on moving in with an old vaudevillian-turned-drunkard sales-man, becomes obsessed with his beautiful daughter. Although the movie was a box office disaster, the soundtrack LP contained all the main themes composed for the film together with other standards by artists such as Louis Armstrong, whose 'Jeeper's Creepers' opens the action.

CHAPTER 17

BRITAIN – MAJORCA – AMERICA

In 1974 John Barry made the decision to leave his Thames-side penthouse for the peace of a remote villa he was having built in Majorca. He had recently finished a rapid succession of film scores as well as the major writing necessary for his third and immensely successful musical, *Billy*. His constant work in composing had made him a rich man, and like several of his contemporaries in the entertainment world, he might also have been influenced by the recent election of a Labour Government committed to a punitive taxation system. However, Barry clearly also needed time to recharge his creative batteries, and the island where he had found the solitude and inspiration to write much of his recent work seemed the ideal solution.

He had been living there for about a year — turning down all film scoring opportunities, opting to record a solitary non-soundtrack album, *Americans*, for Polydor — before he received an invitation to write the score for the American TV movie *Eleanor And Franklin*. To accomplish this task he booked into the Beverly Hills Hotel for just six weeks in October, 1975, but once in Hollywood he was swamped with work opportunities, and was offered *Robin And Marian* and *King Kong* in quick succession. In the end, he lived and worked in the hotel for almost a year, as yet more assignments were accepted, and eventually his stay on America's West Coast lasted almost five years, during which time he met and married his current wife, Laurie. For a while they rented a Beverly Hills residence, but in 1980 they moved to their present home in the US in Oyster Bay, a few miles from New York, where Barry has built his own studio.

Not particularly well received on release, *Robin And Marian* has since won critical acclaim from many quarters. This could be attributed to the reappraisal of the careers of Sean Connery and Audrey Hepburn, who were a magical pairing in the title roles. There were also fine performances from Robert Shaw, Nicol Williamson and Denholm Elliott, not to mention a rare film appearance from Ronnie Barker as Friar Tuck. Richard Lester, the director, recently revealed that after producer Ray Stark's rejection of Michel Legrand's original score, other composers were invited to compete for the assignment by writing a theme.

Barry's was judged to be the best, and he duly wrote the score at the Beverly Hills Hotel. Away in England at the time, Lester, in turn, deemed Barry's score totally inappropriate, and what was more, he found his attitude very arrogant. He had originally commissioned a score from Legrand after running the film with extracts from orchestral pieces by the modern classical composer Michael Tippett. Legrand's score was written for violin, cello and string orchestra, but it failed to work in various places, and Lester simply asked producer Stark if they could try to rectify matters. He was horrified to come back to a completely new treatment: 'I was left with no score, and in the middle of shooting in England. John Barry came in and did the score in America while I was still in England. I thought the score was deficient in many areas. It was totally foreign to the kind of score that we had planned – something more classical and less filmic. Michel had written a score that was very like Tippett and very early string Shostakovich, and John wrote a Hollywood score.'

Almost two decades later, it is hard to imagine John Barry submitting to the indignity of entering a competition to score a movie, particularly as he has often stressed that he 'never goes after a film'. It seems more likely that having submitted a main theme for Stark's approval, he was not aware that the producer had also commissioned themes from other composers; Maurice Jarre was thought to be one them. Perhaps it is no surprise that Barry, who knew that he had been hired by Stark to write a more traditional film score and was doubtless aware of his reaction to Legrand's efforts, was not going to take much notice of telephoned instructions from Lester, who wanted him to retain Legrand's approach. Besides, Lester, who had had disagreements with Barry over his music for *The Knack,* seems to be in a minority in his low opinion of Barry's score for *Robin and Marian.* The soundtrack was issued originally only in limited form as part of an in-house cinema promotion pack, followed by a most unsatisfactory bootleg.

When Barry accepted an invitation to score the remake of *King Kong,* he was not in the least concerned about the inevitable comparisons with the original movie. He deliberately did not view the old film again, to make absolutely certain of avoiding its style: 'No, I didn't go back and listen to it. I only remembered the original *King Kong* from my earlier viewings. Every film has its own life, its own specifics, its own period of time, so that was never a problem. What I did was a reaction to what was on the screen. The film was scored reel by reel as it was shot, the first time Barry had written a film score in this unusual fashion; it was considered necessary because of the race to bring out the film between Barry's producer Dino de Laurentiis and Universal. 'At the time, Universal were planning a remake of their own, which really put the pressure on Dino and the rest of us,' Barry recalls. Universal eventually withdrew, but JB was not able to see the completed film until after the score was finished.

He was satisfied with the end result, and with its album sales around the world, although these were not as great as the producer had hoped. At the time of release the film was one of the most expensive ever made, but Barry refused to be overawed: 'Well, you hopefully rise to the occasion and deliver a marvellous score for them.

You have to go in and do your best. There is always that commercial aspect, but you must go along with the mood of the film. If there is a lot of excitement, you want to keep the momentum going. It rubs off on you. The real pressure is time.'

Apart from the soundtrack album release on the Reprise label in the US and the UK, a single was later put out, with lyrics added to the love theme sung by Andy Williams – 'Are You In There?' The Williams delivery was in typically smooth ballad style, but the flip side was very different – a disco version, complete with the most extraordinary instrumental effects apparently based on the moment in the film when Kong arrives to accept his human sacrifice. Issued only in the States, Japan and Italy, it sold surprisingly well. Another single appeared based on the love theme, this time sung by Demis Roussos, who also wrote the lyrics. Another instrumental version of the theme was recorded by Roger Williams on piano, while a very popular and lengthy disco version in two parts by Barry White's Love Unlimited Orchestra was titled 'Love Theme from King Kong'.

Most film critics did not receive the King Kong score kindly, one commenting on its similarity to *Walkabout* and *Mary Queen Of Scots*. Another complained that parts were scored with 'low droning tones'. According to Barry, there are shades of 'Ave Maria' in the cue 'Kong Hits the Big Apple', as featured on the soundtrack album. This cut is in fact unique in that it is completely different from the rest of the music in the film and on the album; coincidentally, it is Barry's favourite piece from the score.

The American magazine *High Fidelity*, reviewing the soundtrack album of *The Deep*, claimed that Barry was under pressure because he was brought in after John Williams had left the project. Barry has since denied this, saying he believes Williams was doing *Star Wars* at the time, but a book on the making of the film includes quotes from the producers confirming that he was not the original choice. They had not been impressed with the original writer, but were happy with Barry's finished score. Barry later claimed this was the most difficult film he had scored to date, particularly the underwater action, where he was conscious of the challenge of relaying the terror of being in such a situation.

Commenting on the soundtrack album, he said that as the film contained nearly an hour of music, it was necessary to leave out a certain amount on disc. Most of the underwater material was cut into a ballet suite which took up the second side of the album, but this did not include the memorable 'shark attack' sequence which was the musical highlight of the film. The other side contained an instrumental version of the main theme; two vocal versions by Donna Summer, one disco-style, one ballad; and more disco music as featured in the film but not written or performed by Barry. The album was released on the Casablanca label with some US copies appearing in blue vinyl; in the UK it was a standard pressing, but both were issued with a film poster. There was also a single which combined the Donna Summer disco-style vocal with Barry's main theme, and this sold heavily in the UK, peaking at number five. In America, the main theme was coupled with Barry's 'The White House Years' theme.

It was Christmas, 1976, just after Barry had completed *King Kong* for producer Dino de Laurentiis, when he was asked to work on his next film, *The White Buffalo*. The main reason was that the director, Richard Sale, had been dissatisfied with the original score, from a different composer, so de Laurentiis had promised to call Barry in. Unfortunately, it was not a happy experience all round. Barry liked the film he was originally shown and composed specifically for it, but there were a lot of changes to the released print, and the composer felt the music had been tampered with. Once again Barry had been faced with a rush to complete the score, this time because of a delivery date in a foreign market. No album was ever planned, as there was not enough variety of music in the film to warrant it. Barry discussed the possibility of an album later, by developing themes, but as the film was not particularly successful the idea was not pursued.

John Barry at the piano during recording of *The Deep*.

First Love (1977), which starred William Katt, Susan Dey, Beverly d'Angelo and Robert Loggia was based on campus life and modern attitudes towards love and sex. Originally, director Joan Darling wanted a song score, but invited Barry to step in as soon as she realised the original blue print wasn't working. After watching the film, Barry wrote music which he felt gave the production more emotional depth. It was after he had finished the score that further doubts began to emerge. In particular, one of the Paramount executives, while liking it, felt it was too mature for the film; which Barry thought one of the strangest criticisms he had ever heard. The makers eventually decided to compromise by reinstating some of the original songs while retaining some of Barry's music, at which stage he asked for his name to be removed from the credits. When he later saw the film, he heard fragments of his music; no main love theme, just secondary motifs. Some classical pieces had also crept in, and the main titles were accompanied by a Cat Stevens song.

A Harold Robbins novel, *The Betsy* (1977), was made into a film starring Sir Laurence Olivier. It must rank as one of the great actor's unhappiest choices. The critics panned it almost without exception, although the score was one of its few saving graces. There was a lot of music in the film, but the main theme was not considered commercial enough to merit either album or single release. Barry, at pains to point out that, despite this, the theme was considered quite satisfactory for the film, feels the commercial aspect is 'a dilemma we constantly go through'. His view is that it could have been released if the main theme had been reframed in a commercial vein, as happened with *Love Story* in 1970. Part of the score contained a song written especially for a party sequence, but it became too intrusive against the dialogue and was removed. On this occasion Barry agreed with the decision. So far, the only release of the main theme in any form has been on a bootleg compilation album in 1985, apparently taken direct from the soundtrack. *Films And Filming* described it as a 'charmingly (if unsuitably) delicate composition'.

Reading a list of Barry's film scores during his time on the West Coast, one is immediately struck by some unusual assignments. Among them were two films for Golden Harvest, *Game Of Death* and *Night Games*. The first began filming in 1973 but was temporarily abandoned due to the death of its star, Bruce Lee. A replacement was eventually found, but the few brief clips featuring Lee were left in the completed film as a selling pitch. Lee, a Chinese-American, became an overnight cult figure when he abandoned a short-lived attempt at making it in Hollywood and moved to Hong Kong. There he made a rapid succession of films designed to show off his martial arts skills although, ironically, the best known of these, *Enter The Dragon*, was a Hollywood co-production. Both the screenplay and direction of *Game Of Death* was by Robert Clouse, who also directed *Enter The Dragon*. In an interview shortly after the release of the film, Barry revealed that occasionally he is attracted to scoring a film if he believes he can have some fun with it. He went on to confirm that *Game Of Death* was just such a film: 'It was just fun to do a Bruce Lee movie. It was a strange type of film to do, and he's kind of a cult figure, you know. And so it was interesting to do.'

More recently, Barry has admitted that the job was something of a financial breakthrough. He was not being offered much and did not particularly want to do it: 'A Hong Kong producer rang to ask if I'd score it. I named an impossibly exorbitant sum. The producer agreed. Then what happens is that Hollywood companies ask "What did John get paid for his last picture?" You name this price and they pay.' The film was very successful in Japan, resulting in Tam releasing an album, while a few years later, the Victor label followed suit. While the soundtrack album reflected the score well enough, the individual track titles were somewhat odd, bearing little relation to the scenes they accompanied, and assembled in no particular order. Fortunately, a Silva Screen CD release put the record straight, with the restoration of the cue titles originally chosen by Barry.

While no main title theme song was written, Barry composed 'Will This Be The

Song I'll Be Singing Tomorrow', sung on the soundtrack by actress Colleen Camp. At that time he had no regular lyricist, since Don Black, his most recent collaborator, still lived in England. He solved the problem by writing the words himself – probably the only time he has written both music and lyrics for a film song. The music tended to resurface throughout the film, most notably as the love theme for Billy and Ann. Barry's 'Main Title Theme', also known on the original soundtrack album as 'The Bruce Lee Theme', forms the film's second major motif, reappearing at regular intervals. Anyone unfamiliar with the Bruce Lee film *genre* can get some indication of its flavour by listening to the final track, 'Stick Fight/Main Title Reprise', on which the sound effects of the fight can be heard without the accompaniment of music.

Also known as *The Adventures Of Stella Star*, the movie *Starcrash*, a futuristic film starring Christopher Plummer, Caroline Munro and a pre-Bay Watch David Hasselhof, was made to cash in on the success of *Star Wars* a year earlier. Not a lot was different except for the acting, which was of the lowest standard, and the film received only a partial cinema release in the UK. Barry's music did help it, and the space music he wrote for it was a good grounding for his later work on *The Black Hole* and *Moonraker*. The film was a success in France and Italy and won an award for its score at the Festival Du Cinema Fantastique in Paris. Barry composed a pulsating main title theme which recurred during the end credits, and some other varied music to match the action sequences. The score was released on record in Germany, Italy and France, and although the music was the same on each release, the artwork for all three covers was different. In the Italian version of the film, Cher Winz provided a vocal.

Written following a string of TV movies, *Hanover Street* is one of Barry's finest scores of the late seventies. This is an unashamedly sentimental film, starring Harrison Ford and Lesley-Anne Down as a bomber pilot and Red Cross nurse who meet by chance in London during World War II. It was written and directed by Peter Hyams, beautifully photographed by David Watkin and scored with empathy by Barry. His main theme comes in a full orchestral arrangement conducted by Harry Rabinowitz, and was a welcome return to Barry's best scoring after *Game Of Death* and *Starcrash*. Films And *Filming's* reviewer said the movie was 'underlaid with a lush, but ultimately overused, John Barry score'. Regrettably, there was no disc, though there would have been plenty of good music to fill a soundtrack album.

Barry's score for *The Black Hole* followed hard on the heels of his two other space outings, *Starcrash* and *Moonraker*; and as with the latter, Danny Wallin was his sound engineer. A typically spectacular Disney production, *The Black Hole* related the story of a research team's discovery of a survey ship manned by robots poised on the edge of a black hole through which it is finally dragged. It starred big name veterans Maximilian Schell, Anthony Perkins and Ernest Borgnine, but despite some elaborate special effects, a rather dull story line combined with weak direction by Gary Nelson to make this rather a second-rate *Star Wars*. It was the first soundtrack album to be recorded using digital techniques, with Barry enjoying the luxury of working with a 94-piece orchestra. He wrote two principal themes, 'The Overture' and 'Main Title', and reflecting on his inspiration, said: 'The concept of this bottomless three-quarters swirling thing, the black hole, was the film's central image for me, and the thought behind the movement of the main theme.'

The Black Hole was an odd entry into the new niche of space opera that had exploded on to the scene after the unprecedented success of *Star Wars*. Disney studios had no space fantasy scripts, so they dusted off an old tale that had worked for them before – *Twenty Thousand Leagues Under The Sea*! They gave the characters new names and changed the setting, but little else was significantly new. For the overture Barry took a tongue-in-cheek stab at the expected *Star Wars* fanfare by using a retrograde inversion of the John Williams theme for that film; Williams's theme itself had been an alteration of Eric Korngold's *King's Row*, with which George Lucas had temp-tracked his movie. *The Black Hole* score is a kind of weird waltz-time vortex spinning on the foundation of an effective musical device known as the ostinato, a hypnotic repeated figure that impels the listener into the swarm of brass and violins; it is all very unsettling, and strikingly evocative of the mysterious and dangerous phenomenon of the black hole.

It is interesting to speculate why Barry agreed to score *Night Games*. Perhaps he again decided it would be a 'fun' movie, or maybe it was the opportunity to work with the controversial French director Roger Vadim. Whatever the reason, the film itself, best described as a sex fantasy, was an unmitigated disaster. Starring newcomer Cindy Pickett as a Beverly Hills housewife haunted by a childhood rape, along with Joanna Cassidy and Barry Primus, it united reviewers in their condemnation; one described it as 'nothing more than an insult to adult minds'. One of Barry's strengths, however, has always been his ability to produce work infinitely more memorable than the film it accompanies. This was again the case here, where his score comfortably transcended the mediocrity of the film, and would no doubt have been released on record at the time had the movie been more successful. In 1993, however, Silva Screen did manage a première CD release which coupled 30 minutes of the score with music from *Game Of Death* – an interesting pairing.

This successfully encompasses all the main cues from the original score, apart from the opening music, which was Barry's adaptation of the traditional tune 'Skip To My Lou'. JB needed to be at his most creative to breathe life into what turned out to be a ludicrous plot, and among the highlights are the piano-based 'Descent Into Decadence', which forms a love theme reminiscent in tone and technique to Barry's main theme to the otherwise chilling *Jagged Edge* score. The remainder of the score includes the occasional use of a choir – something Barry has never been afraid to use when he feels it is appropriate. *Night Games* was his last score of the seventies, a decade during which he built strongly on his reputation as a composer able to adapt quickly and skilfully to any situation.

CHAPTER 18

THE EIGHTIES AND SUDDEN ILLNESS

Originally titled *To Elvis With Love*, the film *Touched By Love*, from director Gus Trikonis and producer Michael Viner, was a moving story of a woman (played by Viner's wife, Deborah Raffin), whose life caring for a small child suffering from cerebral palsy is illuminated by her love for Elvis Presley and his music. Appropriately enough, Barry based parts of his score on musical themes taken from Presley's 'Love Me Tender'.

Barry was next engaged to write the score for a time travel film, *Somewhere In Time*. He was the ideal choice to work on this romantic fantasy for director Jeannot Szwarc, given his considerable previous experience in the *genre*. Christopher Reeve and Jane Seymour were the leading stars in a film that also featured Christopher Plummer, Reeve playing a young playwright who manages to find a way back in time for a reunion with the girl he loved and lost in a previous existence. Although 'Time' was not a major success at first, its later showing on cable television in the States resulted in a clamour for the reissue of a soundtrack album which eventually won a gold disc. To complement his own score, Barry used Rachmaninoff's 'Rhapsody On A Theme Of Paganini', though this was not the original choice. Richard Matheson, the screenplay writer, suggested Mahler, and it was only when Barry found he could not integrate his score with the chosen music that there was a change of mind. It was Barry himself who eventually suggested Rachmaninoff, and in the words of Szwarc: 'It was unbelievable. The length, the feeling, the tempo were perfect. The music fitted the images beautifully. We had our theme, and John set to work and proceeded to write one of the most beautiful scores I have ever heard.'

The film has since gained something of a cult following, and has even inspired a society dedicated to its memory, with close on a thousand members. Barry has said that of all his scores, he has received more letters of appreciation for *Somewhere In Time* than for any others. Curiously, as in the case of *Midnight Cowboy* the theme from *Somewhere in Time* enjoyed so much air play on BBC Radio 2 some six years after its release that MCA felt obliged to put out a single.

Inside Moves (1980) was an emotional story about a man who tries to commit suicide but survives, though now lame, to eventually make friends with other handicapped people at Max's Bar. Barry wrote just two themes which were expanded upon in the film. Also used were songs by popular artists of the day such as Ambrosia, Leo Sayer and the Eagles. Produced by Richard Donner, the film starred John Savage and Diana Scarwid, the latter entirely deserving her Academy Award nomination. Barry's two themes feature on the accompanying Warner Brothers soundtrack album, which otherwise consisted mainly of pop songs.

It has been jokingly reported that Lew Grade spent more on *Raise The Titanic* than it would have cost to bring up the ship itself. Although cleverly made, the movie was damned by the critics and was a box office disaster. John Barry's score deserved a better film, for as usual it successfully created the appropriate atmosphere for every scene. An interesting Cold War sub-plot about recovering rare Byzanium from the sunken ship only partially lifts the film. Because of the huge production losses, there was no chance of a soundtrack album, and a rare Japanese single of the main theme only partially satisfied Barry fans.

Many of those fans regard *Body Heat* as one of his finest scores. Written in a sultry jazz idiom for director Lawrence Kasdan, Barry's score perfectly fitted the oppressively hot climate depicted and the subsequent crime of passion that gradually unfolds. The plot (A *Double Indemnity* for the 1980s) related the way in which an unfulfilled and frustrated *femme fatale* entraps and then lures a shallow philandering lawyer into murdering her rich husband. The film made stars of its leading players, William Hurt and Kathleen Turner. The soundtrack has since been released, albeit in expensive limited edition format, and is still eagerly sought-after.

Despite his problems with *Titanic*, producer Lew Grade clearly appreciated Barry's fine symphonic score, since he then asked him to work on his next picture, *The Legend Of The Lone Ranger*, directed by William A Fraker. This became JB's second Western in the wake of the quirky *Monte Walsh*, which was also a Fraker movie. In this story, a young Texan played by Klinton Spilsbury assumes the identity of the masked lone ranger after he recovers from an almost fatal ambush, perpetrated by the Cavendish gang. It is interesting to reflect that in *Monte Walsh*, Fraker was working on a project that at the time was seen as the final nail in the coffin of Western movies! *Lone Ranger* turned out to be another film that did not fare particularly well at the box office, but an album materialised, clocking in at a mere 30 minutes long.

Bells (1981) was a horror film, and the first of its kind for Barry. The score consisted almost entirely of synthesizers – another new field for him – with the music orchestrated and performed on them by experts Jonathan Elias and John Petersen. The movie reunited Barry and director Michael Anderson, with whom he had worked on *The Quiller Memorandum*. No music was recorded for commercial release, once again probably because of the film's limited appeal. A tense thriller starring Richard Chamberlain, it did not rate a British cinema release, but appeared very quickly on video. Other titles for this film were *The Calling* and *Murder By Phone*.

Hammett (1982) emanated from the Francis Ford Coppola stable. At first, the choice of Barry as composer was foisted upon Wim Wenders at the insistence of producer Coppola, when neither party seemed particularly interested in working with the other. In fact it took a well-constructed piano/clarinet demo to convince Wenders otherwise. So delighted was he on hearing it that he immediately telephoned Barry to tell him so – at 3 o'clock in the morning! In the film, Dashiel Hammett relates a mystery as one unfolds before his eyes – the plot on which he is currently working. The score is brief yet concise, with Cantonese inflections to evoke the Chinatown setting. With this in mind, Barry called in Lucia Hwong for cross-cultural authenticity. The score relies largely on extrapolations of the main title – a languorous, rolling blues arranged for piano and clarinet played by Michael and Ronnie Lang. Frederic Forrest, Peter Boyle and Marilu Henner were the stars, with supporting roles from Roy Kinnear, Elisha Cook Junior and Richard Bradford.

Jessica Lange starred with Kim Stanley and Sam Shepard in *Frances*, a movie directed by Graeme Clifford about the life of actress Frances Farmer. The two leading ladies were nominated for Academy Awards for their impressive performances. John Barry was not nominated, but his dramatic score spoke volumes about Farmer's turbulent life, and as with *Somewhere In Time*, he combined his own music with a well known classical piece, this time, Mozart's *Sonata in A major K331*, played on the film soundtrack by Chet Swiatkowski. Graeme Clifford, for whom Barry was always first choice to score his first film, said: 'I needed music that was at once romantic and yet underscored the severe emotional stress that pervaded Frances Farmer's life. John achieved this brilliantly with his haunting melodies and beautifully evocative themes, tinged with an undefinable uneasiness.' Barry also wrote a song based on the main theme, 'Close Your Eyes', specifically for the film. Although a demo exists with him accompanying Sarah Brightman on piano, it failed to make the final cut.

In an attempt to exploit his success in the *Magnum PI* TV series, *High Road To China* gave Tom Selleck his first starring film role as a down-and-out alcoholic pilot who is hired by a young socialite (Beth Armstrong) to help locate her missing father. The search opens the door for some stunning aerial photography and the kind of out-and-out adventure one would expect from the director of *Where Eagles Dare* and *Kelly's Heroes*, Brian G Hutton. Barry, well versed in combining full-blown action with lyrical romanticism through his Bond work, proved an inspired choice of composer, while he captured the 1920s masterfully with the use of Jonson and Mack's 'Charleston' as source music. Most of the score is to be found in the soundtrack album issued by Silva Screen; the American issue on the Southern Cross label contains the same music, but the sleeve has different artwork. The movie was well received, and distributed widely through Europe.

The Golden Seal (1983), a Samuel Goldwyn Junior production, told of a small boy's attempts at stopping hunters killing a seal thought to be mythical. Barry collaborated with Dana Kaproff to score this overtly sentimental film, shot in the Aleutian Islands and starring Steve Railsbeck and Michael Beck. The musicians worked together in much the same way Barry had done with Ken Thorne; he composed the main themes while Kaproff scored the remainder of the music. Some prints of the film included a song over the end credits called 'Letting Go', with lyrics by Don Black, which was sung by Glen Campbell and released in Britain as a single. The flip side was an instrumental by Barry and Kaproff, 'Face To Face'. The disc did not sell well enough to trouble the chart statisticians, although an album of the score recorded at Olympic Studios in London was released by Compleat Records.

With Debra Winger in the lead role, *Mike's Murder* (1983) was another film that found its way into the video shops rather than the cinema when it was released in Britain. The score consisted of a main theme written for piano and saxophone, developed in different guises throughout the film. A soundtrack album was released with just the pop music written for the movie and played as source music over the radio and so on by Joe Jackson, who received a credit for the additional music. The film was directed by James Bridges.

Until September (1984), an unashamedly romantic drama set in Paris, gave Barry the perfect vehicle to demonstrate his gift for melody. Director Richard Marquand was thrilled with the result – an understated yet exquisitely evocative score which captured the joy, tenderness and passion of a flowering love affair. This was a marvellous example of a composer underscoring the plot, with tenor sax, flugelhorn, horn and guitar used as lead instruments against a sparse orchestral backdrop to enrich the intensity of the relationship developing on screen. Varese Sarabande were astute enough to issue an LP in America; Silva Screen were equally far-sighted in issuing the CD.

Director Francis Ford Coppola had started *The Cotton Club* (1984) many years earlier, eventually completing it only after the collapse of the Zeotrobe Studios at a cost of over 50 million dollars. John Barry wrote the original music and also acted as music supervisor, but it was Bob Wilbur who was responsible for recreating the Duke Ellington sound used liberally throughout the film. Set in the famous New York night-club during the 1930s, the drama homed in on those who frequented it, particularly the musicians and gangster fraternity. Full of lush songs and arrangements, it even featured star Richard Gere playing cornet solos. The soundtrack album on Geffen Records brought many of the vocals and instrumentals from the film, though to present them all would have called for the double album originally planned. Also included were just two instrumentals composed by Barry, 'Dixie Kidnaps Vera' and 'The Depression Hits'/'Best Beats Sandman'.

Barry was irritated when Coppola changed his mind about the score after it had been recorded, reminding him that the two of them had agreed to the format adopted – an orchestral score to counter the many jazz songs and instrumentals. In the end, Coppola wanted these orchestrations toned down, so rather than changing anything he had written, Barry simply re-recorded the tracks with just a small band. A compact disc was issued with a booklet insert including full colour photographs from the film, both in the UK and Japan, at a time when CDs were relatively new to the market. Both were quickly deleted, but recent reissues have materialised in

America and the UK.

Jagged Edge (1985), a thriller, was Richard Marquand's follow-up to *Until September*. A tense courtroom drama in which a lawyer (Glenn Close) defends a newspaper publisher (Jeff Bridges) accused of murdering his wife, the movie is a labyrinth of red herrings cleverly accompanied by a multi-layered synthesizer score set against the most melodious of main themes written for piano and flute. Despite minimal orchestral music in the film, Varese Sarabande decided to release an album in the form of two suites, later issued as a limited edition CD in 1993. TER picked up the rights to issue the score in Britain, but only on LP.

My Sister's Keeper (1986) was yet another film given its première on video. Originally titled *Monday, Tuesday, Wednesday* and now occasionally *The Killing Affair*, it starred Peter Weller, Kathy Baker, John Glover and Bill Smitrovichin in an intriguing tale of murder and mystery set in West Virginia in 1943; as the original title suggests, it tells of events over just three days. In spite of its excellence, Barry's 30-minute score was never released on record, and remains unfamiliar even to his most fervent admirers; no doubt the video-only release did not help. The score also contained synthesizers provided by Jonathan Elias, with electronic realisations by Elias and Barry.

After their problems on *The Cotton Club*, Barry let Coppola persuade him back to score *Peggy Sue Got Married* (1986), a fantasy time travel film with Kathleen Turner and Nicholas Cage. She played a woman at her high school 25th anniversary reunion who finds herself living her young life again – with the benefit of hindsight – after banging her head in a fall. Buddy Holly's original demo version of 'Peggy Sue Got Married' was used for the opening titles. For the rest of his score, Barry used plenty of guitar and strings, but Varese Sarabande omitted some of this music from the album in favour of pop material including a song sung by Cage, even though Barry's score was good enough to win him a BMI award in 1987. Although the British album used different artwork compared to its US counterpart, the music remained unaltered. Two end titles were written for the film, but of course only one was used in the final print, and this ends up on the album entitled 'Charlie, I Had The Strangest Experience'. Barry revealed how the score, which relied heavily on piano, strings and guitars, took him back to his roots.

The *Howard The Duck* (1986) portrayed in this full-length feature bore no resemblance to *Marvel* comic's cigar-chewing private detective anti-hero, and was severely panned by the critics. Despite its lack of success, MCA released the soundtrack album, which also contained music performed in the film by Dolby's Cube, featuring Cherry Bomb. The original songs were produced by Thomas Dolby, while additional music for the film was composed by Sylvester Levay. A characteristic Barry score occupied the second side. Lea Thompson was the star, while director and producer were Willard Huyck and George Lucas. It was the prospect of working with Lucas for the first time that attracted Barry to the deal, but in the event they never met, and he felt he was misled into writing music for scenes with special effects which at that stage were not even finished. The US edition of the album contained a full colour poster from the film.

Michael Ritchie directed *The Golden Child*, casting Eddie Murphy in the unlikely role of a social worker assigned to look for a mystic child thought able to bring peace to the Earth. Apart from scoring the film, Barry co-wrote the song 'Best Man In The World' which features in the film and on the subsequent album sung by Ann Wilson; but as with so many movies, life was not easy for its makers. Changes before its release included the omission of 40 minutes of footage, and when asked to re-score, Barry refused. Only segments of his music now remain, since Michael Columbier eventually completed the task, but Barry is still credited for 'The Wisdom Of The Ages'. Capitol in America released the Ann Wilson song on a single, while the B-side was a four-minute instrumental version by Barry not left in the film. This instrumental was split in two distinct parts, and perhaps gives some idea of how the rest of his score might have sounded.

After their success on *Jagged Edge*, director Richard Marquand called on Barry to provide the background score for *Hearts Of Fire*, a film set firmly in the rock world. In truth, the movie was dominated by songs by stars Bob Dylan, Rupert Everett and Fiona Flanagan, so Barry's score was sparse, to say the least, and his participation might have been a mark of his respect for the director. There was no question of his score being issued on record, though the rock music did achieve an album release. Of more significance is the fact that this lacklustre film was a very sad end to Marquand's distinguished career, as he died shortly after it was completed.

Masquerade (1988) was Barry's final film before a debilitating illness temporarily laid him low. Meg Tilly and Rob Lowe starred in this Bob Swain production – a tale of romance, murder and betrayal. The haunting main theme was repeated frequently throughout, but a planned soundtrack album was scrapped because of the film's disappointing box office performance. In the UK it was released quickly onto video, a familiar tale; but there was better news when one of Barry's early London associates, John Scott, recorded his version of the main theme with the Royal Philharmonic Orchestra for his 1988 *Screen Themes* compilation album.

For Barry, ill health brought the eighties to a miserable and premature end, culminating in an enforced two-year spell of rest and recuperation. They were dire times, but in hindsight it can be seen that the lay-off served to rejuvenate his artistic muse; come the start of the new decade, he was again at the very top of the tree, clutching another Oscar for his brilliant and innovative work on *Dances With Wolves* . . .

CHAPTER 19

THE NINETIES

My *Life* (1992) was the story of an upwardly mobile professional whose wife is pregnant with their first baby when he finds he is dying of cancer. Desperate to leave some legacy of himself for his child, who will presumably be born after his demise, he adopts a clever plan – he starts taping a video scrapbook of homilies, advice, man-to-man talk and so on for each stage of the newcomer's development. Along with this, he embarks on a discovery mission for spiritual healing, which even if it does not save his life, might at least give him peace of mind. The mood of the film is strongly influenced in a realistic and positive way by Barry's careful and exquisitely sculptured melodies and wistful backdrops. The dying man finds peace with his estranged family, an unbreakable bond with his wife, and briefly, a powerful and beautiful gift of prolonged life through the birth of his baby.

A talented young architect with a plan to build his dream house finds that a financial upset leaves the enterprise in jeopardy. He and his wife borrow money from parents and then, still short of their goal, decide to risk everything on a weekend's gambling in Las Vegas. While her husband is at the tables, his gorgeous wife attracts the attention of a playboy billionaire. His accurate assessment of their plight when the husband suffers a loss at the gaming tables leads him to suggest an *Indecent Proposal* – a million dollars tax free in exchange for a night of lovemaking with the woman.

Its morally controversial story line made *Indecent Proposal* one of the most talked-about films of 1993. Barry certainly found it one of his most difficult assignments, telling author Tom Soter that the changing and ambivalent relationship of the three central characters caused him real problems: 'It was a question of the balance of how you play them off together, and come out at the movie's end feeling good about all of them. Writing the music for that, it was hard to keep that balance – because if you pushed the Robert Redford character too much one way, then you're tipping the scale the wrong way. It was like walking on eggshells on a tightrope, keeping the emotional balance of the melodies in control. How does one interplay all these moments? Believe me, it was a nightmare getting there.'

Barry wrote two principal themes for the film, one of which was layered with a lyric written by the English singer Lisa Stansfield, who recorded the song 'In All The Right Places', taking it into the British Top Ten on its release as a single. That performance, together with an array of other pop standards not written by Barry, made up the soundtrack album, alongside a 25-minute suite of Barry's original score divided into 14 segments. The other principal theme recurs through the suite in a variety of arrangements.

In *Ruby Cairo* (1993) a wife learns of her husband's mysterious death and sets about investigating who he really was after finding that among his possessions nothing seems to fit who he claimed to be. A set of baseball cards holds the key, leading to a worldwide tour of exotic countries and hidden bank accounts, secret codes and mysterious strangers who have removed the money just ahead of her. She learns her husband was a smuggler who arranged his own 'death' to cheat his colleagues and live to tell the tale – but they are reunited too late for either of them to reclaim their marriage, his fortune, or a bungled script that drifts away into a disappointing climax. Andie McDowell took the starring role in a film that marked Barry's return to his style of the sixties with a melodic score.

Two mercenaries become bitter enemies. Years later the one with a conscience (Sylvester Stallone) exacts revenge on former colleagues who had caused him to murder a child. *The Specialist* sets about creating personal bombs that blow only the targeted victim to bits, rather than innocent bystanders. Into this world of vengeance arrives a mysterious woman asking for help. She wants revenge against the very people Stallone is pursuing. He must protect her by killing her lover and his father, a Mafia kingpin who will not allow her to leave a brutal relationship. The plot turns on the growing passion Stallone feels for his unseen employer and his hatred of the mercenary partner who betrayed him. In the end, the silliness of this plot is barely balanced against the excellence of the character actors. Where the movie does work, it is immeasurably aided by Barry's dramatic and powerful action music, in which he eschews his Bond format for a psychological *film-noir* style that hangs a sinister and tense frame around the picture. An action adventure film that could have led to self-parody instead finds Barry always ahead of the game, by holding back instead of laying it on with a trowel. Unhappily, the producers remixed more of the action style of music into scenes where JB had deliberately chosen not to use it; and while his exquisite end titles contain his first use of a muted trumpet in a score in 12 years, it is removed in favour of a raucous and mind-bending rock song.

The director had almost decided to call his film (A) *Scarlet Letter* according to co-composer Peter Buffet, such was the porridge the script made of the old American classic by Nathaniel Hawthorne. Hester, a strictly 1990s-style of woman, arrives in a religious community unaccustomed to assertive females and stirs up resentment among the male leaders as well as driving a wedge between the female residents. Her husband fails to join her because he is captured and tortured by Indians, who make him one of their own. While he suffers, she dallies with a sexually repressed preacher who is 'awakened' by her bold nature. Hester becomes his lover, falls pregnant and when she refuses to divulge his identity as the father, she is imprisoned for destroying public morality. At last her husband returns without divulging his identity, spies on his wife and secretly vows revenge on her. When the child is born, neither the preacher nor Hester will name names, and in the final reckoning they are both to be publicly hanged. Luckily for them, the Christianised Indians conveniently choose this moment to arrive, and the lovers buggy merrily away free as birds. In addition to Barry's exquisite and tender music, some claim to have heard another background sound: that of Hawthorne rotating in his grave.

Looking on the bright side, *Scarlet Letter* is the kind of film that will always be one of JB's fortés, a costume drama with a love story at its centre. The theme melody is simple and beautiful, with horns, strings and full orchestra doing what many would see as more than full justice to the noble and courageous love of Hester and her tragic clergyman.

'I've known the story *Cry, the Beloved Country* for a long time, and it has always appealed to me,' said Barry. 'I found this production quite magnificent, and it was quite wonderful to work on this kind of material, this kind of strength. This is entirely different from the 1952 British production, because it is shot entirely in South Africa by South Africans. It deals with it in a more powerful way, it's got a strength to it that the other never had. *Cry, the Beloved Country* was the basis of a Broadway show, *Lost in the Stars*, which itself had quite a magnificent score. It is something I've been very fortunate with, subjects set in Africa.

One of the themes in *Cry, the Beloved Country* is a hunting scene, and this is a dramatic score in a cinematic sense; there's no real indigenous African music in it. We have some wonderful source music in the movie – all jazz music played by a South African jazz group who were around in the 1940s and fifties. It's fascinating stuff. Apparently this was all the music that was coming from the radio stations during this time, it was all jazz, not African music. But it's strange, when I did *Out Of Africa* there was only one scene in the whole film that had an African music score.

'In *Cry, the Beloved Country* we are dealing with characters in a situation, and the score tends to go with the people, as opposed to the spectacle of it. I love doing lyric pieces, and this is a lyric piece. It's all hard work, some harder than others, but if you have a wonderful screenplay and the movie has been beautifully directed and you have a high performance level, as this has, then life is really a lot easier, because people are not asking you if the music helps the film. This is a fascinating story. Particularly powerful is the scene when the two fathers meet. I needed to create power in the score, and in the sense of the men on the screen, a fascinating interplay of what you can do with music, and the dimensions that music can touch. It's also the interaction between the characters on the screen and the audience, what the characters know and what the audience doesn't know. That's the kind of crossover that music can deal with, and there's no other element in the world that can do this.' Barry clearly enjoyed himself on this film. He even managed to playfully incorporate a musical quotation from his own *Zulu* theme during some of the cues.

Across The Sea Of Time is the second dramatic film from Sony Pictures Entertainment and Sony New Technologies to be presented in the revolutionary

IMAX 3D format. It is the touching story of Tomas, an 11-year-old Russian boy who journeys to New York on a seemingly impossible quest. Guided by postcards of the city with stereoscopic photographs – a primitive forerunner of today's 3D – mailed to Russia 80 years ago, he seeks to recreate his ancestors' travels. He is aided in his great adventure by a variety of helpful New Yorkers, and succeeds in finding not only the old brownstone terraced house on one of the pictures, identifiable only by its street number 117, but the American branch of his family. Cue for weepy reunion.

Director/producer Stephen Low, whose father Colin made the first IMAX 3D film for Expo '86 in Vancouver, created in *Across The Sea Of Time* an ideal vehicle for the breathtaking sight and sound realism made possible by the IMAX format. Visually, the film is built around the contrast between New York City landmarks – Central Park, Coney Island, Times Square, Broadway – as they are today and as they were 80 years ago. Musically, Barry's genius harmonises these contrasting images through a score whose grandeur and emotional depth recall the best of the great romantic composers. The contrast between the sophisticated, suavely contemporary sound of the James Bond soundtracks and the timeless romanticism of *Across The Sea Of Time* tells us all we need to know about Barry's astonishing versatility. It is little wonder he was chosen to score for a film that is simultaneously travelogue, mystery, history and adventure.

'I always go for a melody first, because it's the most direct form of communication dramatically,' Barry told writer Paul Tonks. 'It has to be versatile, though. In *Swept From The Sea* (aka *Amy Foster*), the love theme is used about four times without much change. But 'Yanko's Theme' is used a number of times. He leaves his homeland on the train from Russia through Germany. Then the authentic dance. Then his reminiscences. Again when he dances with a little boy. It's that one theme being used in many different ways. I remember Shostakovich saying about music to "keep the emotion intact". Once you capture that essence, everything else springs from that daddy, the master file. You grow with other harmonic material. Maybe take fractions of the melody. That starts to dictate the rest of the score for you. I do love having a theme that works throughout – it's not possible on every film.'

Barry was reunited with lyricist Tim Rice for a song, 'To Love And Be Loved', which, though not in the film itself, was on the soundtrack album. It was sung by 19-year old newcomer, Corina Brouder, discovered by Barry in rather unusual circumstances. Her sister, Christina takes up the story: 'Corina is our oldest sibling and she is 19. We have had our own family band called The Spirits of Gilbride for 10 years and have performed all over the US and Canada together. We have always known that Corina was the talented one in the group and were just hoping that someday the right person would hear her and know it too.

'The way that came about was a story in itself. Our Dad was renovating part of John Barry's house in Oyster Bay, New York. One day they were chatting and Dad mentioned that Corina could sing. John said for Dad to bring him a tape of her voice and he loved it. He said he would love to have her sing on an upcoming project and true to his word – he did. As well as being a singer Corina is an extraordinary musician and can play the harp, piano, violin and accordion. In her non-musical life she is a licensed hairdresser and a nurse. The very best thing about Corina is that she is really down to earth, has no airs about herself and has a great sense of humour.'

Nine-year-old Simon Lynch (Miko Hughes) is an autistic savant in *Mercury Rising*. Barely able to communicate with the outside world, he spends his time solving puzzles with amazing speed and ease. After deciphering a top-secret military code, nicknamed Mercury, that had been placed in a puzzle magazine for last-minute, redundant quality control, however, Simon's world suddenly changes forever. He calls in with the answer, and the shocked writers immediately report the breach to their supervisor, Nicholas Kudrow (Alec Baldwin), a high-ranking NSA official, who orders that the boy and his family be assassinated to ensure national security.

The boy's parents are murdered, but Simon manages to hide until he's later found by F.B.I. agent Art Jeffries (Bruce Willis). Formerly an undercover agent, Jeffries has recently been relegated to routine operations after being labelled as delusional by his superiors. Assigned to investigate the double homicide, Jeffries intuitively knows the boy is also in danger. After learning that someone ordered the police surveillance dropped at the local hospital, Jeffries takes Simon and goes on the run. From this moment on, the plot revolves around his attempt to protect the boy, expose the NSA officials, and keep from being killed by Burell, Kudrow's assassin.

For his opening to the score, Barry used low piano notes in unison with celli against strings/flutes in a tense and terse understatement of struggle. The mood is appropriately dark, brooding, nervous and dangerous. His other main theme is for Simon and appears in various places throughout the movie. It features flute figures in short phrases against a piano figure over low, tense celli and chording in the strings suggesting innocence and discomfort.

Barry told film music writer Paul Tonks: 'When I heard about Bruce I had reservations. You see this *Die Hard* image. But they sent me a script which has an action sequence at beginning and end, but the middle is this wonderfully drawn character with a little boy. An almost Hitchcockian mystery. It's not an action movie. The opening sets up this guy's response to violence and the end is where the bad guy gets it! So that's something I can get inside. You're constantly looking for scripts where you can do that.'

CHAPTER 20
$\mathcal{S}$TAGE MUSICALS

An item in the music press in September, 1964 reported that Barry was working on a musical version of Grahame Greene's novel *Brighton Rock*. 'Greene gave permission for it to be used, and agreed to help in the writing, which will be handled by Wolf Mankowitz. The difficulty in getting the Boultings to release their hold on the film rights is expected to be resolved.'

This project was something Barry had wanted to do for a long time and had worked on at length, writing many songs. 'In the end nothing came of it, because we couldn't get round the fact that the central character was a very despicable person, and to have this in a musical show appeared to be a problem. It was never staged anywhere. When certain problems appear insurmountable, personality difficulties and so on, it's not an easy undertaking.'

Grahame Greene himself submitted a few lyrics for Brighton Rock, but many years later, in 1987, it was Don Black who was to consider a further attempt at a musical version, this time with fellow sixties survivor Lionel Bart. In the end he opted for *Budgie*, written with Mort Shuman.

Barry's move to CBS coincided with an upsurge in the number of films he was offered and felt able to accept. Many of these scores spawned album releases, although not all on the CBS label. What is more, he found time to work on his first stage musical, *Passion Flower Hotel*, which opened at the Prince of Wales, London in August, 1965. It received mixed reviews, ran for six months and included two or three excellent songs. Critics generally could not decide who was to blame for this rather short run. The *Sunday Telegraph*, under the heading 'Silly and smutty', thought 'Barry seemed more at ease writing the production numbers for Peter Gordeno's lively hot foot if derivative choreography than the melodies for Trevor Peacock's static, repetitive, clumsily contrived lyrics.' On the other hand, Hugh Leonard, writing in *Plays And Players*, thought that 'Trevor Peacock is a most talented lyricist and leaves the composer, John Barry lagging behind.' Leonard disliked almost everything about the show, and was particularly scathing about Francesca Annis, one of the female leads: 'There is only one solo song number in the course of the evening. This goes unaccountably to Francesca Annis, who either cannot or will not sing or dance. She seems to loathe the show, and goes through the evening very much on her dignity, being a good sport about the entire nasty proceedings.'

Leonard did enjoy two of the songs, 'What A Question' and 'I Love My Love', but even these were ruined for him by 'the appalling amplification system in the Prince of Wales'. Herbert Kretzmer, for the *Daily Express*, liked Annis's version of 'How Much of the Dream Comes True', but complained in general about the quality of all the singers. The show featured many young actors and actresses who have since made their mark, including Jeremy Clyde, Nicky Henson, Jane Birkin, who became the second Mrs Barry, Pauline Collins and a very young Michael Cashman, who eventually became well known through BBC TV's *Eastenders*. Barry thought years later that 'over confidence could have been the trouble'. Another problem was the spirit of the play, rooted very much in the new moral outlook of the sixties at a time when West End audiences were still largely conventional and staid.

Alan Jay Lerner first contacted Barry because Katharine Hepburn, a mutual friend, had told him that JB shared his interest in the children's book *The Little Prince*. During the course of this discussion Lerner asked if Barry would be interested in doing *Lolita My Love* (1971) for the American stage. They met in London in May, 1970, but as Barry was still busy scoring films, they wrote only two or three songs, and loosely at that. It was not until October that they got into the heavy writing. In this instance, about 90 per cent of the music was written first, after they had discussed the tempo, mood, title and attitude. Lerner would then add the lyrics, in the opposite fashion to Rodgers and Hammerstein, who started with the lyrics. It meant that all the song titles were written by Lerner – normal practice except when it is the title of a film or show. *Lolita* was a disaster, and says Barry: 'We opened in Philadelphia on February 16th, 1971 to very bad reviews, and closed on February 27th.' The cast returned to New York for a month to go back to the drawing board, and the show resurfaced – with changes in script and personnel – at the Schubert Theatre in Boston on March 23rd; it closed five days later. The hoped-for Broadway opening at the Mark Hellinger Theatre never came to pass and, not surprisingly, neither did a planned original cast album for Columbia Records.

Looking back, Barry says: 'It was getting into better shape. At least the first act was an improvement, and Mike Nichols came to see it and would have liked to direct it. Unfortunately, he had other commitments, so I wanted to put it on the shelf for a while until he could sort out the problems with me.' This proved impossible, and the show closed with losses of $900,000. Barry believed the style of the show had not gone down well with the critics: 'It was a black musical comedy, but when they killed off Lolita's mother in the first act, it upset the American theatre party set. So many American musicals seem to glorify middle-aged American women. Although no original cast album materialised, two or three of the songs were later recorded, notably 'Going Going Gone' by Shirley Bassey and 'In The Broken Promised Land Of Fifteen' by Robert Goulet. There were also a couple of non-commercial recordings on the Mediasound label featuring those two songs and 'How Far Is It To The Next Town?' Then, in 1987, quite out of the blue, an album was released of a complete recording of one of those handful of performances at the Schubert in Boston. Since it was recorded quite unofficially through the theatre's sound system, the quality is by no means perfect, but it gives a fair idea of the style and nature of the show.

Later in the seventies, Barry wrote another musical, and, unlike *Lolita My Love*, the very English *Billy* was an unqualified success. Barry first conceived the idea of staging a musical version of *Billy Liar*, a popular novel and film of the sixties, in 1971. His friend and lyricist Don Black recalls: 'John was always going on about the book, saying how great it was, so we ran the film, re-read it all, and I had to agree it was marvellous. A great story and very funny, which is a thing I miss in musicals these days; you don't get much humour.' Convinced they had enough material to embark on Barry's most ambitious project to date, the two went ahead. At this stage JB did the next best thing to putting up money by securing the rights from the book's writer Keith Waterhouse and Willis Hall. He then persuaded Michael Crawford to take on the title role, and Peter Witt agreed to produce. With TV scriptwriters Dick Clement and Ian La Frenais hired to adapt the play and Patrick Garland at the director's helm – fresh from a recent collaboration with Barry on the film *A Doll's House* – an extremely promising team was complete.

In spite of this coming together of talents, *Billy* was still considered a risky venture at the time, as only Barry had ever worked on a musical before. Possibly with this in mind he and Black spent the best part of 1973 working to perfect the music, all at JB's half-finished villa in Majorca, where he believes splendid isolation helps him write more easily: 'We get up at around six or seven in the morning and work very hard in separate rooms before having a late lunch. Then we talk things over.' The Barry/Black partnership is certainly flexible, for inspiration is equally likely to stem from lyric or music: 'You go through several phases. There are areas where it's obvious where songs should go. There are also highly technical areas where there is no real cause for a song, but the structure needs music to make an idea work. What we have come up with is a traditional musical, as opposed to *Hair*, *Godspell* and *Jesus Christ Superstar*.

The show opened for a three-week trial run at the Palace Theatre, Manchester on Monday, March 25th, 1974, for which Barry brought in orchestrator Bobby Richards and musical director Alfred Ralston. Talking just before the London West End opening, he admitted to being nervous, particularly after the relative failure of *Passion Flower Hotel*. Of the score he said: 'It's a total brass band approach for the scenes that represent reality to Billy; we have no violins at all, just brass, woodwinds and percussion. But when we go into fantasy – Billy dreams he goes to Hollywood and dances like Fred Astaire and Gene Kelly – we drift into an MGM type orchestration.' In fact Barry need not have worried. The show opened to rapturous reviews, and was to run for two years at the Theatre Royal, Drury Lane. It was given a Royal Gala Première in the presence of Princess Margaret on Monday, April 29th, two days before its official first night. Critics were more or less unanimous in their praise of Michael Crawford in the lead role, and this time the music, too, seemed to be everything they were looking for. For the *Daily Express*, Herbert Kretzmer wrote: 'The songs are always suitably dashing or sentimental, always right for the moment, if lacking any obvious hit. 'Some Of Us Belong to the Stars' is one of the show's best songs. For Michael Crawford the title is prophetic.' The *Guardian* noted especially 'John Barry's catchy score and Don Black's pointed lyrics'. Jack Tinker in the *Daily Mail* praised almost everything about the show, but neglected to mention the music; and Milton Schulman, in the *London Evening Standard*, felt that 'John Barry's music was more practical than melodic, though I suspect that songs like 'Billy' and 'I Missed the Last Rainbow' could catch on. Don Black's lyrics were sharp and bright.'

After Crawford had spent nearly two years as Billy, he was succeeded by the multi-talented but older Roy Castle, but nobody wanted to see the show without Michael, and it closed within a few weeks. An original cast album was issued in the UK on CBS and went silver; and Sony reissued the album on CD and cassette in the early nineties. Ambitious plans to take the show to Broadway failed to materialise. It closed at the end of 1976, and three years later Barry and Black were reported to be working on an American version. They intended to rework the score, adding some new songs, and adapt it for an American audience that might not have homed in on the resonances of, say, life in Northern England and brass band music. Again, nothing materialised, but revivals of *Billy* are always on the cards.

In November, 1987, when he was working with Mort Shuman on *Budgie*, Don Black discussed just such a revival: "We never did anything with *Billy* originally. It never went to America; it never went anywhere. It was just one of those things. Somehow we all got involved in different projects and we didn't pursue it. But plans are now at an advanced stage to revive it. We've got some exciting thoughts about recasting, and I really think it could happen all over again.' In 1989 Don Black still intended to revive the show, but said the stumbling block was finding someone suitable to play Billy. John Barry also mentioned this problem in a radio interview in 1987, but he was optimistic that most of the original writing and production team would be available for the revival.

Late in 1989 the original director, Patrick Garland, also talked about a proposed revival. He said the idea was to bring the show up to date, enabling the young English comedian and singer Gary Wilmot to play the lead. Nothing materialised, but late in 1992 things got off the ground in the form of a two-week National Youth Music Theatre production at the Edinburgh Festival. Black and Barry wrote two new songs, 'My Heart Is Ready When You Are', a duet for Liz and Billy, and 'One Man Can Make A Difference', sung by Billy. TV comedian Andrew O'Connor took the lead and Don Black hoped to attract West End producers with a view to a new London run, but the continuing recession and the recent failure of other musicals combined to put the venture on ice once more.

The Little Prince And The Aviator, Barry's second musical in collaboration with Don Black, was due to open at the Alvin Theatre on Wednesday, January 20th, 1982. It had started rehearsals in the November, and previewed at the same theatre from New Year's Day. Poor reaction to these trial runs led to low ticket demand for the opening, and producer A Joseph Tandet ran into financial difficulties. Sadly, the musical failed to open. Unusually for a production of this kind, up-front finance was raised by forming a public company, Little Prince Productions Ltd, and selling 750,000 shares to the public at two dollars each. The musical's book was by Hugh Wheeler, an adaptation of Antoine de Saint-Exupery's fable about an airman who makes a forced landing in the Sahara Desert. Here he meets a little boy who has been transported there by birds from another planet.

Anthony Rapp played the title role, Michael York was Toni, the aviator (actually Saint-Exupery), and Ellen Greene was Suzanne. This was not the first attempt at a musical version of the book, as there had been an unsuccessful 1974 film version, featuring songs by Lerner and Loewe.

CHAPTER 21

THE OSCARS

One day in April, 1967, Barry was awoken at 5.15 a.m. by a phone call from Michael Crawford, who was watching the *Oscar* awards on television in New York. JB had picked up awards for best original score and for best song – with lyricist Don Black – for the film *Born Free*. It was the first time an Englishman had won both awards, but Barry, though obviously aware of his nomination, was unable to be present as his second wife, Jane Birkin, was expecting their first child. Kate was born just an hour later at a London clinic. Curiously, Barry had not wanted to honour his commitment to score the film, feeling that he had been misled by the director James Hill, whose vision of the movie's dramatic mood contrasted very sharply with his own. Much to the director's chagrin, Barry thought it had a lot in common with a sentimental Disney feature. He argued bitterly about having to score the film, but by that time he was already contracted to the project. According to Barry, the governing team on the picture were at odds between themselves and with him over how the score would fit the film. The producer, Carl Foreman, at first decided to omit Matt Monro's vocal main theme, but once Roger Williams' cover version was successful it was hastily reinstated.

Apart from the *Oscars*, the score won an *Ivor Novello* award and *Born Free* was chosen for the Royal Film Performance of 1966, opening at the Odeon, Leicester Square on Monday, March 14th. Barry was the first British composer to be presented to the Queen on such an occasion. Strangely, the song was destined to become a standard, yet it was only a minor chart hit for Matt Monro.

In complete contrast to *Born Free*, Barry's other Oscar during the sixties, won for his score for *The Lion In Winter*, remains a personal favourite from that decade. Normally Barry prefers to orchestrate all his own work, finding this the most enjoyable part of the job. For this film, however, he was faced with the strictest of deadlines – just three weeks in all for both scoring and recording; because of this he turned for assistance to Bobby Richards, an English orchestrator. On the plus side, JB was clearly delighted with the opportunity to return to one of his early passions – choral music – to illustrate the English Royal Family of the twelfth century, and their domination by the Church of Rome. He later said the music 'went with the picture' in only two places – the slaying sequences, the only two areas of exact dramatic music. His work won him not only his second Oscar for best original score,

John Barry meets The Queen at the Royal Première of *Born Free*.

but also the prestigious Anthony Asquith Award from the British Film Academy. An interesting footnote is that Colin Miles, the owner of See For Miles Records, passed a singing audition with Barry for a part in the film. He was to be one of a group portraying the King's subjects, but as with many other young hopefuls, his part in the film ended up on the cutting room floor.

Mary, Queen Of Scots (1971) was an epic production telling the story of Mary Stuart's opposition to Elizabeth I and her imprisonment and execution. An all-star cast of Vanessa Redgrave, Glenda Jackson, Trevor Howard, Patrick McGoohan and a youthful Timothy Dalton certainly made sense at the box office. A soundtrack album was released in Britain and America with a theme that became so popular that is spawned a vocal version. 'This Way Mary' was recorded by a number of artists including Johnny Mathis and Matt Monro, the latter with the aid of John Barry and released as a single with another song based on a theme used in the film, 'Wish Now Was Then', with lyrics by Don Black. The Australian reissue of the album contained two extra tracks which were uncredited, although one was merely a repeat of the main theme. A studio version was not only made for Polydor on the

Christopher Lee, John Barry and their wives at the Royal Première of *Born Free* in 1966.

Producer and Director with John Barry for *Mary Queen of Scots* reading.

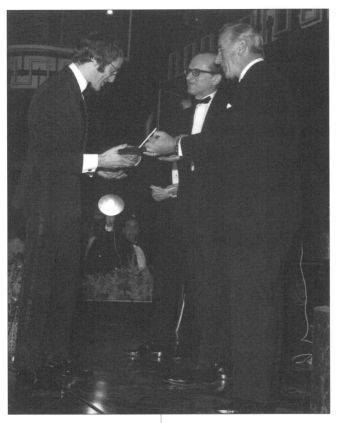

Above left: Lord Mountbatten presents John Barry with the Anthony Asquith Award for Best Score for *The Lion in Winter,* at the Grosvenor House Hotel in March 1969.

Above right: John Barry at CTS Studios for the recording of *Mary Queen of Scots* in 1971.

Concert album, but recorded again in 1972 for release as a single, a more pop orientated version released back-to-back with 'Diamonds Are Forever' as the flip side. Barry won an Academy Award nomination for his excellent period score, but was beaten by Michel Legrand's music for *The Summer of '42*.

Winning an Oscar is a highlight in any composer's career; to win a fourth is a remarkable feat, yet this is what Barry achieved with *Out Of Africa* in 1986. In winning again, he had to beat off strong opposition from Bruce Broughton's *Silverado*, Georges Delerue's *Agnes of God*, Maurice Jarre's *Witness* and Quincy Jones's *The Color Purple*.

It's true to say that this film had a lot going for it before Barry got involved. For example, a script based on Karen Blixen's best-selling book, outstanding photography by David Watkin and two of the most popular actors of the day: Robert Redford & Meryl Streep. But despite these obvious advantages, director Sydney Pollack had designed *Out of Africa* with the deliberate intention of letting music play an important part. 'I need a great score, or I'm dead,' he told Barry. Barry duly obliged, but later said that despite appearances to the contrary, there was only 35 minutes of music in the entire film. He felt credit was due to Pollack's production technique, which deceptively gave the impression of a much lengthier score. The film won a total of six Oscars, including best picture and best direction, although the only nominated actors, Meryl Streep and Klaus Maria Brandauer, missed out.

Serious illness saw off most of the rest of the eighties for Barry, who has since laughingly claimed that everybody needs to take a sabbatical when they get to his age – though he did not necessarily recommend his method, a ruptured oesophagus! His comeback score, *Dances With Wolves*, won him another Academy Award for best score in 1991. That means that to date, Barry has received an impressive seven nominations, winning five times – a record that will take some beating. Barry wrote one and a half-hour's music for *Dances*, making it his longest score to date. For first-time director Kevin Costner, having Barry on the team proved to be an educational experience. After initially perceiving the score in the tradition of 'The Great American Western', Barry persuaded him to approach it differently: more specifically from the point of view of the leading character, John Dunbar, in much the same way the screen-play did. By taking Dunbar's perspective, Barry was able to compose a moving and lyrical score, which drew on Dunbar's own sense of loss at seeing, as an outsider, the last vestiges of a peaceful indigenous culture – 'How The West Was Lost' rather than won, in effect. His was a priceless piece of advice, for the score succeeded in underpinning the emotional *gravitas* perfectly. Never was an Oscar so richly deserved. Interest in 'The John Dunbar Theme' became so intense in the UK that a single was issued exclusively there. Infused with a contemporary backing

Far left: Recording *Chaplin* at Abbey Road Studios in 1991.

Left: John Barry with Sir Richard Attenborough at the *Chaplin* recording sesions.

track, it attracted considerable air-play.

During the past few years, Sir Richard Attenborough has forged a fine partnership with composer George Fenton, who has written the music for most of his recent films. However, when *Chaplin* was in production, Fenton was already committed to another project, forcing Sir Richard to look elsewhere. It was no surprise to find him teaming up with Barry, for they had worked together on *The L-Shaped Room*, an Attenborough co-production, and on *Seance On A Wet Afternoon*, in which Attenborough had a starring role as well as co-production credit. According to Sir Richard, he wanted a score that would capture the heartbreak and humour, as well as the romance and drama of Chaplin's extraordinary life. The outcome, which gained Barry another Oscar nomination in 1993, delighted Attenborough, and did much to enhance a film that failed to win the wholehearted approval of either critics or public. Barry's poignant main theme crops up in various guises on the sound-track album – piano-led, and interpolating Chaplin's own composition 'Smile'.

CHAPTER 22

WORKING IN TELEVISION

John Barry's small screen appearances with his Seven began as early as 1957 – on August 30th, when they made their debut on *Teddy Johnson's Music Box* for ATV. Other shows for Independent Television followed during the next five or six years, including several appearances on Jack Good's *Oh Boy!* throughout 1958 and 1959. In fact, after Good had fallen out with Harry Robinson over the rights of ownership of the Lord Rockingham's XI name, he was lined up to take over as musical director of the show, only to be beckoned by the BBC with *Drumbeat*.

Rehearsals for the first *Oh Boy!* took place at the Four Provinces Club in Islington on September 8th and 9th, 1958, before the show embarked on a highly successful and lengthy run. *The Jack Jackson Show, Boy Meets Girl* and *Sunday Break* were other ITV series with appearances by the group during 1959/60, but the highlight was undoubtedly *The Royal Variety Show*, televised for the first time ever on May 16th, 1960, and broadcast six days later. Throughout 1961, the Seven made appearances on *Big Night Out, Sunday Night at the London Palladium, Thank Your Lucky Stars* and *All That Jazz*, in the last of which they appeared in further guest spots during 1962.

Apart from *Drumbeat*, there were many other shows for the BBC, mainly on guest spots. They appeared with a well loved veteran comedian on *The Ted Ray Show*, but far better for their 'street cred' was the *Juke Box Jury* on February 6th, 1960, when Barry was a guest in 'the hot seat' while 'Hit And Miss' was played, discussed and rightly voted a resounding hit. On November 2nd, 1962, he took part in a tele-recorded pilot of a new BBC pop show that incorporated *Juke Box Jury*. A 19-strong John Barry Orchestra was involved in this ambitious project which, if the go-ahead had been given, would have resulted in a six-week run beginning on December 29th. Barry was given £381.50 for this, presumably out of which he had to pay the orchestra, but later was awarded a further payment of £125 'for conducting two arrangements and assisting the producer'. The pilot failed to find favour with the top brass, but nevertheless, two weeks later the JB7 recorded an appearance in *Christmas Night With The Stars*, peak time viewing for December 25th. The following year, the BBC needed to fill the awkward spot just before the evening's viewing got off the ground, and they hit on the idea of a 30-minute show called *Around Seven*. On November 6th, John Barry appeared conducting a small group that included Vic Flick and Johnny Scott, who also backed guest appearances from Chad and Jeremy and Annie Ross. Ember boss Jeffrey Kruger had a big hand in arranging the line-up, as all were artists under contract to his label at the time.

On May 10th, 1966, the BBC broadcast a programme of folk music with Nina and Frederik. The orchestra was directed by John Barry, and songs included 'If Dreams Came True', 'Charade', 'Mr Noah', 'That's My Song', 'Little Boxes', 'Maladie D'Amour', 'Les Enfants', 'Daddy', 'What If', 'There But For Fortune', 'Inch Worm', 'The One On The Right Is The One On The Left' and 'Norwegian Wood'. Barry and the orchestra played the theme from *The Knack* while the great Danes were changing their costumes.

The highlight, perhaps, of Barry's BBC career was broadcast on December 17th, 1972, in a programme entitled *John Barry and His Music,* introduced by Michael Parkinson with guests Michael Crawford and Fiona Fullerton. Barry was not only interviewed at some length by Parkinson, but also conducted various movie themes against the backdrop of scenes from the films. The musical content was based firmly on Barry's recent programme at the 1972 Filmharmonic concert at the Albert Hall.

In 1995, the BBC recorded a series of 'shorts' for a series called *Close-Up,* to coincide with 100 years of cinema. Various film celebrities were invited to choose a scene from a movie they considered memorable, and on April 1st, John Barry was the featured guest and selected the ballet scene from *An American In Paris*.

Despite these on-screen appearances, Barry's strength on television, as elsewhere in his professional life, lay in composing. 'Hit And Miss', the very first TV theme written and recorded by Barry, was not originally commissioned as a theme. The John Barry Seven Plus Four had recorded it as their debut record for Columbia, and after it was voted a unanimous hit on *Juke Box Jury*, host David Jacobs liked it so much that the following week, February 13th, 1960, it replaced 'Juke Box Fury' by Tony Osborne's Ozzie Warlock and the Wizards as the programme's signature tune. It remained for the show's entire nine-year run, and was later rearranged when it resurfaced in 1979, and again in 1989. It reached number 10 in the British charts.

Girl On A Roof (1961), a television play from the BBC in Manchester about a young girl's obsession with a fictitious pop singer Red Mayne, was originally intended as a vehicle for Adam Faith, but he pulled out to be replaced by Ray Brooks (complete with dyed hair). Johnny De Little was cast in a supporting role, while the John Barry Seven were seen and heard on stage backing these two actors and in their own concert performance. The numbers they played were 'Bees Knees', 'Black Stockings', 'I Want You Baby', 'Kid's Stuff', 'Mad Mab', 'Not Guilty', 'Saturday's Child', 'Skid Row' and 'Walk Don't Run'. Orchestrations were by Barry.

Ray Brooks performed two songs, 'Flea Brain' and 'I Want You Baby', while Johnny De Little sang 'I Did What You Told Me' and his own version of 'I Want You Baby', all of which were backed by the Seven. Waveney Lee played the young fan. The play, which was transmitted on February 16th, was written by former BBC TV producer Stuart Douglass, who also supplied the lyrics for 'I Want You Baby'. The producer was Chloe Gibson.

Falling In Love (1961) was a documentary study of young love, narrated by

Michael Flanders, for which Barry wrote the complete score. For the recording, he used the Seven, augmented with musicians such as Johnny Scott and Ike Isaacs.

The Betrayers (1962) was a play for ATV which starred Erica Rogers, and Barry was merely responsible for writing the theme, which was not recorded.

Dateline London (1962) was a daily news programme for the London ITV region which used the theme Barry had recorded with the John Barry Seven and Orchestra as 'Cutty Sark'. It climbed to 35 in the British charts.

The score for *The Human Jungle* (1963), an intriguing ABC series about psychiatrist Dr Roger Corder's case-book, was written by Bernard Ebbinghouse. It was played, however by John Barry and his Orchestra and recorded, although not in its original format, on Columbia. It was not until the eighties that the television version was released as part of a collection of TV themes on the Filmtrax label, and in 1994 Play It Again included the even rarer stereo version on another TV themes compilation.

Elizabeth Taylor in London (1963) was a television special made in England by the American TV company ABC. Barry thought one of the reasons behind the original approach to him was pure convenience; producers Philip D'Antoni and Norman Baer were renting an apartment in the same London square where he was living. He gained an Emmy nomination for the score to a programme seen by more than 80 million viewers in America on October 6th, 1963, when it was networked by CBS. In Britain, BBC Television showed it on Christmas Eve of the same year. The recording of the score, which featured Johnny Spence and his Orchestra, took place at CTS Studios in Bayswater on August 12th, with John Barry producing. Apart from the Ember single discussed earlier in the book, the complete score with dialogue was released by Colpix Records, both in Britain and America – the latter including an extra track, 'The Churchill Speech'. In 1992, Play It Again re-issued the score only on CD, but included both sides of the Ember single as bonus tracks.

Following their success with *Elizabeth Taylor*, producers Baer and D'Antoni had no hesitation in turning once more to John Barry for the score for *Sophia Loren In Rome* (1964). They played his *Taylor* score to Loren, who, although liking it very much, wondered whether Barry was conversant enough with Rome to catch its exciting flavour. They knew he would be able to cope, but without telling her, flew him down to Rome for a few days so the three of them could soak up its ambience. A week after Barry had flown back to London he produced a tape of a theme which the producers played to Loren. They did not tell her in advance who had composed it, but it won her immediate approval. The song was 'Secrets of Rome', which Loren eventually sang on the soundtrack. The complete score was issued only in America on Columbia, who also put out Loren's vocal as a single. Curiously, six tracks from the score were later issued together with material from an advertising campaign for Yolande, which had no connection with Barry. Music from both occupied each side of an LP on the Chemstrand label.

Barry, as usual, made great use of his main theme, 'Secrets Of Rome', which appeared four times in various guises on the LP; another track, 'Marcello', appeared twice. Not all the score was composed specifically for the programme; possibly to boost its length, Barry went back to his EMI days and reused 'March Of The Mandarins', slightly rearranging and extending as well as re-titling it 'The Ballet'. He also used a previously unissued EMI recording, 'The Aggressor', retitled in the plural. EMI have recently released the original on their *John Barry – The EMI Years Volume Two*.

The music was recorded in Rome, with Barry issuing instructions to the Italian orchestra through an interpreter. Even so, according to the producers, the session still encountered one problem. After an hour had elapsed, the entire orchestra got up and walked out. A baffled Barry shouted 'Where are you going?' at which one of the musicians shouted back in Italian that they were going to change the parking meter time cards on their cars. When the producers walked into the empty studio, Barry improbably explained that these artistic Latins were taking a tea break! The album was reissued in the eighties on CBS in Australia only, but was released for the first time on CD in 1998.

A popular soap opera, *The Newcomers* (1965) starred Maggie Fitzgibbon, Alan Browning and Gladys Henson as the Cooper family, as well as a host of well known British character actors including Wendy Richards and Campbell Singer. The series, which also introduced Judy Geeson as the Coopers' young daughter, was screened twice a week on BBC TV and ran for almost three years. It used John Barry's 'Fancy Dance' as its theme, the record having been made for Ember a year or so earlier.

Barry wrote both the main theme for *Vendetta* and 'The Danny Scipio Theme', the latter recorded by Gary Blake on a single. This 1966 BBC offering, which starred Stelio Candelli as Scipio, was an adventure series about a lone Italian battling against the Mafia. Barry recorded the two themes for single release on CBS.

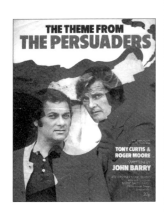

Barry's theme for the ITC show, *The Persuaders*, was once described by the *New Musical Express* as the best TV theme ever written. Sweeping statements like that are always open to argument, but there is no denying its long-standing impact. The show featured two of the most popular stars of the time, England's Roger Moore, who was reputedly committed to his role of Lord Brett Sinclair by ITC's Lord Grade before he had even consulted him, and America's Tony Curtis, who played Danny Wilde. Despite great popularity in England, its premature demise after only 24 episodes reflected indifference in America, the very market where success was imperative. With Barry commissioned to write only the theme, it was left to Ken Thorne to compose most of the incidental music. The theme was released as a single and became an instant hit, reaching number 13 in the charts, Barry's most successful solo single to date. A new arrangement was included in his programme for the 1972 Filmharmonic concert, but was omitted from the album that followed.

Talking much later about the popularity of the theme, Barry told *The Daily Telegraph's* James Delingpole: 'It's strange because it's in three/four time, and all rock 'n' roll is in four/four. I suppose people like the strong, driving bassline and the simple melody. I was always looking for a fresh sound, so I went to this friend of mine called John Leach, who travelled all over the world collecting strange instruments.

He came up trumps by over-dubbing the sound of a cimbalom with a kantele, the zither-like national instrument of Finland.'

The Adventurer (1972), ITC's follow-up series, was also filmed on location, and Barry was again asked to compose the theme tune. Starring Gene Barry as a debonair villain catcher, it was again created with an eye for an American prime time slot – but despite the jet set backgrounds this, too, failed to impress, and ran for only 24 episodes. Polydor released a re-recording of the theme as a single, which was in slightly slower vein than the original TV version. A symphonic arrangement was also part of the repertoire of the Philharmonic Concert that year, and was released on the record *Concert,* a studio recording of some of its highlights. Even Barry's theme and supporting roles from Barry Morse, Stuart Damon and Catherine Schell could not save the series.

Made by Anglia TV, *Orson Welles' Great Mysteries* (1973) was indeed introduced by Welles, but he did not appear in any of the episodes. The series was not syndicated in the UK and so had a limited audience, but it became very popular in Japan, and Polydor took the option to release the theme as a single. In Britain it appeared on the 1974 album *Play It Again.* A total of 26 episodes were made, and Barry's haunting theme, using synthesizers and guitar, was the last British TV theme he composed.

Although originally an American made-for-television movie, *Love Among The Ruins* (1973), directed by George Cukor, was given a theatre release in the UK. It starred Sir Laurence Olivier opposite Katharine Hepburn, who played an elderly and affluent widowed actress seeking the services of a past lover (Olivier) for legal counsel in a breach of promise case. When he accepts the case she is disturbed by his failure to recognise her. Olivier half sung, half talked a few lines from the song 'Love Among the Ruins', with lyrics by Don Black. It was not recorded, but Barry laid down the instrumental in 1974 for the *Play It Again* album, and this recording was as faithful to the original as one could get.

Hot on the heels of Anthony Harvey's last film with John Barry, *They Might Be Giants,* was *The Glass Menagerie* (1973), a movie made in America for TV. The film, which received a theatre release in the UK, again starred Hepburn, this time as an aristocratic mother who with her invalid daughter (Joanna Miles) lives in the hope of something turning up to improve their circumstances. The main theme was simply scored on the high notes of a piano, actually played by Barry on the soundtrack, and the only music recorded was a remake of the theme, somewhat toned down, for release on the *Play it Again* album.

Eleanor And Franklin (1976) might well be Barry's finest score for a made-for-television film. His uncanny instinct for choosing prestigious projects stood him in good stead once again, for this adaptation of Joseph P Lash's Pulitzer Prize-winning biography of the Roosevelts eventually won ten *Emmys.* The fact that Barry's music was not even nominated caused a major upset at the time. The film told the story of the Roosevelts before Franklin became President through the recollections of the widowed Eleanor, with Jane Alexander and Edward Herrman in the title roles. The

'Eleanor and Franklin' theme had an admirable dignity and strength touched with a hint of sadness, and is among the most memorable television music of the decade.

For the sequel *Eleanor And Franklin: The White House Years* (1977), Barry reprised his original main theme – and this time he was rewarded with an *Emmy* nomination, although in the end he lost to Leonard Rosenman's score for *Sybil*. American film music critic Tony Thomas described Barry's theme as 'simple yet wistful ... essentially American in character, and yet one that has universal regret for the past as it fades into memory. It is a prime example of the eloquence of music when written as an extra dimension to visual experience.' The success of the two productions led to the release in the US of the main theme on a Casablanca single, as the flip side of Barry's 'Theme From The Deep'. In the UK, a Donna Summer vocal took the place of 'The White House Years'.

A small town college professor's wife (Elizabeth Ashley) discovers her husband is having an affair with one of his students in *The War Between The Tates* (1977). Richard Crenna starred as Brian Tate, who is forced to resolve this crisis in his normally orderly life. Barbara Turner's adaptation of Alison Lurie's book won her an Emmy nomination, but no music from the film was commercially recorded.

Barry returned to the world of American politics for *Young Joe, The Forgotten Kennedy* (1977). Peter Strauss played Joe, the eldest of the Kennedy brothers, who undertook a dangerous World War II mission that it was hoped would bring him home a hero and see him achieve the family dream of a Kennedy in the White House. The film won an *Outstanding Special Emmy* nomination for 1977-78, but lost out to *The Gathering* – Barry's next assignment. Again, no music materialised on record.

The Gathering (1977) starred Edward Asner as a dying businessman facing his last Christmas. He makes an 11th-hour attempt to pull together the family he left several years earlier, having allowed his work to take precedence. Maureen Stapleton as his wife was nominated for an *Emmy*, as were director Randall Kleiser and three other of the production team, but it was the movie itself that won the only *Emmy* as that Outstanding Special of '77-'78. This was a Hanna-Barbera production for which Barry was signed by Harry R Sherman, the producer of *Eleanor And Franklin*. No music was released, and when H-B produced a second part two years later, Barry was not involved.

George Cukor's version of Emlyn Williams's classic play *The Corn Is Green* (1978) marked his tenth collaboration with his favourite actress, Katharine Hepburn. She plays the indomitable schoolmistress, Miss Moffatt, who is determined to stamp out illiteracy in a Welsh mining village. Ian Saynor co-stars as Morgan, a brilliant pupil she is determined will win a scholarship to Oxford, and Bill Fraser, Patricia Hayes, Anna Massey and Toyah Willcox feature in a fine supporting cast. Most of Barry's score consisted of short cues, and there was not sufficient material to be released.

Deborah Raffin won the plaudits of the US critics for her role as *Willa* (1979), the waitress who turns to truck driving to support her three children. This was the last in a run of TV movies for Barry, an engaging story which also starred Clu Gulager.

The music set the scene immediately, with the main titles encapsulating the speed of the trucks. This was another film in which Barry used a harmonica theme, while other songs were written especially for the film and sung by various artists, including the Incredible Bongo Band and the Bellamy Brothers.

Svengali (1983) was an updating of the classic story of power and obsession, with Peter O'Toole as music teacher Anton Bosnyak and Jodie Foster as Zoe Alexander, a young rock singer who comes under his spell. After the disappointment of their failed musical, *The Little Prince And The Aviator*, Barry and Don Black wrote three excellent songs for this Anthony Harvey-directed movie. There were plans to issue a recording of Foster's 'Getting Some Feeling Back In My Heart', possibly coupled with 'One Dream At A Time', but no record company was interested.

Barry was recommended for *USA Today: The Television Show* (1988), the networked early evening news programme, by graphics designer Richard Greenberg, who had worked with him on the film *Inside Moves* in 1980. According to film music journalist Jon Burlingame, executive producer Steve Friedman wanted music that was 'viewer friendly', and was quick to point out that he was not interested in the type of theme John Williams had written for *NBC News* – he thought it was too jarring, too serious. Barry recalled Friedman's directive: 'He wanted something very different, not a pretentious opening title theme, but something very distinctive that would be recognised when you heard it.' He worked without the benefit of seeing Greenberg's titles, recalling that this had also been the case with 'The James Bond Theme', when the main title designer was Maurice Binder: 'A thing like this sometimes works because it's two totally different energies going – and when they come together, it sparks.' Barry remembered the cries of the street corner newspaper sellers back in his home town of York, when they always seemed to carry a little tune of their own. He took that as a basic idea, and his theme was a three-note descending melody that suggested a musical 'USA'. Producer Friedman liked it, believing it set the tone of the programme. Unfortunately, the critics did not care for the format of the show, and four months after its September début, Friedman was replaced by Jim Bellows. He in turn decided to replace both the graphics and the music, saying it was 'sleepy'.

SUNNY GIRL
de geweldige filme muziek van de Sunsilk Shampoo TV-films

Chapter 23

TV Commercials

In the early sixties John Barry composed the music for the Milk Marketing Board's famous 'Drinka pinta milka day' campaign, which he followed with an advertisement for Ingersol watches and Izal toilet paper. He continued in this medium until 1967, composing for a whole string of British TV commercials. In fact, most of the population absorbed Barry's *oeuvre* during this decade, whether conscious of it or not. His Sunsilk shampoo theme became even more widely known when Barry recorded it commercially as 'The Girl With The Sun In Her Hair'. Don Black later added a lyric, and the song was recorded by Davy Clinton on the NEMS label, and was included on Play It Again's *Don Black Songbook* compilation CD in 1993.

In America, Barry composed music for White Owl Cigars in 1965 and Eastern Airlines in 1968.

More recently he wrote the music for a Kodak film campaign, which was seen in Britain and America to coincide with the screening of the 1992 Olympic Games.

CHAPTER 24

WORKING IN RADIO

John Barry's work on radio in Britain was almost exclusively for the BBC, commercial radio in the late 1950s and early 1960s being limited to Radio Luxembourg. At one time he was negotiating for a series of half-hour shows for the latter, but according to Vic Flick, he was unhappy with the recording facilities offered, and declined after just one programme was broadcast. So after early difficulty in breaking into TV, how did Barry go about getting the band some radio exposure? It was their agent, Harold Fielding, who first wrote to the assistant head of variety, Jim Davidson, seeking an audition for them. This was arranged for September 18th, 1957, just days before their first appearance on *Six-Five Special*. Producer Jimmy Grant was in charge of the audition, before which he had received a request from Fielding to set up facilities for the Seven's instruments, to which they added a vibraphone.

Two weeks later, Fielding received a response from Donald Maclean, BBC Radio's variety music organiser. He turned them down, saying that 'the reports on the audition recording indicate that they are not acceptable for broadcasting.' It seems they remained 'unacceptable' for a couple of years, because it was not until September 28th, 1959 that they made the first of several appearances on Brian Matthew's *Saturday Club* – produced, ironically, by Jimmy Grant. Their fee for this date was £47, which increased to £59 the following year, when two of the broadcasts were 'Specials' from the Royal Albert Hall.

Actor and broadcaster Brian Matthew.

Brian Matthew was impressed by the group, and when he became responsible for producing and compering a new programme, *Easy Beat,* he lost no time in engaging them as resident band. The Seven were augmented by four violins, and Barry received £73.98 per show, plus a £5 supplementary fee for himself. Apart from their own spot the group also accompanied the bubbly Welsh singer Maureen Evans, and their repertoire consisted of both their own work and hits by other artists. 'Peter Gunn', 'Bonnie Came Back' and 'Rebel Rouser' are examples, but more surprisingly, Barry included instrumental versions of classic songs such as 'What Is This Thing Called Love?', 'I Remember You', 'Easy To Love', 'How High The Moon' and 'Black Bottom'. Barry composed the *Easy Beat* signature tune, later recorded by the guitarist Bert Weedon, and the group's run on the show lasted from January to June, 1960. It would have been longer, but the Seven were needed for a summer show with Adam Faith in Blackpool, and had to stand down. Weedon took over their spot.

In 1961, Matthew was responsible for yet another weekly programme, *Music With A Beat,* on which the Seven again had their own spot and backed Kay McKinley. The emphasis was on easy-listening music, with Barry including numbers such as 'St Louis Blues', 'Lonesome Road' and 'Tuxedo Junction', as well as accompanying McKinley on 'How Wonderful To Know', 'Half Of My Heart' and 'Little Boy Sad'. Barry also used the opportunity to play his latest record releases, 'The Menace', 'Starfire' and its flip side, 'A Matter Of Who'.

During his time in England, Barry was often in demand for radio interviews, appearing on *Let's Go, Late Night Saturday, Movie Go Round, Be My Guest, Roundabout* and *Late Night Extra* in the 1960s. On his return to Britain in the 1980s and 1990s he was frequently a guest of Gloria Hunniford and of Brian Matthew, the latter presenting a two-hour celebration of his life and music.

On May 22nd, 1967, Barry joined the select band of people who appeared as guests on *Desert Island Discs* with its original host Roy Plumley. His eight castaway records were a fair reflection of his musical tastes at the time, and ran as follows:

1. *Symphony No.5 Opus 100,* Second movement: 'allegro marcato', Prokofiev
2. 'It Never Entered My Mind', Frank Sinatra
3. 'La Suerte de los Tontos', Stan Kenton and his Orchestra
4. *Symphony No.9,* Fourth movement: 'adagio', Mahler
5. 'The Gypsy', Kodaly Girls' Choir of Budapest
6. *Cello Concerto in E flat Opus 107,* First movement, Shostakovich, with Mstislav Rostropovich on cello
7. *Concerto for Orchestra,* Third movement: 'Ellegid', Bartok
8. *Alexander Nevsky Opus 78, the Crusades in Pskov,* Prokofiev

His luxury item was an upright piano, and his book *The Imitation of Christ* by the fifteenth-century German philosopher monk Thomas à Kempis, probably the best known devotional work ever written.

CHAPTER 25

JOHN BARRY IN CONCERT

John Barry concert appearances began more than forty years ago, when as one of the JB7 he toured regularly throughout the British Isles. The highlight of those early days was always the annual *New Musical Express* Poll Winner's Concert. These concerts began in 1953, just after the journal itself made the newstands, and participants were traditionally those artists who had figured high in the yearly *NME* polls.

In 1958, the JB7 finished a creditable third behind Lonnie Donegan and Chris Barber in the small groups section, particularly bearing in mind their lack of a hit record at that time. Thus they were included in the line-up for the 1959 concert, held at the Royal Albert Hall, London, in January. They actually opened the bill, as the *NME's* James Wynn reported: 'Some torrid playing by the powerhouse JB7 – highlighted by a big beat version of the time-worn "The Saints" – got the show off to a good start.'

The following year, the JB7 fared one better in the poll, finishing second to Donegan. They were invited to partcipate in the 1960 programme and were joined by Adam Faith, who was a late replacement for Alma Cogan, accompanying him when he sang 'Poor Me' and 'What do you Want?' The concert venue had changed to the vast Wembley Empire Pool, which could seat 10,000. The *NME's* Keith Goodwin was impressed by the JB7. 'When it comes to beat music, the JB7 is unrivalled in Britain, and the outfit's own driving performance – including "The Saints" and John's latest composition "Hit And Miss" – told us why it is held so high in the estimation of fans.'

March 5th, 1961 saw the final Poll Winner's concert appearance for The Seven. Once again finishing runners-up, this time to The Shadows, they also backed Adam Faith, appearing this time as a Poll Winner himself. The concert was the first to be televised, albeit three weeks later, by ATV. Faith had a lengthy set, singing 'Wonderful Time', 'Singin' In The Rain', 'What Do You Want?', 'Worried Man', 'Lonesome Traveller', 'Who Am I?' and 'When Johnny Comes Marching Home'. Keith Goodwin admired his performance and stage presence, but singled out The Seven for even more praise: 'The big beaty sound created by The John Barry Seven is the sort of thing that makes teenagers want to clap their hands and stamp their feet, which is just what they did when the multi-talented Barry led his men through hits like "Hit And Miss" and "Walk Don't Run". For big beat music at its best, Barry is undoubtedly the tops!'

John Barry's solo concert performances have been few and far between. They began in January, 1964, when with a 23-piece orchestra he toured the country in a series of shows with Shirley Bassey. Presented by the Vic Lewis Organisation, they followed a successful concert in the singer's home city of Cardiff on December 21st, 1963. Matt Monro joined the package in the second week, withdrew due to a death in the family, and returned from Copenhagen towards the end of March to rejoin from April 10th. The concerts were very popular and ran for months in halls up and down the country, with the first at the Odeon, Leicester Square. The show then visited Birmingham, Manchester, Bradford, Nottingham, Brighton, Bristol and Sheffield among others, and featured a selection of standards and hits by Bassey and Monro, accompanied by the Barry orchestra.

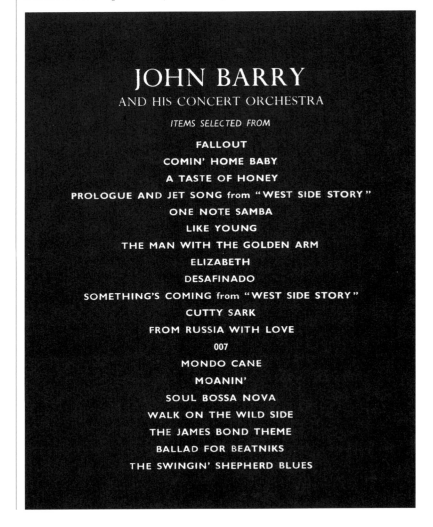

JOHN BARRY
AND HIS CONCERT ORCHESTRA
ITEMS SELECTED FROM
FALLOUT
COMIN' HOME BABY
A TASTE OF HONEY
PROLOGUE AND JET SONG from "WEST SIDE STORY"
ONE NOTE SAMBA
LIKE YOUNG
THE MAN WITH THE GOLDEN ARM
ELIZABETH
DESAFINADO
SOMETHING'S COMING from "WEST SIDE STORY"
CUTTY SARK
FROM RUSSIA WITH LOVE
007
MONDO CANE
MOANIN'
SOUL BOSSA NOVA
WALK ON THE WILD SIDE
THE JAMES BOND THEME
BALLAD FOR BEATNIKS
THE SWINGIN' SHEPHERD BLUES

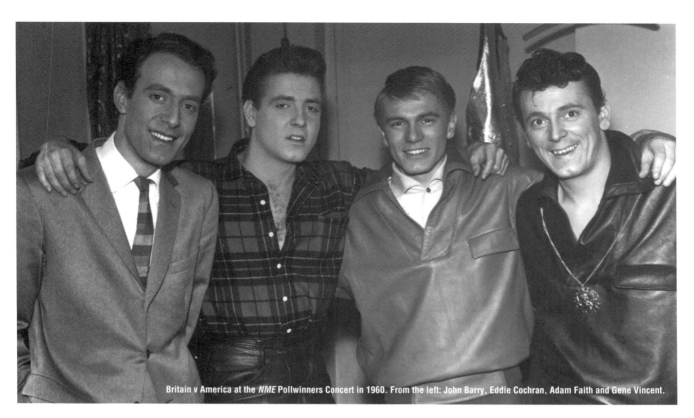

Britain v America at the *NME* Pollwinners Concert in 1960. From the left: John Barry, Eddie Cochran, Adam Faith and Gene Vincent.

The John Barry Seven with their *NME* runners-up award for best small group.

Right: Pete Murray presents an award to John Barry at the 1960 *NME* Pollwinners Concert.

Below: Barry looks on, as the rest of JB7 accompany Adam Faith at the 1961 *NME* Pollwinners Concert, Wembley, London

Frank Chacksfield, John Barry and Sydney Samuelson at the 1971 Filmharmonic reception on the Martini Terrace.

Michael Crawford (as the White Rabbit), Fiona Fullerton (as Alice) and John Barry at the 1972 Filmharmonic.

John Barry at the 1972 Filmharmonic, Royal Albert Hall.

Barry conducts the Royal Philharmonic Orchestra at Filmharmonic '72

The orchestra also had its own spot, in which its programme included standards such as 'A Taste Of Honey', 'Like Young', 'The Man With The Golden Arm', 'Walk On The Wild Side' and music from *West Side Story* – *Prologue,* 'Jet Song' and 'Something's Coming'. The set also included Barry's most requested tunes – 'Elizabeth' from the TV documentary starring Elizabeth Taylor, 'Cutty Sark', 'From Russia With Love', '007' and of course 'The James Bond Theme'. The package took three days to get from one location to another, and an *NME* reviewer described it as 'a refined, classy package show'. 'Desafinado', 'Elizabeth' and 'Coming Home Baby' were Barry's best-received numbers.

Bassey's 45-minute slot included a powerful rendition of 'I Who Have Nothing'. Other songs ranged from 'Stop The World', 'Typically English', 'What Now My Love', 'Gone', 'If I Were A Bell', 'Second Time Around', 'Fly Me To The Moon', 'All The Things You Are', 'No Regrets', 'I Could Have Danced All Night' and 'Climb Every Mountain' to 'You'll Never Walk Alone'. Monro opened with 'Let Me Sing And I'm Happy', followed by his recent hits 'I Love The Little Things', 'My Love And Devotion', 'Portrait Of My Love', 'My Kind Of Girl', together with covers of 'Around the World', 'Bill Bailey', 'It's A Matter Of Association', 'Somewhere' and 'This Land Is Mine'. He closed with the standard 'If I Had A Hammer'.

Promoter Vic Lewis recalls an occasion at the Brighton Dome when Barry phoned to say that he was unable to make the gig as his car had broken down. Lewis had to conduct the orchestra himself, but this was no hardship as he was a renowned band-leader and conductor. Shirley Bassey recalls a more exciting mishap: 'As I hit a top note, my strap broke and out came my left boob. I didn't miss a beat as I kept my hand there and looked to the wings to ask for another dress, but there wasn't any-body there. So I sang "will somebody please bring me another dress", but nobody did, and I finished the song still holding on. My husband, in the audience, suddenly realised what was wrong, and got them to bring another dress to the side of the stage. I said to John Barry, who was playing for me at the time, "Busk it, I'm off", and I did the quickest change I've ever done in my life. I came on in another gown and everyone applauded.'

Barry toured with many other artists, and in the same year the Seven backed Brenda Lee over three weeks. This included 17 concerts and four ballroom dates, opening on November 16th and covering venues in Birmingham, Dunstable, Belfast, Boston, Sheffield, Bristol, Norwich and Blackpool among others. An 11-piece Barry orchestra also backed Billy Fury on his spring tour of 1965, when Fury's group the Gamblers was also on stage. Each band had its own spot on the pro-gramme. The tour opened at Romford on March 2nd and then moved to other venues including Leicester, Bristol, Lincoln, and Blackpool. It finished in Ipswich on the 20th, before resuming, after a month's break, in Gloucester on April 24th.

A highlight of Barry's concert career was when he was asked to appear at the third Filmharmonic, a regular event organised by Sidney Samuelson in aid of the Cinema and Television Benevolent Fund. These concerts started in 1970 and ran regularly until 1980, after which there was a one-off special British Film Year presentation in

1985. Barry conducted his own music during the second half of the concert, after Miklos Rozsa had opened the proceedings, and not surprisingly, the Royal Albert Hall was filled to capacity. It took place on October 7th, 1972, just after Barry had completed his score for Joseph Shaftel's *Alice's Adventures In Wonderland* – which was soon to open in London's West End. The compère for the evening was Michael Parkinson, who of course later interviewed Barry in a BBC TV special about his work.

The following year Barry was invited back to the Royal Albert Hall for a second concert, this time with Muir Mathieson sharing the billing.

MUSIC FROM THE MOVIES
presented by
BRYAN FORBES and ROGER MOORE

Part I conducted by MUIR MATHIESON

The Dambusters *Eric Coates*
1954 Directed by Michael Anderson. Starring Michael Redgrave and Richard Todd.

Legend of the Glass Mountain *Nino Rota*
1949 Directed by Henry Cass. Starring Michael Denison and Dulcie Gray.

Things to Come *Sir Arthur Bliss*
1935 Directed by William Cameron Menzies. Starring Raymond Massey and Ralph Richardson.

Limelight *Charles Chaplin*   Solo violin, Erich Gruenberg
1952 Directed by Charles Chaplin. Starring Charles Chaplin and Claire Bloom.

The Big Country *Jerome Moross*
1958 Directed by William Wyler. Starring Gregory Peck and Jean Simmons.

The Magnificent Seven *Elmer Bernstein*
1960 Directed by John Sturges. Starring Yul Brynner and Steve McQueen.

Henry V: St Crispin's Day Scene *Sir William Walton, arr. Muir Mathieson*
Spoken by Bryan Forbes
1944 Directed by Laurence Olivier. Starring Laurence Olivier and Leslie Banks.

Interval of twenty minutes

Part II conducted by JOHN BARRY
Featuring John Barry's compositions for Bryan Forbes's films including:

Seance on a Wet Afternoon
1964 Starring Kim Stanley and Richard Attenborough.

The Whisperers
1966 Starring Edith Evans and Eric Portman.

And more John Barry compositions including:
The James Bond films

From Russia with Love
1963 Directed by Terence Young. Starring Sean Connery, Daniella Bianchi and Lotte Lenya.

Goldfinger
1964 Directed by Guy Hamilton. Starring Sean Connery, Honor Blackman and Shirley Eaton.

Thunderball
1965 Directed by Terence Young. Starring Sean Connery, Claudine Auger and Luciana Paluzzi.

On Her Majesty's Secret Service
1969 Directed by Peter Hunt. Starring George Lazenby, Diana Rigg and Ilse Steppat.

Diamonds are Forever
1971 Directed by Guy Hamilton. Starring Sean Connery, Jill St John and Charles Grey.

Born Free
1965 Directed by James Hill. Starring Virginia McKenna.

The Knack
1965 Directed by Richard Lester. Starring Rita Tushingham and Michael Crawford.

Midnight Cowboy
1969 Directed by John Schlesinger. Starring Jon Voight and Dustin Hoffman.

Alice's Adventures in Wonderland
1972 Directed by William Sterling. Starring Fiona Fullerton and Hywel Bennett.

Zulu
1963 Directed by Cy Endfield. Starring Stanley Baker, Jack Hawkins and Michael Caine.

The Persuaders and **The Adventurer:** Themes from the TV series.

Mary Queen of Scots
1971 Directed by Charles Jarrott. Starring Vanessa Redgrave and Glenda Jackson.

The Quiller Memorandum
1966 Directed by Michael Anderson. Starring George Segal and Alec Guinness.

Research: Tony Rayns   Production: Brian Eastman

Also in 1973, Barry went on to conduct a concert at the Hollywood Bowl with the Los Angeles Philharmonic, when Elmer Bernstein & John Green also appeared. Barry's programme was as follows:

LOS ANGELES PHILHARMONIC
August 18th, 1973 at 8.30 p.m.
FILMHARMONIC 73 – THE ACADEMY AT THE BOWL
'The James Bond Theme'
'Goldfinger'
'Born Free' (vocal – Bambi McCormick)
'The Knack'
'Midnight Cowboy'
'Zulu'
'The Big Country' (Moross)
The James Bond Suite:
'From Russia With Love'
'Thunderball'
'007'
'You Only Live Twice'
'OHMSS'
'Diamonds Are Forever'

Barry toured Japan for a series of 30 one-night stands in 1975. Trombonist Don Lusher recalls: 'I was part of an orchestra of 25 players led by John Barry. We had been working for him doing the music for the James Bond films, and when he was asked to do this tour, he said he would only go if he could use the same studio musicians. Eventually it was organised, and we set off on New Year's Day. The tour was over a period of five to six weeks. Eileen, my wife, was not well, and I was reluctant to leave her, but she insisted, as she felt this would be a wonderful experience for me, which indeed it was. Sid Margo was our contractor and manager and did a really fine job. The organisation was first class, and we all had a wonderful time. We started off in Tokyo. We then went right down to the south of the country and then back to Tokyo. We then went up north, and back to Tokyo before returning to London. Travel was by air and bullet-train, and a little by coach. The band was excellent; we had a really interesting time, musically and socially. We brought home many beautiful souvenirs. Japan made a big impression on us. Everything was so well organised, the country and people were so different from England, yet I felt perfectly at home.'

Two subsequent attempts at providing a concert platform for Barry were thwarted. He was due to conduct his music from *Out Of Africa* in a US concert extravaganza in early 1988, but this coincided with his serious illness. More recently, in 1992, he was all set to appear at the Seville Music Festival with the RPO, but the concert was cancelled at the 11th hour, when part of the stage collapsed.

However, on signing a new recording contract with Decca at the beginning of 1998, Barry would soon be raising his public profile to hitherto unimaginable heights. Not since the days of the JB7 was he to appear so regularly on both radio and television and in the national press. To cap it all, a prestigious concert was also arranged in the spring to the delight of those loyal fans who had assumed that Barry had put away his conductor's baton for good.

April 18th, 1998, 8 p.m: As seasoned musicians from the English Chamber Orchestra created a cacophony of discord while tuning up in front of an expectant Albert Hall audience, a familiar bespectacled frame emerged from the back, weaving in and out of music stands, stools wires and instruments. "For those of you who don't know me, my name is Michael Caine," he explained, as if introductions were really necessary. He then proceeded to relate an incident from his formative years with warmth, wit, poise and panache. During the early sixties, while still a struggling actor, he found himself evicted from his digs on account of acute financial embarrassment. With nowhere to lay his head, he decided to chance his arm by calling on a friend, whose flat was situated not far away, in Cadogan Square. Could this be his salvation for the night? Noticing the light still on, he disturbed the occupier, busy entertaining a nubile young lady, to beg a room for the night. The answer, thankfully, was in the affirmative. The young lady beat a hasty retreat. For the next few weeks, Caine became house guest to John Barry, where he soon discovered first hand a fastidious craftsman at work. In the early hours of each night, Caine's beauty sleep was regularly disturbed and curtailed by a composer in full flow. During that very first evening, Barry burned the midnight oil in order to complete the theme for his latest assignment which just happened to be *Goldfinger.*

The relevance of this anecdote was not lost on the attentive audience. Caine finished his recollection, then proudly introduced as one of his 'true friends', John Barry, to a full auditorium, eagerly anticipating his first UK concert since 1973. A rapturous ovation ensued as Barry carefully wended his way through the orchestral obstacle course before reaching the conductor's podium. Nervously, he thanked and embraced Michael Caine, then suggested starting the concert with that annoying tune which once kept Caine awake all those years ago.

'Let's have some fun,' he then remarked. The dramatic introduction to *Goldfinger* stirred the 87-piece orchestra into life and settled the nerves of the conductor. Suddenly, everything seemed to fall into place for three members of the audience sitting on the second row, and the purpose of this book began to make perfect sense.

The concert was an enormous success with even the critics falling over themselves to praise it. The reaction of *The Times'* Caitlin Moran was typical: 'As befits the only popular composer who could run the Beatles close in a My Genius Is Bigger Than Yours competition, John Barry's first concert in 23 years is, as you would expect, An Event. Barry has aged gracefully into a lithe, white-haired wolfhound, and bows sweetly to the roaring worship of the Albert Hall after showbiz pal Michael Caine has weaved his way through the orchestra to introduce him. "The producer hated this first song," Barry says in a fabulous bass rumble, like Alan Rickman eating a tom-tom. "But there wasn't enough time for me to write something else." Pause, "Ha."

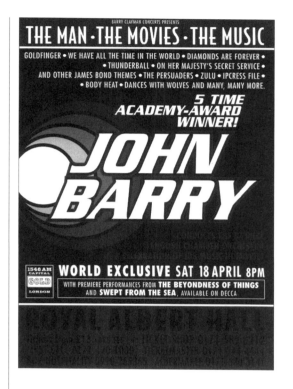

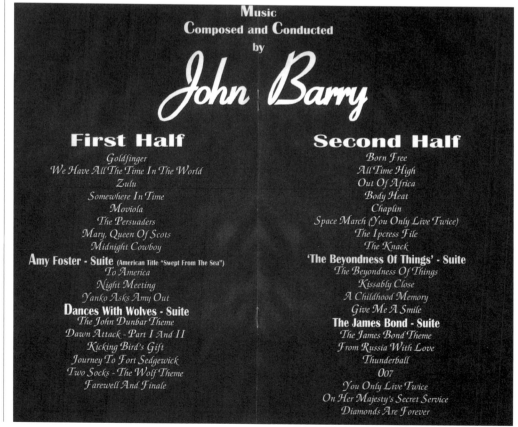

Music
Composed and Conducted
by

John Barry

First Half
Goldfinger
We Have All The Time In The World
Zulu
Somewhere In Time
Moviola
The Persuaders
Mary, Queen Of Scots
Midnight Cowboy
Amy Foster - Suite (American Title "Swept From The Sea")
To America
Night Meeting
Yanko Asks Amy Out
Dances With Wolves - Suite
The John Dunbar Theme
Dawn Attack - Part I And II
Kicking Bird's Gift
Journey To Fort Sedgewick
Two Socks - The Wolf Theme
Farewell And Finale

Second Half
Born Free
All Time High
Out Of Africa
Body Heat
Chaplin
Space March (You Only Live Twice)
The Ipcress File
The Knack
'The Beyondness Of Things' - Suite
The Beyondness Of Things
Kissably Close
A Childhood Memory
Give Me A Smile
The James Bond - Suite
The James Bond Theme
From Russia With Love
Thunderball
007
You Only Live Twice
On Her Majesty's Secret Service
Diamonds Are Forever

John Barry on the beach at
Sheerness, Kent, photographed by
Terry O'Neil in 1998.

'The laughter is still cresting as he brings his baton down for "Goldfinger"; and that filthy stripper's brass rings out like a big Sex Christmas. Barry sways, a beat ahead of the orchestra, like a ballerina in black linen; and coaxes his players along with winks, grins and tiny kisses. When he follows it with the sighing, butterfly-strings of "We Have All The Time In The World", and the colossal, face-shattering brass punches from *Zulu*, you know every audience member is going to be smug about seeing this gig for the rest of their lives. The heart-melting beam on Barry's face as he cues in the harmonica for "Midnight Cowboy" suggests that he might be a little bit, too.

'Of course, it's Barry's big brass Bond stuff that made his name: "Thunderball"; the entirely worshippable "On Her Majesty's Secret Service"; "Diamonds Are Forever". All are played with apocalyptic urgency. Used to the pop-vocal versions, one forgets the dark, shark-like shadows Barry panics his compositions with; the incendiary cellos and asphyxiating brass. However, pure Bond freaks will be surprised to find they also know and adore Barry's other title music: the dark, dancing clavinet from *The Ipcress File*, *The Knack* and *The Persuaders* are all lodged in the thirty-something subconscious, only to tumble forth again during Britpop. Blur's "Sing" – you know, that circular haze from *Trainspotting* – is 'The Persuaders' and nothing else and Pulp's *This Is Hardcore* would simply be Jarvis' rhyming perviness, were it not for Barry.

'Given copious opportunity for laurel-resting, then, it is nothing short of miraculous that the reason for this unicorn-rare show – the world première of *The Beyondness of Things* (Barry's first non-soundtrack album in more than 20 years) – is a possible triumph over his past. A CinemaScopic musical autobiography, *Beyondness* oozes such bittersweet emotional resonance that one can only presume Barry tried to write his biography, but found even the most beautiful of words too pale, dumb and angular, and fled to the rich tidal wash of his orchestra.

'The three standing ovations he received were the most devoted clappings I've ever seen in my life. From up in the circle, it looked like praying. Entirely understandable.'

CHAPTER 26

OTHER ASSIGNMENTS

After his time with EMI and Ember Records, Barry has spent periods recording exclusively for various other labels – notably CBS (now Sony) and Polydor. These produced compilation albums of film music and other material.

His switch from Ember to CBS, which was the first US company to begin operations in the UK in its own right, took place in March, 1965. Although expensive for the company, it was a major breakthrough for Barry, which would bring its rewards as the years unfolded. In a major deal, he was to act as both a performer and producer, and was to record many new artists for the label.

Probably the most rewarding element of Barry's seven-year run with CBS was his success with his first three LP releases, discs that contained specially recorded versions of all his major film themes at a time when movie albums were all the rage. They sometimes contained different arrangements from those heard on the original film soundtracks, and even though the orchestras were rather small compared with modern standards, the recordings still seemed to have a 'richness'. The sessions were produced by Barry at CTS Recording Studios in Bayswater, London and mixed by engineer John Richards on to three-track tapes.

Barry's first collection album in 1966 – *Great Movie Sounds Of John Barry* – contained faithful versions of his themes for *The Chase, The Whisperers, The Knack* and *Seance On A Wet Afternoon*, a different arrangement of his theme from *The Ipcress File* and an extended version of 'The James Bond Theme'. There were also numerous single releases that year, including a special picture bag edition of 'The James Bond Theme' issued by CBS Special Products in conjunction with Fry's Chocolate, and three picture cover EPs – *Themes From James Bond Films, Big Themes From The Big Screen* and *Great Screen Themes* – each containing two titles from the first two albums and specially created by Carr's Biscuits, Walls and Lyons Bakery respectively.

1967 saw the release of the main theme from the latest James Bond extravaganza *You Only Live Twice*, an orchestral version which appeared on his second album, *John Barry Conducts His Greatest Movie Hits*, released in the same year. This album contained the usual batch of themes with the added bonus of a first recording of his music from *Dutchman*. This remains the only version commercially available. The flip was the Sunsilk theme, better known as 'The Girl With The Sun In Her Hair', and it was perhaps a mistake for CBS not to issue this as the topside.

As his film assignments increased, Barry had fewer chances to visit a recording studio for non-film work. He did, however, manage to record a completely different arrangement of the Oscar-winning theme from *The Lion In Winter* for single release, and it later appeared on his third compilation album, *Ready When You Are, JB*, released in 1970. The LP contained his popular 'Theme From Romance For Guitar and Orchestra' from *Deadfall*, and a version of his theme from *The Appointment*. Another single was released in 1969, featuring two tracks from the Oscar-nominated *Midnight Cowboy*, on which Barry worked as musical director. This version of the main theme with harmonica plus 'Fun City', which was not used in the final film, were again different from the original soundtrack versions. Jean 'Toots' Thielemans played harmonica on the original soundtrack and was invited back for this remake.

Although CBS found some of Barry's major themes good sellers, they had yet to score a hit. His fortunes did not change with the release in November, 1969, of the main title from *On Her Majesty's Secret Service*, which was backed by an instrumental version of 'We Have All The Time In The World'. A second release from the film contained two vocals by Nina, who with Frederik had earlier recorded with Barry for Columbia Records. Hal David supplied the lyrics for the tune 'Do You Know How Christmas Trees Are Grown?', used as source music in the film, and 'The More Things Change', which was also recorded by Barry and his Orchestra for *Ready When You Are, JB*. Two other tracks appeared on this album only, 'Afternoon and 'Who Will Buy My Yesterdays?', the latter based on a theme used in the film *OHMSS*. The album provided a selection of sleeve notes, including some by his friend and colleague Bryan Forbes and the American composer Quincy Jones.

In 1971 Barry was asked to write the theme music for the series *The Persuaders*, with Roger Moore and Tony Curtis. As we recalled earlier, this was a lavish production from Lord Grade's ITC, with splendid locations and the need for an appropriate signature tune. The theme was released on CBS and became so popular that it reached Number 13 in Britain and sold well worldwide. The American demo issue contained not only the mono version, which was the norm for singles at that time, but also the stereo, later to appear on the album *The Persuaders*, released in February, 1972. This was basically a reissue of some of the themes released previously, with the addition of this one track and a full colour sleeve picturing Curtis and Moore. The flip side was a re-release of 'The Girl With The Sun In Her Hair', since the Sunsilk advertisement was still showing on British TV. *The Persuaders* remains one of the most sought-after themes by Barry, and was available for some years after the disc's release. It was ironic that Barry's first chart hit with CBS turned out to be his last recording before his switch in 1972 to another of Britain's major companies, Polydor.

Not surprisingly, CBS pressed various reissues in the following years, beginning with a double LP set in 1976 called *The Music Of John Barry*; this is now quite sought-after. It was not until 1988 that CBS, or more accurately its parent company Columbia, released some tracks on compact disc which included a far superior and alternative version of the theme from *The Chase*. This used a completely different

John Barry pictured for *The Concert* album (Dezo Hoffman/Rex Features)

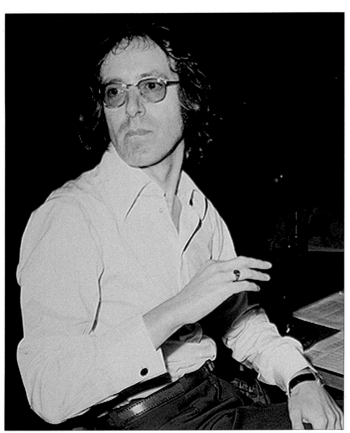

John Barry recording *Diamonds Are Forever* (© John Glanvill).

VOCAL SELECTIONS from BILLY

H. M. Tennent Ltd presents
THE PETER WITT PRODUCTION

MICHAEL CRAWFORD

in

A New Musical

Adapted by DICK CLEMENT & IAN LA FRENAIS
(Based on "Billy Liar" by Keith Waterhouse and Willis Hall)

Music by
JOHN BARRY

Lyrics by
DON BLACK

With
BRYAN PRINGLE   AVIS BUNNAGE   CHRISTOPHER HANCOCK
DIANA QUICK   GAY SOPER   ELAINE PAIGE
LOCKWOOD WEST   BETTY TURNER   BILLY BOYLE
Barry James   Elsie Winsor

Costumes by
ANNENA STUBBS

Production Designed by
RALPH KOLTAI

Lighting Designed by
JULES FISHER

Vocal & Dance arrangement by
RAY HOLDER

Music arranged & Orchestrated by
JOHN BARRY and BOBBY RICHARDS

Dance Orchestrations by
KEN CLAYTON

Musical Director
ALFRED RALSTON

Dances & Musical numbers staged by
ONNA WHITE

Directed by
PATRICK GARLAND

Charles Hansen
EDUCATIONAL SHEET MUSIC & books
1860 Broadway / New York, New York 10023

a publication of
EDWIN H. MORRIS & COMPANY, INC.

John Barry signs for Terry Walstrom (Terry Walstrom).

John Barry signs for Martyn Crosthwaite (Martyn Crosthwaite).

John Scott (John Scott).

Barry, Wayne Kramer and Richard Kraft (Wayne Kramer).

Vic Flick (Vic Flick).

Eric Tomlinson (Eric Tomlinson).

John Barry at CTS, Wembley (courtesy CTS).

John Barry and Richard Lewzey at CTS, Wembley (courtesy CTS).

John Barry and Richard Lewzey at CTS, Wembley (courtesy CTS).

John Barry at CTS, Wembley (courtesy CTS).

John Barry at the Gstaad Film Music Festival with Leslie Bricusse (©Lydia Pawelak).

John Barry at the Gstaad Film Music Festival.

John Barry at the Gstaad Film Music Festival.

John Barry at the Gstaad Film Music Festival with Michael Caine (©Lydia Pawelak).

Barry and Maryam d'Abo on the set of *The Living Daylights* (© 1987 Danjaq, LLC and United Artists Corporation. All rights reserved.)

John Barry on the set of *The Living Daylights* (© 1987 Danjaq, LLC and United Artists Corporation. All rights reserved).

Above: The Centenary of Cinema British Film Institute commemorative (copy) plaque (the original plaque already affixed to the house in York where he was born in 1933) being presented by cinema historian Ronald Curry MBE to John Barry at the Royal Albert Hall concert rehearsals, Saturday 18th April 1998. (© Ronald Curry MBE).

Above right: John Barry at the podium (© Irene Cooper).

Below: Laurie Barry with John's agents: Richard Kraft and Lyn Benjamin (London Features International).

Below right: John Barry at the podium (Chris Taylor/Decca Records Ltd).

John Barry at the podium receiving flowers after the concert (Chris Taylor/Decca Records Ltd.)

John Barry at the podium with Michael Caine and the replica plaque (Chris Taylor/Decca Records Ltd.)

John Barry conducts the English Chamber Orchestra at the Royal Albert Hall concert (Chris Taylor/Decca Records Ltd).

The lighting effects at the Royal Albert Hall concert (© Irene Cooper).

John Barry at the podium acknowledging applause (Chris Taylor/Decca Records Ltd.)

John Barry pictured at his Cadogan Square residence in 1998 (© Jonathan Eeles).

John and Laurie Barry at the BASCA awards ceremony.

John Barry with Chris Roberts of Polydor Classics (Chris Roberts).

John Barry and Don Black at the BASCA awards ceremony.

John & Laurie Barry, Lyn Benjamin, Richard Kraft, Basil & Bobbie Poledouris at the concert reception (Paul Tonks).

John Barry & Basil Poledouris at the concert reception (Paul Tonks).

John Barry at the HMV signing in Oxford Street, London (Ley Bricknell).

Fulford House - now the York Pavilion Hotel (© Mrs Roe).

Abbey Road Studios (Dave Howell).

introduction, which aptly depicted the urgency of the scenes on screen, before returning to the format of the previous release. Another reissue album surfaced in January, 1981, *Big Screen Hits Of John Barry*, but this does not contain 'Thunderball', as credited, but 'Capsule In Space', sometimes credited as 'Space March', from the opening sequence to *You Only Live Twice*.

Barry's first release for his new label Polydor came on March 23rd, 1972, with the issue of the themes from the films *Mary Queen Of Scots*, known as 'This Way Mary', and *Diamonds Are Forever*. Both were co-composed by Don Black. The single enjoyed considerable air-play and was followed in the autumn by the release of the theme from the ITV series *The Adventurer*, coupled with 'Follow Follow', Barry's central theme to the film *Follow Me*. These were the only single releases by Barry on the label possibly because sales of TV and film theme singles had generally reached their peak by the early seventies. That said, Polydor in Japan took the option to release a single of the next theme he wrote, for Anglia TV's *Orson Welles' Great Mysteries*. This was coupled with his version of 'Born Free', recorded with the Royal Philharmonic Orchestra.

Barry was originally contracted to two albums a year for Polydor, although this format was not adhered to because of film commitments. The first album was a remake of some of the 1972 Philharmonic concert programme, recorded at Abbey Road Studios in London and engineered by Peter Bown. Released in January, 1973, it contained two medleys, one a suite from his latest film, *Alice's Adventures In Wonderland*, written in collaboration with Don Black, and the other 'The James Bond Suite', taking in themes from *Dr No* through to *Diamonds Are Forever*. Barry also recorded a new version of his theme from *The Adventurer*, together with favourites such as 'Born Free' and 'Midnight Cowboy'.

Barry's next outing for the label was an album of themes from stage, screen and television entitled *Play It Again*, which was also the title of the song from his latest assignment, *The Tamarind Seed*. This album contained 12 themes from his most recent commissions. Utilising only a small orchestra, Barry included many previously unrecorded items, such as *The Glass Menagerie* and *Love Among The Ruins*, both TV movies, 'The Good Times Are Coming' from *Monte Walsh*, *Boom!*, 'Lolita' from the stage musical, *Walkabout* and 'Sail The Summer Winds' from *The Dove*. This last theme was also recorded for Polydor by Lyn Paul, whose single differed slightly from the original soundtrack version. The album, released in November, 1974, was recorded at Air Studios, London and produced by Barry. Engineers were Geoff Emerick and John Middleton.

Barry's third and final album for Polydor, *Americans*, was released in November, 1976, exactly a year after the recordings were made at Glen Glenn Sound Studios, Hollywood, shortly after his arrival to score the TV spectacular *Eleanor And Franklin*. Side one consisted of a lengthy piece entitled 'Yesternight Suite', incorporating 'By Myself', from the Broadway show *Be My Devil*, and 'As Time Goes By', from the 1931 revue *Everybody's Welcome*, while side two contained five more jazz-orientated tracks. The album notes described the LP as 'a personal impression of the

John Barry with Paul Hartnoll from
Orbital at his Cadogan Square
residence.

John Barry presents a BASCA to
George Martin in 1985.

sights and sounds of the United States'. The record was only the second time he had composed music especially for an album.

Barry used key personnel for this album, drawing on outstanding musicians, many of whom had come from jazz backgrounds. However, the album was not widely promoted and did not sell particularly well. It is now one of Barry's most sought-after non-soundtrack releases.

Barry at the piano prior to the Moviola recording.

Although *Americans* was his last non-soundtrack album for Polydor, apart from various reissued collections, it became apparent in the following year or so that other material had been recorded. In October, 1977, they issued a compilation simply called *The Very Best Of John Barry*. The album was so popular that it was reissued at mid price in July, 1981. It contained a completely new version of 'Curiouser And Curiouser' from *Alice's Adventures In Wonderland,* which was presumably recorded at the *Play It Again* sessions, alongside the theme from *A Doll's House,* which up to this day has never been recorded in any other format.

In the early nineties, Barry signed for the Sony label. Apart from a number of original soundtracks which emanated during this period, he also recorded two compilations albums – *Moviola* and *Moviola II*. Harking back to his time with Polydor, he recorded with The Royal Philharmonic Orchestra at Abbey Road Studios. Full details of the tracks included can be found in the discography.

The second of these albums wasn't quite as successful as the first, and in 1998, Barry signed for Decca, part of the Polydor group. Under this deal, he agreed to make three non-soundtrack albums for them. The first of these, 'The Beyondness Of Things' was released in April, to coincide with his Albert Hall concert appearance. He also conducted an album signing session at HMV, Oxford Street, London, where a crowd of several hundred fans stood in line. Again, full track details can be found in the discography.

CHAPTER 27

JOHN BARRY: SOME RANDOM THOUGHTS

Barry is clearly bemused by interest in his earlier work, but accepts it gratefully. 'I've done almost 100 pictures,' he told musician and journalist David Toop, 'so there are many points of reference.' Despite a healthy public interest in cinema soundtracks, composers with the arranging skills, melodic gifts and musical breadth of Barry, Elmer Bernstein, Ennio Morricone or the late Nino Rota may be a vanishing breed. They have often been displaced in recent years by electronic composers or rock soundtracks, assembled from unrelated pop tracks. Barry feels that this last approach has had its day. 'On the last *Rocky* soundtrack album,' he says, 'there were songs that weren't even in the film, and it said "inspired by the movie". The songs were recorded three years ago, before the movie was made. I'd like to know how they do that. Back to the future, I guess.'

'When I first went out to Los Angeles at the beginning of the sixties,' Barry says, 'all those guys who ran the studio departments were composers, like Johnny Green, who was running MGM. They understood music and they would cast a composer as you would cast a star. That aspect is very thin on the ground now.' Now enough of an elder statesman to step off the production line, Barry remains pragmatic, though. 'It's what we do for a living,' he admits. 'Sometimes you run into a dry patch when you're not offered anything extraordinary, so you do something unextraordinary. But I think those days are gone. Hopefully.

'Going abroad to record is not an artistic choice, it's a financial choice', he told Christine Ferrari of *The Hollywood Reporter*. 'To me, the ultimate thing you're going after is the quality of the work. Scoring a film on the Continent is cheaper. But I find the quality of the work lacking. And you usually spend almost twice as much time getting what you want. For instance, I've recorded many of the James Bond scores in London, but when we recorded *Moonraker* in Paris, it took us twice as long. What should have been a four-and-a-half-day schedule in London had to be doubled in Paris due to lack of comprehension and talent. Obviously, Ennio Morricone can communicate more favourably with the Roman musicians than I could when I did a Sophia Loren special many years ago. It was pretty difficult communicating. It is possible, but there are difficulties, which become a time factor. Quite frankly, the places that I really like to record are Los Angeles, New York or London, because of the professionalism there. That's where it exists.

'When I was first involved with *Dances*, they were considering the possibility of scoring in a European situation. I said that I didn't think it would ultimately be beneficial for the production, being that the story was so American. We ended up recording in Los Angeles and I really think the LA musicians were the best choice'. Nothing, however, will ever tempt him to relocate to the heart of Hollywood: 'it just doesn't suit me,' he reflects, less the international composer than the Englishman abroad. 'I guess it's all that nice weather.'

Does anyone still use a Moviola?' asked Fred Karlin and Rayburn Wright in *On The Tracks*, 1990. Marvin Hamlisch does. So does John Barry. They always work with a black-and-white dupe, and Barry is enthusiastic about operating in this way: "I love that lever on the Moviola when you're running it through, and then you don't quite know where you're going to do something, and you can watch and you can hit that lever and you can freeze the picture so when you're writing you know that's the exact frame you're going to make a switch. I'm sure I'll work on the Moviola till I die. People don't like it because it's noisy or whatever, but I love it. I just love it."

'He adds: "I hate clicks; they screw up performance. But sometimes I'll use them just to ease technical things. Otherwise, I love the give and take of free performance.' For the Bond movies, he does not use click on the rhythm cues, and his solution to the ever-present problem of getting the rhythm section and the orchestra to hear well enough with the drums in the isolation booth is to have just the drums in the headset. That said: 'I haven't used drums in the Bond things for quite a while. There's percussion, but not drums. I write the rhythms orchestrally rather than with a dance set. Like in *Body Heat*, it was mostly just bass guitar and guitar. I try to keep away from drums, creating the mood with a string pad and then the guitar creating the rhythmic movement."'

John Barry was quoted in Robert Hoshowsky's transcript of the 1996 Gstaad Cinemusic Conference as saying: 'Time plays fun and games with films. Take the James Bond movies, for instance. I can see the earlier ones, and they hold up much stronger than the later ones. So there's something there that's quite strange. You'd think that the more contemporary the film making was . . . but this is a very unusual example, because there's never been a series of movies made in that way you know? And so I've had some strange bearing on style and what have you, but I think the classic Bond movies were the earlier ones, and therefore they are the ones that hold up. The latter ones became more formula, and they're not half as interesting. I would think that the genesis of the Bond sound . . . I studied two years, a correspondence course with Bill Russo. Bill Russo was Stan Kenton's arranger composer and also an early trombonist. And I was a big, big fan of Stan Kenton's, and I wanted to listen to the early Kenton stuff – that brass sound was predominant, both the high brass – they said he had five trumpets, five trombones – and also the low brass sound, a rich, low sound. I think the genesis of the Bond sound was most certainly that Kentonesque, sharp attack; extreme ranges, top Cs and beyond, and on the low end you'd go right down to the low Fs and below, so you'd have a wall of sound. The typical thing, that Bond thing, is very much this brass sound.

'I used a synthesizer very early on, in *Midnight Cowboy* although you wouldn't recognise it. And it was for the Miami Beach sequence, where he has this fantasy where he goes out to Miami, and I had this flute on the melody, and I had this synthesizer playing off to give a sense of humour that the flute didn't have. So I used it that way. And I used a synthesizer, believe it or not, for *The Lion in Winter*; the low end of the main title theme, "Dah dah dah dum, dah dah dah dah dah dum". That was timpanies and synthesizers. And the scene where Anthony Hopkins was going to slaughter all his enemies, and they do that beat, and use the Latin chant. The whole emphasis of that was to use the orchestra and the synthesizer, but the edge came from the synthesizer, which was buried in with the orchestra. I love using it that way.

'Conducting your own music is terribly important. It's trying to make it happen. You spot the music, you compose the music, you orchestrate it, and then you get into that studio and the whole thing takes on its life for the first time, really. That's what the performance works out, although you work, watching that orchestra in the studio, those who make the shift – I mean, I'm not talking of rock, maybe three seconds – maybe you'll hit something, but when you're writing it, you've hidden it for a certain time. You might get a recoil effect. The performance is the real fun. And that's also another problem that's happening today. Many of the young composers are not conducting their own music. I think you have to have composed it, conduct it, and know every phrase and movement, and then you're in the master driving seat, where you make all those subtle changes which will finalise your piece of music. And if you have to explain to somebody, the conductor, it loses a lot.

'A good working relationship with the director is essential. First of all, all the conversations you have with the director are very important, choosing what will have music. You discuss the scenes, and if there are any pertinent points that the director brings up, you make side notes on what those relevant remarks are. So I always have that. Any time during the process of writing, if I have any doubt or a question, I will phone the director and say "Look, I'm working on this scene or this cue or whatever, and I have a question". And you clear that up, and once you get that cleared, from the director's point of view, you're still very free. People seem to think that the director has this control over his film, but within the music areas you're still unbelievably free. I mean, look at one of the finest dramatic composers of this century, Stravinsky, and all the ballets he wrote – he was working within dramatic confines.

'I would absolutely refuse to work on a project where the director made it clear that he wanted me to compose every day under his thumb. I was asked by Barbra Streisand to do *The Prince of Tides*. I live in New York, she lives in Los Angeles, and I went and met with her, and she showed me some footage and she said "Why aren't you moving to Los Angeles?" and I said "Absolutely not". And she said "Well, I like to know what's going on" – Barbra's an extreme case, by the way – and I said "Even if I did move to Los Angeles, I have no desire to meet with you once I know what I'm going to do." I can't work with someone over my shoulder, absolutely no way.'

CHAPTER 28

POSTSCRIPT: WHATEVER HAPPENED TO THE SEVEN?

Most of the original JB7 returned to their home roots in the North of England. Ken Golder and Fred Kirk still live in their home town of Scarborough, and Ken plays drums in a couple of local orchestras. Jack Oliver and Mike Cox returned to Leeds, where the latter still teaches and plays. Derek Myers left England and is believed to be in Hong Kong. Sadly, after going back to teaching, Ken Richards died from a heart attack while performing on stage with his friends Golder and Kirk. Keith Kelly's career as a solo singer blossomed briefly in 1960, with three Top Fifty hits before he faded back into obscurity.

Of the classic JB7 line-up, Les Reed turned to writing and producing notably in partnership with Barry Mason. He had several major chart successes including 'It's Not Unusual' and 'Delilah' (Tom Jones), 'The Last Waltz' and 'Les Bicyclettes de Belsize' (Engelbert Humperdinck), There's A Kind Of Hush' (Herman's Hermits/The Carpenters), 'Here It Comes Again' (The Fortunes). He now owns several publishing companies, which his daughter, Donna, helps to run. Recently he was working on a musical he hopes is destined for the West End.

After leaving the JB7 and session work, Vic Flick began to concentrate on writing for TV and films, a field in which he is still involved at the time of writing. Unfortunately for Vic, during his years with the Seven, their A and R manager John Burgess was under the mistaken impression that he was contracted exclusively to John Barry. This misunderstanding prevented Vic from being asked to make records in his own right. However, in 1989 he very nearly emerged into the limelight once again when he was chosen to play Michael Kamen's arrangement of 'The James Bond Theme' for the new Bond film *Licence To Kill*, alongside Eric Clapton. Although the theme was recorded and both musicians were filmed performing it on location in London, the producers eventually decided not to use it, preferring to commission a song that was performed by Gladys Knight. Vic now lives and works in Santa Monica, California.

Dougie Wright left the band in July, 1962 and then joined the Ted Taylor Four, which eventually became the Bob Rodgers Four. He started doing a lot of session work and was on many hits of the sixties. In the seventies he joined a jazz group, the Eddie Thompson Trio, and also played for Harry Stoneham's Band, often appearing on TV in *The Michael Parkinson Show*. He now teaches percussion at colleges in the Leicester area.

Jimmy Stead became a hairdressing salon owner and now lives in Luton. Mike Peters is a TV and video repair man, working and living in Leeds. Dennis King died on December 26th, 1992. Another tragic death was that of Bobby Carr, who was murdered by a crazed drug addict he had taken in as a lodger shortly after he was drafted into the band to take Barry's place on tour. Keyboardist Brian Hazelby is still playing in the Midlands.

Of the later line-ups, Bobby Graham became a top session drummer and now owns a video production company and composes music for television. Guitarist Ray Russell also turned to writing music for TV after a career which saw him featuring in a number of groups. Tony Ashton went on to form Ashton, Gardener and Dyke, who are chiefly remembered for their minor classic 'Resurrection Shuffle', and later linked with Deep Purple members in Ashton and Lord and then Paice, Ashton and Lord.

Keyboardist Ron Edgeworth became involved in arranging for the Seekers and later married their vocalist, Judith Durham. He sadly died a few years ago of motor neurone disease after a long illness through which Judith nursed him.

Mike O'Neill left in 1965. While still with the JB7 he had formed a band called Crawdaddies with the Seven's road manager, Tony Colton, and at one time was using the Seven's van and gear to fulfil Crawdaddie bookings! Later in the sixties, the two friends were in Poet and the One Man Band. O'Neill has continued to play in various bands up to the present day.

Kenny Sammon and Bob Downes are still active jazz musicians, it is believed, the latter based in Germany. Terry Childs became a local Musicians Union representative. Alan Bown went on to form the Alan Bown Set, which also included ex-Seven members Dave Green, Jeff Bannister and Stan Haldane. In the early seventies he joined Jonesy and is now involved in the management side of the business. Dave Richmond is still doing the odd session for both TV and films, and is currently playing bass guitar with the Joe Loss and Burt Kaempfert bands.

John Scott, who often augmented the Seven for recording sessions on flute and alto sax, is now a renowned composer for film and television. He splits his time between Los Angeles and London.

John Barry lives and works in Oyster Bay, New York. When in England he operates from an apartment in Cadogan Square. He is reported to have no regrets about leaving the band; in fact he is believed to be doing rather well on his own.

DISCOGRAPHY
PART ONE

All items are listed in catalogue/release date order within each label. Main labels are listed first followed by releases on other labels and all entries are UK releases unless otherwise stated. Please refer to the 'Key' in Part 2 on page 221 of the Discography for details of the country of origin. Generally only original UK releases are quoted but occasionally American; other releases may be listed if the musical content or sleeve are different. Most imports, and single/EP releases from the late 60s/early 70s onwards, however, are listed in Part 2 if they relate to Film or TV and are thus not repeated here.

John Barry singles and EPs are listed first followed by singles and EPs for those artists he accompanied.

78r.p.m. releases are given for John Barry singles only. The release date is given in the right hand column.

If only one title is listed for an entry under 'Singles' this indicates the other track was not connected with John Barry.

Items which were written/co-written by John Barry but which were not arranged, conducted or produced by him have been ignored for the purposes of these listings unless they are of special interest. In any case, details of some cover versions of special interest are referred to in the main text of Part 2.

(M) = Mono
(S) = Stereo
* = Accompaniment directed by John Barry
** = With John Barry & His Orchestra
Earlier releases are annotated as follows:
(1) – John Barry & The Seven
(2) – John Barry Seven
(3) – John Barry Seven Plus 4
(4) – John Barry & His Orchestra
(5) – John Barry Seven & Orchestra
(6) – Michael Angelo & His Orchestra
(P) – Picture cover release
All other items are by John Barry/John Barry (& His) Orchestra unless stated.

JOHN BARRY SINGLES

Catalogue No	Titles	Composer(s)	Release date

PARLOPHONE

R 4363 (*)	ZIP ZIP (1) THREE LITTLE FISHES (1)	(Kaye-Booros) (Dowell)	OCT 57
R 4394 (*)	EVERY WHICH WAY (2) YOU'VE GOTTA WAY (2)	(Torme) (Barry)	JAN 58
R 4418 (*)	BIG GUITAR (2) RODEO (2)	(De Rosa-Genovese) (Barry)	MCH 58
R 4453 (*)	PANCHO (2) HIDEAWAY (2) With Latin-American rhythm accompaniment	(Barry) (Barry)	JUL 58
R 4488 (*)	FARRAGO (2) BEE'S KNEES (2)	(White) (Barry)	NOV 58
R 4530 (*)	LONG JOHN (2) SNAP 'N' WHISTLE (2)	(White) (Barry)	FEB 59
R 4560 (*)	LITTLE JOHN (2) FOR PETE'S SAKE (2)	(Barry) (Barry)	JUN 59
R 4580	TWELFTH STREET RAG (2) CHRISTELLA (2) (*) Also released on 78 r.p.m.	(O'Bowman) (Barry)	SEP 59

COLUMBIA

DB 4414	HIT & MISS (3) ROCKIN' ALREADY (3)	(Barry) (Trad. arranged: Barry)	FEB 60
DB 4446	BEAT FOR BEATNIKS (4) BIG FELLA (4)	(Barry) (Barry)	APR 60
DB 4480	BLUEBERRY HILL (4) NEVER LET GO (4)	(Lewis-Stock-Rose) (Barry)	JUN 60
DB 4505	WALK DON'T RUN (2) I'M MOVIN' ON (3)	(Smith) (Snow)	SEP 60
DB 4554	BLACK STOCKINGS (2) GET LOST JACK FROST (2)	(Barry) (Barry)	DEC 60

DB 4598	MAGNIFICENT SEVEN (2) SKID ROW (2)	(Bernstein) (Barry)	FEB 61
DB 4659	THE MENACE (4) RODEO (4)	(Barry) (Barry)	JUN 61
DB 4699	STARFIRE (2) * A MATTER OF WHO (3)	(Lordan) (Russell)	SEP 61
DB 4705	ROCCO'S THEME (6) SPINNEREE (6)	(Rota) (Barry)	SEP 61
DB 4746	WATCH YOUR STEP (2) TWIST IT (2)	(Parker) (Barry)	NOV 61
DB 4800	THEME FROM 'THE ROMAN SPRING OF MRS STONE' (6) TEARS (6)	(Addinsell) (Maxwell)	MCH 62
DB 4806	CUTTY SARK (5) LOST PATROL (5)	(Barry) (Maxwell)	MCH 62
DB 4898	THE JAMES BOND THEME (5) THE BLACKSMITH BLUES (5) Released on both Green, and later Black, labels. All future releases on this label featured a Black label.	(Norman) (Holmes)	SEP 62
DB 4941	THE LOLLY THEME (5) MARCH OF THE MANDARINS (5)	(Barry) (Barry)	NOV 62
DB 7003	THE HUMAN JUNGLE (5) ONWARD, CHRISTIAN SPACEMEN (5)	(Ebbinghouse) (P) (Barry)	MCH 63
DB 7414	TWENTY HOURS AGO (2) SEVEN FACES (2)	(Suede) (Bown-Mansfield)	DEC 64

EMBER

EMB S 178	KINKY (5) FANCY DANCE (5)	(Scott) (Barry)	AUG 63
EMB S 181	007 (5) FROM RUSSIA WITH LOVE (5) *	(Barry) (P) (Bart)	OCT 63
EMB S 183	ELIZABETH (5) THE LONDON THEME (5)	(Barry) (Barry)	DEC 63
EMB S 185	ZULU STAMP (2) MONKEY FEATHERS (2)	(Barry) (P) (Barry)	JAN 64
EMB S 243	007 (4) ** LONELINESS OF AUTUMN (NON SAPEVO) (4)	(Barry) (P) (Calvi/Pallase)	NOV 67

UNITED ARTISTS

UP 1060	SEANCE ON A WET AFTERNOON (4) OUBLIE CA (4)	(Barry) (Barry)	JUL 64
UP 1068	GOLDFINGER (4) TROUBADOUR (4)	(Barry-Bricusse-Newley) (Barry)	OCT 64
UP 634	MIDNIGHT COWBOY * FUN CITY * * Original Soundtrack recordings.	(Barry) (P) (Barry)	OCT 80

CBS

201747	A MAN ALONE (4) BARBRA'S THEME (4)	(Barry) (Barry)	APR 65
201822	THE SYNDICATE (4) WHAT A QUESTION (4)	(Barry-Peacock) (Barry-Peacock)	OCT 65
202390	VENDETTA THE DANNY SCIPIO THEME	(Barry) (Barry)	OCT 66
202451	THEME FROM 'THE QUILLER MEMORANDUM' (Wednesday's Child) SLEEP WELL MY DARLING	(Barry-David) (Barry-David)	NOV 66
WB 730	THE JAMES BOND THEME	(Norman) (P)	NOV 66
2825	YOU ONLY LIVE TWICE THE GIRL WITH THE SUN IN HER HAIR	(Barry-Bricusse) (Barry-Black)	APR 67

3935	THE LION IN WINTER (Part 1) THE LION IN WINTER (Part 2) (Organist: Alan Haven)	(Barry) (Barry)	JAN 69
4468	MIDNIGHT COWBOY * FUN CITY * Harmonica: Jean 'Toots' Thielemans.	(Barry) (Barry)	AUG 69
4680	ON HER MAJESTY'S SECRET SERVICE WE HAVE ALL THE TIME IN THE WORLD	(Barry) (Barry)	NOV 69
7469	THEME FROM 'THE PERSUADERS' THE GIRL WITH THE SUN IN HER HAIR	(Barry) (Barry-Black)	SEP 71

POLYDOR

2058 216	THIS WAY MARY DIAMONDS ARE FOREVER	(Barry-Black) (Barry-Black)	MAY 72
2058 275	THE ADVENTURER FOLLOW, FOLLOW	(Barry) (Barry-Black)	JUL 72

CAPITOL (USA)

F 4212	LONG JOHN (2) SNAP 'N WHISTLE (2) USA Debut record.	(White) (Barry)	1959

JOHN BARRY EPs

PARLOPHONE

GEP 8737	THE BIG BEAT (2) FARRAGO PANCHO* HIDEAWAY* RODEO * With Latin-American Rhythm Accompaniment.	(White) (Barry) (Barry) (Barry)	JUL 58

COLUMBIA

SEG 8069	THE JOHN BARRY SOUND (3) except * – (2) HIT & MISS ROCKIN' ALREADY WALK DON'T RUN * I'M MOVIN' ON	(Barry) (Trad. arranged: Barry) (Smith) (Snow)	FEB 61
SEG 8138	BEAT GIRL (Original Soundtrack) I DID WHAT YOU TOLD ME* THE STRIPPER MADE YOU* MAIN TITLE – BEAT GIRL * Vocals by Adam Faith	(Barry-Peacock) (Barry) (Barry-Peacock) (Barry)	MCH 62
SEG 8255	JOHN BARRY THEME SUCCESSES (5) THE HUMAN JUNGLE CUTTY SARK THE JAMES BOND THEME THE LOLLY THEME	(Ebbinghouse) (Barry) (Norman) (Barry)	JUL 63

EMBER

EMB EP 4544	LONELINESS OF AUTUMN LONELINESS OF AUTUMN FANCY DANCE ELIZABETH THE LONDON THEME	(Calvi) (Barry) (Barry) (Barry)	FEB 64
EMB EP 4551	JAMES BOND IS BACK FROM RUSSIA WITH LOVE (5) 007 (5) MONKEY FEATHERS (2) ZULU STAMP (2)	(Bart) (Barry) (Barry) (Barry)	AUG 64

UNITED ARTISTS

UEP 1011	FROM RUSSIA WITH LOVE OPENING TITLES – JAMES BOND IS BACK FROM RUSSIA WITH LOVE JAMES BOND THEME	(Film Soundtrack) (Barry) (Bart) (Norman)	
	007 GIRL TROUBLE LEILA DANCES DEATH OF KERIM Arranged & Conducted by John Barry.	(Barry) (Barry) (Barry) (Barry-Bart)	NOV 63
UEP 1012	GOLDFINGER (Original Motion Picture Score) MAIN THEME GOLDFINGER (Instrumental Version) PUSSY GALORE'S FLYING CIRCUS DAWN RAID ON FORT KNOX Music Composed, Arranged & Conducted by John Barry.		NOV 64
UEP 1015	THUNDERBALL (Original Motion Picture Score) THUNDERBALL (Instrumental) DEATH OF FIONA BOND BELOW DISCO VOLANTE MR. KISS KISS BANG BANG Music composed, Arranged & Conducted by John Barry.	(Barry-Black) (Barry-Bricusse)	JUL 66

CBS

WEP 1126	THEMES FROM JAMES BOND FILMS YOU ONLY LIVE TWICE GOLDFINGER Specially created for Carr's SPORTS biscuits by CBS SPECIAL PRODUCTS	(Barry-Bricusse) (Barry-Bricusse-Newley)	NOV 67
WEP 1129	BIG THEMES FROM THE BIG SCREEN THE JAMES BOND THEME THEME FROM 'BORN FREE' Created exclusively for WALL'S by CBS SPECIAL PRODUCTS	(Norman) (Barry-Black)	DEC 67
WEP 1131	GREAT SCREEN THEMES WEDNESDAY'S CHILD GOLDFINGER Created exclusively for LYONS BAKERY by CBS SPECIAL PRODUCTS	(Barry) (Barry-Bricusse-Newley)	DEC 67

RAINBOW ADVENTURE FILMS INC (USA)

PRO 543	ALICE'S ADVENTURES IN WONDERLAND CURIOUSER & CURIOUSER (Instrumental) * YOU'VE GOTTA KNOW WHEN TO STOP * THE LAST WORD IS MINE * THE PUN SONG Promo only – not issued in picture sleeve. * 3 songs from the Original Soundtrack.	(Barry-Black) (Barry-Black) (Barry-Black) (Barry-Black)	DEC 72

JOHN BARRY ACCOMPANIMENT SINGLES

PARLOPHONE

ADAM FAITH

R 4591 *	WHAT DO YOU WANT? FROM NOW UNTIL FOREVER	(Vandyke) (M/H Nesbitt-Venis)	OCT 59
R 4623 *	POOR ME THE REASON	(Vandyke) (Barry)	JAN 60
R 4643 *	SOMEONE ELSE'S BABY BIG TIME	(Vandyke-Ford) (Bart)	APR 60
R 4665 **	JOHNNY COMES MARCHING HOME MADE YOU	(Trad. Arr. Barry-Maitland) (Barry-Peacock)	JUN 60
R 4689 **	HOW ABOUT THAT! WITH OPEN ARMS	(Vandyke) (Bacharach-David)	SEP 60
R 4708 *	LONELY PUP (IN A CHRISTMAS SHOP) (*) GREENFINGER (*) Accompaniment and children directed by John Barry.	(Alexander) (Lewis)	OCT 60
R 4735 *	WHO AM I? THIS IS IT	(Vandyke) (Vandyke)	FEB 61
R 4766 *	EASY GOING ME WONDERIN'	(Bart) (Vandyke)	APR 61
R 4807 *	DON'T YOU KNOW IT? MY LAST WISH	(Vandyke) (Barry-Vandyke)	JUL 61
R 4837 *	THE TIME HAS COME A HELP-EACH-OTHER ROMANCE	(Vandyke) (Singleton)	OCT 61

R 4864 **	LONESOME	(Pellish)		
	WATCH YOUR STEP	(Parker)	JAN 62	
R 4896 **	AS YOU LIKE IT	(Vandyke)		
	FACE TO FACE	(Vandyke)	APR 62	

OTHER ARTISTS

BILL & BRET LANDIS *
R 4570   BABY TALK   (Schwartz)   JUL 59

JOHNNY GAVOTTE *
R 4631   CAN'T FORGET   (Hawker-Shakespeare)
         IT'S NOT TOO LATE   (Sheridan)   FEB 60

DANNY DAVIS **
R 4657   YOU'RE MY ONLY GIRL   (O'Mahoney)
         LOVE ME   (Stoller-Leiber)   MAY 60

GERRY DORSEY *
R 4739   BIG WHEEL   (Vandyke)   FEB 61

DIZ DISLEY & THE DOWNBEATS *
R 4767   DJANGO'S CASTLE   (Reinhardt)   APR 61

BOB MILLER & THE MILLERMAN
R 4779   TROUBLE SHOOTER   (Barry)   JUN 61
         Not accompanied and directed by John Barry

ANITA HARRIS **
R 4830   I HAVEN'T GOT YOU   (Bart)
         MR. ONE AND ONLY   (Lordan)   OCT 61

PETER GORDENO **
R 4862   YOU'RE FOLLOWING ME   (Hilliard-Bacharach)
         I GOT EYES   (Smith-Jones-
                        Dixon-Keyes)   JAN 62

BOBBY SHAFTO *
R 4870   OVER AND OVER   (Bart)
         I WANT MY BED   (Bart)   FEB 62

TONY ROCCO *
R 4886   STALEMATE   (Martin-Rocco)
         KEEP A WALKIN'   (Sedaka-Greenfield)   MCH 62

PETER GORDENO **
R 4913   UPTOWN   (Mann-Weil)
         THE MAKINGS OF A MAN   (Stallman-Jacobson)   MAY 62

DARREN YOUNG **
R 4919   MY TEARS WILL TURN TO LAUGHTER   (Askew)
         I'VE JUST FALLEN FOR SOMEONE   (Askew)   JUN 62

PETER GORDENO **
R 4931   DOWN BY THE RIVERSIDE   (Trad. Arr: Barry)   SEP 62

MARK TRACEY **
R 4944   CARAVAN OF LONELY MEN   (Barry-Pretlow)
         NEVER ENDING   (Carr-Newell)   SEP 62

PETER GORDENO **
R 4999   YOU CAN DO IT IF YOU TRY   (Vandyke)   FEB 63

THE BOYS
R 5027   POLARIS   (Frere-Manston)
         JUMPIN'   (Frere-Manston)   JUN 63
         Produced by John Barry

COLUMBIA

THE FIVE DALLAS BOYS **
DB 4445   BOSTON TEA PARTY   (Vandyke)
          RAMONA   (Wayne-Gilbert)   MCH 60

RUSS CONWAY **
DB 4564   PEPE   (Wittstart)
          MATADOR FROM TRINIDAD*   (Boyd-Stanford)   DEC 60

JOHNNY DE LITTLE **
DB 4578   NOT GUILTY   (Peacock)
          THEY   (Barry-Russell)   JAN 61

DENNIS LOTIS **
DB 4626   WHERE YOU ARE   (Ornadel-West)
          LOVE'S A SECRET GAME   (Wakley-Inman)   APR 61

JOHNNY WORTH *
DB 4811   YOU KNOW WHAT I MEAN   (Vandyke)
          ALL THESE THINGS   (Vandyke)   MCH 62

BILL COTTON (*) & KATHIE KAY **
DB 4843   OPPOSITES   (Bart)
          IF THE YOUNG ONES CAN BE HAPPY (*)   (Bart)   JUN 62

MARION RYAN **
DB 4857   NO LOVE BUT YOUR LOVE   (Scharfenberger-West-Busch)   SEP 62

KATHIE KAY & BILL COTTON **
DB 4896   SOMEONE NICE LIKE YOU   (Newley-Bricusse)   SEP 62
          With The Rita Williams Singers

JOHNNIE DE LITTLE **
DB 4907   LOVER   (Rodgers-Hart)
          YOU MADE ME LOVE YOU   (Monaco-McCarthy)   OCT 62

NINA & FREDERIK **
DB 4936   WHITE CHRISTMAS   (Berlin)
          SILENT NIGHT   (Gruber)   NOV 62

NINA & FREDERIK **
DB 4953   THERE ONCE WAS A TIME OF MAN   (Edmonson)
          INCH WORM   (Loesser)   JAN 63

MARTY WILDE **
DB 4980   LONELY AVENUE   (Pomus)
          BRAND NEW LOVE   (Fielding-Wilde)   FEB 63

JOHNNY DE LITTLE *
DB 7023   DAYS OF WINE & ROSES   (Mancini-Mercer)
          RIDE ON   (Pratt-Horan)   APR 63

JOHNNY DE LITTLE *
DB 7044   THE WIND & THE RAIN   (Green-Newell)
          UNCHAINED MELODY   (North-Zaret)   JUN 63

TOMMY STEELE **
DB 7070   EGG & CHIPS   (Green-Newell)
          THE DREAM MAKER   (Green-Newell)   JUL 63

TOMMY STEELE & MARION RYAN **
DB 7070   MAXIMUM PLUS   (Green-Newell)   JUL 63
          Demo release only – B-side of 'The Dream Maker'

NINA & FREDERIK **
DB 7172   PUFF (THE MAGIC DRAGON)   (Yarrow-Lipton)   NOV 63

SHIRLEY BASSEY *
DB 7360   GOLDFINGER   (Barry-Bricusse-Newley)   SEP 64

MATT MONRO
DB 8860   THIS WAY MARY   (Barry-Black)
          WISH NOW WAS THEN   (Barry-Black)   FEB 72
          Orchestra Arranged & Conducted by John Barry.

EMBER

MISS X (Joyce Blair)
EMB S175   CHRISTINE   (Count Jaine-de-Mora y Aaragon-Bricusse)
           S-E-X   (Bricusse)   JUL 63
           Mainly a White label release.

STEVE CASSIDY
EMB S177   ECSTASY   (Manston-Kaye-Pratt)
           I'M A WORRYIN'   (Haven)   SEP 63
           Accompaniment Arranged and Directed; Produced by John Barry.

PHILIP LOWRIE
EMB S179   I MIGHT HAVE KNOWN (BEFORE)   (Cawtheray)
           I MIGHT HAVE KNOWN (AFTER)   (Cawtheray)   SEP 63
           Arranged & Directed by Gordon Franks; Produced by John Barry.

CHAD STUART & JEREMY CLYDE
EMB S180   YESTERDAY'S GONE   (Stuart-Kidd)
           LEMON TREE   (Holt)   SEP 63
           Produced by John Barry

ANNIE ROSS
EMB S182   A LOT OF LIVIN' TO DO   (Strouse-Adams)
           BYE BYE BLUES   (Hamm-Bennett-Lawn)   NOV 63
           With Johnny Spence & His Orchestra. Produced by John Barry.

CHAD STUART & JEREMY CLYDE
EMB S186   LIKE I LOVE YOU TODAY   (Alquist-Stuart)
           EARLY IN THE MORNING   (Stookey)   FEB 64
           Produced by John Barry

UNITED ARTISTS

THE COUNTDOWNS
UP 1024 — MOUSE ON THE MOON (Grainer); THE BIG SAFARI (Norman) — Directed by John Barry. — MAY 63

A BAND OF ANGELS
UP 1049 — ME (Baker-d'Abo); NOT TRUE AS YET (Baker-d'Abo) — Produced by John Barry. — APR 64

ALAN HAVEN
UP 1057 — THEME FROM 'A JOLLY BAD FELLOW' (Barry); JEE BEE'S (Haven) — JUL 64

A BAND OF ANGELS
UP 1066 — SHE'LL NEVER BE YOU (Sedaka-Greenfield); GONNA MAKE A WOMAN OF YOU (d'Abo-Baker) — SEP 64

SHIRLEY BASSEY
UP 2254 — MY LOVE HAS TWO FACES (Barry-Lawrence) — Arranged & Conducted by John Barry. — NOV 68

LOUIS ARMSTRONG
UP 35059 — ALL THE TIME IN THE WORLD (Barry-David) — Arranged & Conducted by John Barry. Produced by Phil Ramone. — DEC 69

SHIRLEY BASSEY
UP 35293 — DIAMONDS ARE FOREVER (Barry-Black) — Arranged & Conducted by John Barry. — NOV 71

SHIRLEY BASSEY
UP 602 — MOONRAKER (MAIN TITLE) (Barry-David); MOONRAKER (END TITLE) (Barry-David) — Produced & Conducted by John Barry. Labels on this release were inadvertently reversed. — DEC 79

CBS

JOHNNIE DE LITTLE *
201790 — THE KNACK (Barry-Bricusse); WHAT TO DO WITH LAURIE (Leiber-Stoller-Wheeler) — Produced by John Barry. — JUL 65

JEREMY CLYDE *
201823 — I LOVE MY LOVE (Barry-Peacock); ANYTIME (Clyde) — Produced by John Barry. — OCT 65

NINA
4681 — DO YOU KNOW HOW CHRISTMAS TREES ARE GROWN? (Barry-David); THE MORE THINGS CHANGE (Barry-David) — Arranged, Conducted & Produced by John Barry. — NOV 69

VARIOUS LABELS

CAPITOL

MATT MONRO *
CL 15436 — BORN FREE (Barry-Black) — MCH 66

MATT MONRO *
CL 15477 — WEDNESDAY'S CHILD (Barry-David) — NOV 66

DECCA

THE THREE BARRY SISTERS
F 11118 — TALL PAUL (Roberts-B & D Sherman); TILL THEN (Seiler, Marcus, Wood) — With The Johnny Prendy Orchestra. — MCH 59

DERRY HART & THE HARTBEATS
F 11138 — NOWHERE IN THIS WORLD (Hart); COME ON BABY (Baldock-King) — Accompaniment Directed by Johnny Prendy. — MAR 59

THE THREE BARRY SISTERS
F 11141 — JO-JO THE DOG-FACED BOY (D & B Sherman-Roberts); I-AY OVE-LAY OO-YAY (Brout-Lasky) — With The Johnny Prendy Orchestra. — MAR 59

LITTLE TONY AND HIS BROTHERS
F 11164 — ARRIVEDERCI BABY (Barry-Dawn) — Composed by John Barry. — MAY 59

TOM JONES
F 12292 — THUNDERBALL (Barry-Black) — NOV 65

FONTANA

ALAN HAVEN *
TF 590 — THE KNACK (Barry) — JUL 65

HMV

DANNY WILLIAMS **
POP 703 — YOUTHFUL YEARS (Napper); IT DOESN'T MATTER (Raysor-Barrett) — APR 60

THE ENGLAND SISTERS *
POP 710 — LITTLE CHILD (Cowen); HEARTBEAT (Montgomery-Petty) — JUN 60

VAN DOREN **
POP 1040 — THE COFFEE GRINDER (Manzo) — JUL 62

DICK KALLMAN **
POP 1118 — SAY IT ISN'T SO (Berlin) — FEB 63

DON, DAVID & DEAN *
POP 1159 — WELL YOU STARTED IT (Ford-Hillier-Hillier); NEVERTHELESS (I'M IN LOVE WITH YOU) (Kalmar-Ruby) — MAY 63

PYE

LANCE FORTUNE
7N 15240 — BE MINE (Menke-Panas-Luth-Stellman); ACTION (Barry-Peacock) — Accompaniment Directed by Johnny Prendy. — MAR 60

SAGA

LARRY PAGE
SAG 2902 — BIG BLON' BABY (Roberts-Jacobson); I VIBRATE (Twitty) — OCT 59

LARRY PAGE
SAG 2903 — HOW'M I DOING, HEY, HEY (Fowler-Redman); THROW ALL YOUR LOVIN' MY WAY (Barry) — OCT 59

LARRY PAGE
SAG 2904 — LITTLE OLD FASHIONED LOVE (Barry); MARILYN (White) — All tracks accompanied by The Saga Satellites, directed by John Barry. — OCT 59

TOP RANK

ADAM FAITH
JAR 126 — AH, POOR LITTLE BABY! (Falk-Koury) — Accompaniment arranged by John Barry. Released on both Blue/silver and (later) Red/White (Top Rank International *) labels. * Reissue — JUN 59

DES LANE *
JAR 203 — MOONBIRD (Barry); THE CLANGER MARCH (Braden) — OCT 59

JOHN BARRY ACCOMPANIMENT EPs

PARLOPHONE

NINA & FREDERIK
SEG 8215 ** — WHITE CHRISTMAS; WHITE CHRISTMAS (Berlin); SANTA CLAUS IS COMING TO TOWN (Coots); AWAY IN A MANGER (Kirkpatrick); SILENT NIGHT (Kruber) — NOV 62

NINA & FREDERIK
SEG 8301 ** — SING FOR THE YOUNG IN HEART; PUFF THE MAGIC DRAGON (Yarrow-Lipton); INCH WORM (Loesser); 207 — SEP 63

EMBER

CHAD STUART & JEREMY CLYDE

EMB EP 4543	YESTERDAY'S GONE		
	YESTERDAY'S GONE	(Stuart-Kidd)	
	LEMON TREE	(Holt)	
	LIKE I LOVE YOU TODAY	(Alquist-Stuart)	FEB 64
	EARLY IN THE MORNING	(Stookey)	
	Produced by John Barry		

OTHER ARTISTS – LPs

The following albums feature artists accompanied/produced by John Barry. Only those tracks featuring John Barry are listed

1960	ADAM		
	12 tracks arranged and conducted by John Barry	UK 33	PARLOPHONE PMC 1128 (M)
	* Reissues with different sleeve artwork	UK 33	PARLOPHONE PCS 3010 (S)
	Wonderful Time/Diamond Ring/Summertime/	US 33	MGM E 3951
	Greenfinger/Piper Of Love/A Girl Like You/	UK 33	MFP 1002 (M)*
	Turn Me Loose/So Many Ways/Singin' In The Rain/	UK 33	REGAL ZONOPHONE
	Fare Thee Well My Pretty Maid/I'm A Man/Hit The Road To Dreamland		SREG 1033 (S) *

1961	ADAM FAITH		
	14 tracks arranged and conducted by John Barry	UK 33	PARLOPHONE PMC 1162 (M)
	* Reissue with different sleeve artwork	UK 33	PARLOPHONE PCS 3025 (S)
	Watch Your Step/I've Just Fallen For Someone/	UK 33	WORLD RECORDS ST 486 (S)*
	I'm Coming Home/All These Things/It's All Over Now/		
	Come To Me/If I Had A Hammer/A-Help-Each-Other Romance/		
	Sho' Know A Lot About Love/Second Time/I'm Gonna Love You Too/		
	Little Yellow Roses/As Long As You Keep Loving Me/		
	You And Me And The Gang		

1963	ANNIE ROSS SINGS A HANDFUL OF SONGS		
	12 tracks arranged and conducted by Johnnie Spence	UK 33	EMBER NR 5008 (M)
	Produced John Barry. Sound Engineer: Eric Tomlinson	UK 33	BULLDOG BDL 1049 (M) *
	Recorded at CTS Studios, London	US 33	DECCA DL 4922 (M) **
	* Like Someone In Love	SP 33	EVEREST 1227 (FSR 550) (S)
	** Fill My Heart With Song		

1963	SATURDAY NIGHT SING-A-LONG WITH THE BILLY COTTON LOT		
	(Billy Cotton & His Orchestra)	UK 33	EMBER CEL 901 (M)
	Reissued as Let's All Join In – different sleeve artwork	UK 33	EMBER SE 8011 (M)
	Arrangements by Pete Moore/Jackie Brown		
	Sound Engineer: Eric Tomlinson		
	Produced by John Barry. Recorded at CTS Studios, London		

1963	FOOL BRITANNIA		
	Non-music album written and devised by Leslie Bricusse/Anthony Newley	UK 33	EMBER CEL 902 (M)
	Starring:- Peter Sellers, Joan Collins, Anthony Newley, Leslie Bricusse,		
	Daniel Massey, Michael Lipton		
	Recorded at RCA Victor Studios, New York – 6. 8. 63.	UK EP	EMBER EMB EP 4530 *
	Directed by Martin Holtzman	UK EP	EMBER EMB EP 4531 **
	Edited at CTS Studios, London by Eric Tomlinson		
	Supervising editor for UK release only – John Barry		
	Also released on 2 EPs:		
	* Fool Britannia; ** More Fool Britannia		

1963	SPEAK SOFTLY		
	(Dick Kallman)	UK 33	HMV CLP 1642 (M)
	Includes Deed I Do/My Romance/Mam'selle/	UK 33	HMV CSD 1493 (S)
	Glory Of Love/Say It Isn't So with John Barry & His Orchestra		

1965	CHAD & JEREMY SING FOR YOU		
	Yesterday's Gone/Like I Love You Today	UK 33	EMBER NR 5021 (M)
		UK 33	EMBER STNR 5021 (S)

1965	YESTERDAY'S GONE		
	(Chad & Jeremy)	US 33	WORLD ARTISTS WAM 2002(M)
	Yesterday's Gone/Like I Love You Today	US 33	WORLD ARTISTS WAS 3002 (S)

1966	JOHN BARRY MEETS CHAD & JEREMY		
		UK 33	EMBER NR 5032 (M)
		CA 33	CAPITOL (S)T 6126 (S/M)
	Yesterday's Gone/Lemon Tree/Like I Love You Today		

1966	THE BEST OF CHAD & JEREMY		
		UK 33	EMBER NR 5036 (M)
		UK 33	EMBER STNR 5036 (S)
	Yesterday's Gone/Like I Love You Today	US 33	CAPITOL ST 2470 (S)

1966	MORE CHAD & JEREMY		
	Lemon Tree	US 33	CAPITOL TT 2546 (M)
		US 33	CAPITOL ST 2546 (S)

1978	THE TWO BEST SIDES OF ADAM FAITH		
	First LP release of Ah, Poor Little Baby! (Mono)	UK 33	EMI NUTM 16 (S/M)

JOHN BARRY – COLLECTION COMPACT DISCS

The following CD releases give details of collections featuring John Barry only. Details of any film or series for which titles were used are given in Part 2.

1988	HIT AND MISS Hit & Miss/Big Guitar/Rodeo/Big Fella/Walk Don't Run/Bee's Knees/ Every Which Way/Main Title – Beat Girl/Human Jungle/I'm Movin' On/ Zapata/Like Waltz/Black Stockings/James Bond Theme/Lost Patrol/ Magnificent Seven/Hideaway/The Menace/Never Let Go/The Sharks	UK CD	C5 CD 516
1988	ZULU & OTHER THEMES Main Title Theme -Isandhlwana 1879/News Of The Massacre – Rorke's Drift Threatened/Wagons Over/First Zulu Appearance & Assault/Durnford's Horses Arrive And Depart – The Third Assault/Zulu's Final Appearance And Salute/ The V.C. Roll and Men Of Harlech/Elizabeth Theme/From Russia With Love/ Four In The Morning/007 Theme/Monkey Feathers/Fancy Dance/Judi Comes Back/ The London Theme/Tetha Leyanto/High Grass/Zulu Stamp/Big Shield/ Ngenzini/Kinky/Yesterday's Gone */No Tears For Johnny */Aliki/ The Loneliness Of Autumn * Chad & Jeremy with John Barry & His Orchestra	UK CD	SILVA SCREEN FILMCD 022
1988	THE FILM MUSIC OF JOHN BARRY The James Bond Theme/Born Free/Fun City/The Lion In Winter/ We Have All The Time In The World/Wednesday's Child/ From Russia With Love/Space March/The Wrong Box/The Ipcress File/ Thunderball/The Chase*/The Knack... And How To Get It/The Whisperers/ King Rat/The Appointment/Goldfinger * Alternate, extended version	US CD	COLUMBIA CK 44376
1990	STRINGBEAT It Doesn't Matter Anymore/Sweet Talk/Moody River/There's Life In The Old Boy Yet/A Handful Of Songs/Like Waltz/Rodeo/Donna's Theme/ Starfire/Baubles, Bangles & Beads/Zapata/Rum-Dee-Dum-Dee-Dah/ Spanish Harlem/Man From Madrid/The Challenege Also contains 18 tracks from Beat Girl.	UK CD	PLAY IT AGAIN PLAY 001
1990 1996	AMICALEMENT VOTRE (THE PERSUADERS!) The Persuaders!/Midnight Cowboy/Goldfinger/Danny Scipio Theme/007/ The Girl With The Sun In Her Hair/On Her Majesty's Secret Service/Vendetta/ Thunderball/The Chase/From Russia With Love/The James Bond Theme	FR CD US CD	CBS 466900 2 COLUMBIA WK 36754 2
1991	THEMES BY HOLLYWOOD'S GREAT COMPOSERS James Bond Theme/Dutchman	US CD SONY MUSIC SPECIAL PROJECTS AK 47019	
1991	THE BEST OF JOHN BARRY Goldfinger/Sail The Summer Winds/Love Among The Ruins/Lolita/ A Dolls House/Follow, Follow/Diamonds Are Forever/Boom!/ Midnight Cowboy/This Way Mary/The Glass Menagerie/Thunderball/007/ Play It Again/Orson Welles' Great Mysteries/We Have All The Time In The World/ The Whisperers/Curiouser & Curiouser/Billy/The Good Times Are Coming/ Walkabout/The Adventurer Reissued in 1996 as The Very Best Of John Barry – different sleeve. * Includes full liner notes not present on UK release.	UK CD JA CD	POLYDOR 849 095 2 POLYDOR POCP-2528 *
1991	GREAT TV & FILM HITS OF JOHN BARRY The Persuaders!/Born Free/James Bond Theme/Ipcress File/Goldfinger/ Midnight Cowboy/Space March */The Lion In Winter – Main Title/ From Russia With Love/Vendetta/You Only Live Twice – Theme/The Knack/ On Her Majesty's Secret Service/Danny Scipio Theme/Girl With The Sun In Her Hair/The More Things Change * Miscredited as Thunderball.	NL CD	COLUMBIA 467956 2
1992	ARCHIVE – DRAMA/CRIME 3 Moods 1 & 2* * Full versions plus 29/59 second commercial cuts Recorded in 1959 – Non-Commercial issue.	UK CD	CHAPPELL RECORDED MUSIC LIBRARY CHAP 168
1992	THE BEST OF BIG MOVIE HITS Space March */Theme From Born Free/Theme From The Persuaders!/ Midnight Cowboy/The Ipcress File/We Have All The Time In The World/ The Lion In Winter – Main Title/Goldfinger/You Only Live Twice/ Danny Scipio Theme/Girl With The Sun In Her Hair/The More Things Change/ Fun City/James Bond Theme * Miscredited as Thunderball.	AUS CD	COLUMBIA 471123 2

1992	JOHN BARRY: THE EMBER YEARS VOLUME 2	UK CD	PLAY IT AGAIN PLAY 003

A Lot Of Livin' To Do/Let Me Love You/All The Things You Are/
I'm Gonna Go Fishing/Like Someone In Love/Limehouse Blues/
A Handful Of Songs/All Of You/Fly Me To The Moon/Nature Boy/
What's New/Love For Sale.
All tracks sung by Annie Ross and arranged and conducted by Johnnie Spence
Zulu – Main Title */Monkey Feathers (alternative version)/From Russia With Love/
High Grass/Kinky/Monkey Feathers/Loneliness Of Autumn/Ngenzeni/
Fancy Dance/Big Shield/Zulu Stamp (alternative version)/Aliki/Tetha Leyanto/
Troubadour/Zulu Stamp/007
*Narration: Richard Burton
All Annie Ross tracks are Stereo. All other tracks are Mono

1992	BEST OF JAMES BOND 30th ANNIVERSARY COLLECTION		
		UK CD	EMI 798413 2 (CDBOND 007)
		US CD	EMI USA 798413 2

Goldfinger (Shirley Bassey)/A View To A Kill (Duran Duran)/Mr. Kiss
Kiss Bang Bang (Dionne Warwick) (c)/We Have All The Time In The World
(Louis Armstrong)/All Time High (Rita Coolidge)/The Living Daylights (A-ha)/
Thunderball (Tom Jones)/You Only Live Twice (Nancy Sinatra)/Moonraker
(Shirley Bassey)/On Her Majesty's Secret Service/The Man With The Golden Gun
(Lulu)/Diamonds Are Forever (Shirley Bassey)/007

		US CD	EMI USA 7 98560 2

The double (limited) CD release contains the following extra tracks:-
The James Bond Theme (a)/Goldfinger (Anthony Newley) (b)/
Pussy Galore's Flying Circus/Golden Girl/Death Of Tilly/
The Laser Beam/Thunderball Suite (d)/Mr. Kiss Kiss Bang Bang
(Shirley Bassey) (e)/You Only Live Twice (Julie Rogers) (f)/
You Only Live Twice (g)/Thunderball (h) radio spots

(a) Stereo release
(b) Previously unreleased – recorded May 14th 1964. One of two versions
(c) Previously unreleased -unused title song
(d) Previously unreleased selections from the film (21 mins 10 secs):
1) Bond Meets Domino/2) Lights Out For Paula/3) For King And Country/
4) Bond With SPECTRE Frogmen/5) Leiter To The Rescue/
6) Bond Joins Underwater Battle/7) Death Of Largo/8) End Titles
Selection 2) was not used in the film.
(e) Previously unreleased – alternative version of the song.
(f) Recorded 1.1.66. Previously unreleased and unused main title vocal.
(g) Includes extracts from the soundtrack plus James Bond Theme
and brief extract from Opening Titles/James Bond Is Back.
(h) Includes extract from James Bond Theme & Thunderball.

1992	MOVIOLA	UK CD	EPIC SOUNDTRAX 472490 2
		US CD	EPIC SOUNDTRAX EK 52985 2

Recording Engineer: Shawn Murphy
Recorded at EMI, Abbey Road Studio, London
Out Of Africa/Midnight Cowboy/Body Heat/Somewhere In Time/
Mary, Queen Of Scots/Born Free/Dances With Wolves */Chaplin/
The Cotton Club/Walkabout/Frances/We Have All The Time In The World/
Moviola**
*Combination of The John Dunbar Theme & Journey To Fort Sedgewick
** Composed for Prince Of Tides (Unused)
Performed by The Royal Philharmonic Orchestra

1993	JOHN BARRY: THE EMI YEARS VOLUME 1 (1957-1960)	UK CD	EMI 7 89416 2 (CDEMS 1497)

Let's Have A Wonderful Time/Rock-A-Billy-Boogie/Zip Zip/
Three Little Fishes (USA version)/Every Which Way I/ You've Gotta Way/
Big Guitar/Rodeo/Pancho/Hideaway/Farrago/Bees Knees/When The
Saints Go Marching In/Pancho/Long John/Snap 'N' Whistle/Little John/
For Pete's Sake/Bees Knees/Little John/Rebel Rouser/Mad Mab/
Good Rockin' Tonight/Twelfth Street Rag/Christella/Beat Girl (Main Title)/
Hit & Miss/Rockin' Already/Beat For Beatniks */Big Fella*/Blueberry Hill/
Never Let Go/Walk Don't Run */I'm Movin' On/Saturday's Child/
Black Stockings */Get Lost Jack Frost *
*First Stereo release – All other tracks arc Mono
Tracks 1 & 2 from Six Five Special
Tracks 13 & 14 from Oh Boy! – Announcement: Jimmy Henney
Tracks 19-23 from Drumbeat
Track 35 from Saturday Club
Tracks 19 & 23 with Bob Miller & The Millermen

1993	JOHN BARRY: THE EMI YEARS VOLUME 2 (1961)	UK CD	EMI 7 89586 2 (CDEMS 1501)

The Magnificent Seven */Skid Row */Dark Rider **/Iron Horse **/
The Menace*/A Matter Of Who*/Rocco's Theme */Spinnerree */
It Doesn't Matter Anymore/Sweet Talk/Moody River/There's Life
In The Old Boy Yet/A Handful Of Songs/Like Waltz/Rodeo/Donna's
Theme/Starfire/Baubles, Bangles &Beads/Zapata/Rum-Dee-Dum-Dee-Dah
Spanish Harlem/Man From Madrid/The Challenge/Watch Your Step **/
Twist It/Watch Your Step/Satin Smooth **/The Aggressor **
* First Stereo release. All tracks are Stereo except tracks 25 & 26
** Previously unreleased
Tracks 7 & 8 by Michael Angelo & His Orchestra
Tracks 9-23 released on Stringbeat – See previously (1990)

1994	THE JOHN BARRY COLLECTION (4 CD PACK)	UK CD	FAT BOY FATCD 418

1. Zulu/Zulu Stamps (13 Tracks)
2. Four In The Morning (11 Tracks)
3. From Russia With Love/007/Elizabeth In London/London Theme/
The Loneliness Of Autumn/Zulu – Main Theme/Yesterday's Gone */
Like I Love You Today */Fancy Dance/Lovers/Fire Of London/
Elizabeth Theme/Troubadour
* With Chad & Jeremy. All other tracks – John Barry & His Orchestra
Tracks 3, 4, 10-12 from Elizabeth Taylor In London
4. John Barry & Guests:
Yesterday's Gone */Lemon Tree */Like I Love You Today */
Ecstasy **/I'm A Worryin' **/Might Have Known (Before) (*)/
I Might Have Known (After) (*)/A Lot Of Livin' To Do/
Let Me Love You/All The Things You Are/I'm Gonna Go Fishin'/
Like Someone In Love/Limehouse Blues/A Handful Of Songs/
All Of You/Fly Me To The Moon/Nature Boy/What's New/
Love For Sale
* With Chad & Jeremy. **With Steve Cassidy. (*) With Philip Lowrie
All other tracks with Annie Ross; Johnnie Spence & His Orchestra

1994	THE MUSIC OF JOHN BARRY	UK CD	COLUMBIA 983 379 2
		UK CD	COLUMBIA 476750 2 *
		US CD	COLUMBIA WK 36633 2 **

You Only Live Twice/Born Free/Goldfinger/Whisperers/
From Russia With Love/Wednesday's Child/Space March (Capsule In Space)/
Girl With The Sun In Her Hair/Thunderball/Dutchman/The Wrong Box/
The James Bond Theme/007/Mister Kiss Kiss Bang Bang/The Chase/
King Rat/The Knack/Seance On A Wet Afternoon/The Ipcress File/
Midnight Cowboy/Theme For Romance For Guitar & Orchestra/O.H.M.S.S./
The Appointment/The Lion in Winter
* UK pressing for export to USA (1996)
**US equivalent of above (1996)

1995	007 AND OTHER GREAT SOUNDTRACK THEMES	UK CD	CHARLY CDCD 1225

007/From Russia With Love/Kinky/Fancy Dance/Zulu – Main Title */
Zulu Stamp/Monkey Feathers/Ngenzeni/Aliki/Tetha Leyanto/
Troubadour/Elizabeth Theme/The London Theme/Four In The Morning/
The Loneliness Of Autumn.
* Narration: Richard Burton.

1995	ZULU & OTHER GREAT FILM THEMES OF JOHN BARRY	UK CD	CASTLE MAC CD 221

From Russia With Love/Zulu/The Loneliness Of Autumn/Fancy Dance/
Troubador/Zulu Stamp/007/Kinky/Elizabeth In London/Elizabeth Waltz/
English Garden/London Theme/Lovers/Fire Of London/Elizabeth Theme/
Four In The Morning/River Walk/Lover's Clasp/Norman Leaves/
River Ride/Lover's Tension/First Reconciliation/Norman Returns/
London Waltz
Tracks 9-15, and 24 from Elizabeth Taylor In London
Tracks 16-23 from Four In The Morning

1995	MOVIOLA II: ACTION AND ADVENTURE	UK CD	EPIC SOUNDTRAX EPC 478601 2
		US CD	EPIC SOUNDTRAX EK 66401

Recording Engineer: Shawn Murphy
Recorded at Air Studios, London
Performed by The Royal Philharmonic Orchestra
The James Bond Suite:
Goldfinger/The James Bond Theme/From Russia With Love/
Thunderball/007/You Only Live Twice/On Her Majesty's Secret Service/
Diamonds Are Forever/All Time High (From Octopussy)
Until September/King Kong/Zulu/
Dances With Wolves Suite:
Pawnee Attack Part I & II/Kicking Bird's Gift/Journey To Fort Sedgewick/
Two Socks – The Wolf Theme/Farewell And Finale Part I & II
Did You Call Me (From The Specialist)/The Specialist

1995	CINEMA GOLD	UK CD	HALLMARK 304192

007/From Russia With Love/Kinky/Fancy Dance/Zulu-Main Theme*
Zulu Stamp/Monkey Feathers/Ngenzini/Aliki/Tetha Leyanto/
Troubador/Elizabeth Theme/London Theme/Four In The Morning/
Loneliness Of Autumn
* Narration: Richard Burton

1995	JOHN BARRY: THE EMI YEARS VOLUME 3 (1962-1964)	UK CD	8 35046 2 (CD EMS 1555)

The James Bond Theme/The Blacksmith Blues/Cutty Sark/Lost Patrol*/
Theme From Roman Spring Of Mrs. Stone* (*)/Tears (*)/Blueberry Hill**/
Cherry Pink & Apple Blossom White**/Smokey Joe (X)/Unchained Melody (X)/
The Party's Over (X)/The Lolly Theme*/March Of The Mandarins*/
The Human Jungle (Alternate Version) (X)/The Big Safari (XX)/
Mouse On The Moon (XX)/Twangin' Cheek (X)/I'll Be With You In Apple
Blossom Time**/Volare**/The Human Jungle*/Onward Christian Spacemen*/
Seven Faces/Twenty Four Hours Ago/Theme From A Jolly Bad Fellow (**)/
Oublie Ca/Seance On A Wet Afternoon/That Fatal Kiss
* First Stereo release
**First UK release
(*) Michael Angelo & His Orchestra
(**) Alan Haven
(X) Previously unreleased
(XX) The Countdowns Directed by John Barry
All tracks Stereo except 6, 15, 16, 22-26

1996	JOHN BARRY Zulu (Main Theme) */From Russia With Love/007 Theme/ Kinky/Loneliness Of Autumn/Fancy Dance/Troubador/Four In The Morning/ Elizabeth Theme/London Theme/Elizabeth In London/Monkey Feathers/ Big Shield/Judi Comes Back/River Walk/Norman Leaves/Moment Of Decision/ Aliki/Ngenzeni/Tetha Leyanto/First Reconciliation/Lovers/Lovers Clasp/ Fire Of London/River Ride * Narration by Richard Burton	NL CD	UNITED AUDIO ENTER' UAE 30342
1996	THE VINTAGE COLLECTION 1 Mood 3 (Retitled: Swinging City) – full version. Recorded in 1959 – Non-Commercial issue.	UK CD	BRUTON MUSIC BRO 15
1997	JOHN BARRY EXPERIENCE 007/From Russia With Love/Loneliness Of Autumn/Four In The Morning/ River Walk/Lovers' Tension/First Reconciliation/Judi Comes Home/Elizabeth In London/ The London Theme/The Elizabeth Theme/Lovers/Aliki/Zulu (Main Title Theme) */ First Zulu Appearance And Assault/Zulu Stamp/Monkey Feathers/Tetha Leyanto/ Fancy Dance/Christine ** * Narration: Richard Burton. ** Sung by Miss X (Joyce Blair).	UK CD	CARLTON SOUNDS 30360 00812
1997	HIT AND MISS WITH JOHN BARRY Hideaway (*)/When The Saints Go Marching In (*)/Long John (*)/ Twelfth Street Rag (*)/Hit And Miss (**)/Beat For Beatniks (***)/ Blueberry Hill (***)/Never Let Go (***)/Walk Don't Run (*)/ Black Stockings (*)/The Magnificent Seven (*)/It Doesn't Matter Anymore/ Spanish Harlem/The James Bond Theme (x)/Cutty Sark (x)/ Cherry Pink And Apple Blossom White (***)/Unchained Melody (***)/ I'll Be With You In Apple Blossom Time (***)/Volare (***)/ That Fatal Kiss (***). (*) John Barry Seven (**) John Barry Seven Plus Four (***) John Barry & His Orchestra (x) John Barry Seven & Orchestra All other tracks by John Barry.	UK CD	MUSIC FOR PLEASURE CDMFP 6392 (57697 2)
1997	THE BEST OF JOHN BARRY – THEMEOLOGY Persuaders Theme/Midnight Cowboy/The Ipcress File/The Knack/ Wednesday's Child/Space March (Capsule In Space)/ The Girl With The Sun In Her Hair/Vendetta/The Danny Scipio Theme/ The James Bond Theme/Goldfinger (1)/Diamonds Are Forever (1)/ From Russia With Love (2)/You Only Live Twice/Thunderball/ On Her Majesty's Secret Service/007/Walk Don't Run/Beat For Beatniks/ Hit And Miss/Born Free (2)/Main Title – I Had A Farm In Africa (Out Of Africa)/ The John Dunbar Theme (3) (1) Sung by Shirley Bassey (2) Sung by Matt Monro (3) (Track 13) from the Original Soundtrack. * Limited Edition Digipack ** Different artwork/title	UK CD UK CD FR CD	COLUMBIA 488582 2 COLUMBIA 488582 9 * COLUMBIA COL 488582 6 **
1998	JOHN BARRY – THE HITS & THE MISSES Hit & Miss (3) Walk Don't Run * (2) Rocco's Theme * (6) Cutty Sark (5) The James Bond Theme * (5) * Stereo release. This compilation also includes 45 vocal tracks with accompaniment by John Barry (Orchestra). See Other Artists – Compact Discs for full track listing.	UK CD	PLAY IT AGAIN PLAY 007 (2 CD SET)
1998	THE BEYONDNESS OF THINGS The Beyondness Of Things, Kissably Close, The Heartlands, Give Me A Smile, A Childhood Memory, Nocturnal New York, Meadow Of Delight & Sadness, Gifts Of Nature, The Fictionist, Dawn Chorus, The Day The Earth Fell Silent, Dance With Reality. Perfomed by the English Chamber Orchestra Recording engineer: John Richards Recorded at Abbey Road Studios, London (14-16th October 1997) solo harmonica – Tommy Morgan solo alto sax – David White executive producer – Chris Roberts orchestral management – Christian Rutherford	LONDON	460 009-2 (PY 900)

CHAD & JEREMY – COMPACT DISCS

1988	ZULU & OTHER THEMES Includes Yesterday's Gone & No Tears For Johnnie only - With John Barry & His Orchestra	CD UK	SILVA SCREEN FILM CD 022
1990	BEST OF CHAD & JEREMY Yesterday's Gone – the only track arranged by John Barry	CD US	K-TEL 778-2
1992	CHAD & JEREMY SING FOR YOU Yesterday's Gone */If She Was Mine/Willow Weep For Me/ No Tears Fo Johnny/The Truth Often Hurts The Heart/If I Loved You/ September In The Rain/Like I Love You Today */Donna Donna/A Summer Song/ Dirty Old Town/From A Window/What Do You Want With Me?/ My Colouring Book/If You Gotta Heart/No Other Baby/Now And Forever/ Too Soon/The Girl From Ipanema/Four Strong Winds/Only Those In Love/ You Know What/Sleep Little Boy/My How The Time Goes By/ It Was A Very Good Year BONUS TRACKS: Lemon Tree */Early In The Morning */Your Mother's Out Of Town (*)/The Nearness Of You (*)/A Summer Song (alternative version) (*) (*) Previously unreleased *These tracks only arranged by John Barry NB. This album contains the entire output of Chad & Jeremy recorded for Ember Records and the full track listing is thus quoted	GR CD	REPERTOIRE REP 4286-WY
1994	THE EMBER YEARS VOLUME 3 Not True As Yet (a)/Me (a)/She'll Never Be You (a)/Gonna Make A Woman of You (a)/Christine (b)/I Should Have Known (Before) (c)/ Bye Bye Blues (d)/Ecstasy (e)/I'm A Worryin' (e)/Yesterday's Gone (f)/ Lemon Tree (f)/Early In The Morning (f)/Like I Love You Today (f) All the above tracks are produced by John Barry (a) A Band Of Angels; b) Miss X (Joyce Blair) (c) Philip Lowrie; arranged and conducted by Gordon Franks (d) Annie Ross; arranged and conducted by Johnnie Spence (e) Steve Cassidy; arranged and conducted by John Barry (f) Chad & Jeremy; arranged and conducted by John Barry All above tracks are mono except: I Should Have Known/Like I Love You Today	UK CD	PLAY IT AGAIN PIA 101
1996	BEST OF CHAD & JEREMY Yesterday's Gone/Like I Love You Today/Lemon Tree	US CD	ONE WAY OW 31380

ADAM FAITH – COMPACT DISCS

1989	THE BEST OF ADAM FAITH What Do You Want?/Poor Me/Someone Else's Baby */Johnny Comes Marching Home */Made You/How About That? */Lonely Pup (In A Christmas Shop) */ This Is It */Who Am I? */Easy Going Me */Don't You Know It?/The Time Has Come/Lonesome/As You Like It *Stereo tracks	UK CD	MUSIC FOR PLEASURE CD MFP 6048
1990	THE ADAM FAITH SINGLES COLLECTION What Do You Want?/Poor Me/Someone Else's Baby/Johnny Comes Marching Home/Made You/How About That?/Who Am I?/Easy Going Me/Don't You Know It?/The Time Has Come/Lonesome/ As You Like It All tracks are in Stereo	UK CD	EMI CDP 7936632 (CZ 260)
1991	ADAM FAITH THE E. P. COLLECTION Wonderful Time/Diamond Ring/How About That? */Lonely Pup (In A Christmas Shop) */What Do You Want?/Poor Me/Someone Else's Baby */ The Time Has Come/Piper Of Love/Made You/Did What You Told Me/ Face To Face/Watch Your Step/Turn Me Loose/I'm Coming Home/ I'm A Man *Stereo tracks	UK CD	SEE FOR MILES SEE CD 298
1994	THE BEST OF – THE EMI YEARS What Do You Want? */From Now Until Forever */Ah! Poor Little Baby */ Poor Me */Summertime/Wonderful Time/Someone Else's Baby/When Johnny Comes Marching Home/Made You */Hit The Road To Dreamland/ I'm A Man/How About That?/With Open Arms/Singin' In The Rain/ Fare Thee Well My Pretty Maid/Lonely Pup (In A Christmas Shop)/This Is It/ Who Am I?/Sho' Know A Lot About Love/As Long As You Keep Loving Me/ I'm Gonna Love You Too/Easy Going Me/Wonderin'/Watch Your Step/ Don't You Know It? */The Time Has Come */A Help-Each-Other-Romance/ Lonesome */As You Like It */Face To Face */You Can Do It If You Try (*) All tracks Stereo except * – Mono (*) Previously unreleased	UK CD	EMI 8 28429 2 (CDEM 513) (2 CD Set)

| 1997 | THE VERY BEST OF ADAM FAITH | UK CD | MUSIC FOR PLEASURE |
| | A reissue of the 1989 CD The Best Of Adam Faith. | | CD MFP 6380 (857413 2) |

| 1997 | ADAM | UK CD | EMI DORIG 106 (8 56568 2) |

Wonderful Time/Diamond Ring/Summertime/Greenfinger/Piper Of Love/
A Girl Like You/Turn Me Loose/So Many Ways/Singin' In The Rain/
Fare Thee Well My Pretty Maid/I'm A Man/Hit The Road To Dreamland
Special Gatefold sleeve release featuring all tracks from Adam's first (1960) album in Stereo & Mono.

OTHER ARTISTS – COMPACT DISCS

The following compact discs feature artists accompanied/produced by John Barry.
(x) First CD release.
(s) First Stereo release.

| 1988 | RUSS CONWAY'S GREATEST HITS | UK CD | EMI COMPACTS FOR PLEASURE CDB 7 52030 2 (CC 203) |
| | Pepe (x) (s) | | |

| 1988 | HIT SONGS OF THE 60s | UK CD | PICKWICK PWK 053 |
| | Be Mine (Lance Fortune) (x) | | |

| 1988 | LITTLE TONY AND HIS BROTHERS | FR CD | BIG BEAT 7904072 |
| | Arrivederci Baby (x) | | |

1989	ANNIE ROSS SINGS A HANDFUL OF SONGS	SP CD	FRESH SOUND FSR CD 61
	12 tracks arranged and conducted by Johnnie Spence		
	Produced by John Barry. Sound Engineer: Eric Tomlinson		
	Recorded at CTS Studios, London (x) (s).		

| 1990 | MATT MONRO SINGS DON BLACK | UK CD | EMI CDP 7 93878 2 (CZ 272) |
| | Born Free/Wish Now Was Then (Mary, Queen Of Scots) (x) (s) | | |

1990	JUMPIN' – INSTRUMENTAL DIAMONDS Vol.1	UK CD	SEQUEL NEXCD 149
	(BRITISH 60s INSTRUMENTALS (1961-1964))		
	Polaris (x)/Jumpin' (x) (The Boys)		

| 1993 | DON BLACK SONGBOOK | UK CD | PLAY IT AGAIN PLAY 005 |

Born Free (*) */To Sir With Love (Lulu)/
The Girl With The Sun In Her Hair (Davy Clinton) **/
True Grit (Danny Street)/On Days Like These (*)/
This Way Mary (*) */Wish Now Was Then (*) */
Curiouser And Curiouser (*) **/The Me I Never Knew (*) */
Billy (Lena Martell) **/The Lady From L.A. (Michael Crawford) */
I Missed The Last Rainbow (Michael Crawford) */
Play It Again (Wilma Reading) **/I'll Put You Together Again (Hot Chocolate)/
Tell Me On A Sunday (**)/The Last Man In My Life (**)/
Anyone Can Fall In Love (**)/Always There (**)/
There Is Love And There Is Love (Adam Faith)/
In One Of My Weaker Moments (Anita Dobson)/
Anything But Lonely (**)/Love Changes Everything (**)
(*) Matt Monro
(**)Marti Webb
* Composed, arranged and conducted by John Barry.
This Way Mary (x) (s)/The Lady From L.A. (x)/I Missed The Last Rainbow (x)
**Composed by John Barry.
Lyrics for all titles composed by Don Black.

1994	DOWN MEMORY LANE	UK CD	FAT BOY FAT CD 153
	WITH THE BILLY COTTON SHOW BAND		
	CD release of the 1963 Billy Cotton LP – Saturday Night Sing-A-Long		

1995	RUSS CONWAY – A DOUBLE CELEBRATION	UK CD	EMI CD RUSS 1 (8 34408 2)
	(4 CD BOX SET) – CELEBRATION DAY includes:	UK CD	EMI CD 8 34410 2
	Matador From Trinidad (x) (s)		

| 1998 | JOHN BARRY – THE HITS & THE MISSES | UK CD | PLAY IT AGAIN PLAY 007 |
| | | | (2 CD SET) |

What Do You Want? (Adam Faith)/Can't Forget (Johnny Gavotte)/Hit & Miss (John Barry)/
Boston Tea Party (The Dallas Boy)/Big Time (Adam Faith) */Carve Up (Adam Faith) */
It Doesn't Matter (Danny Williams)/Walk Don't Run (John Barry) */Greenfinger (Adam Faith) *
Pepe (Russ Conway) */Matador From Trinidad (Russ Conway) */Not Guilty (Johnny De Little)/
Big Wheel (Gerry Dorsey)/Where You Are (Denis Lotis)/Django's Castle (Diz Disley & The
Downbeats)/My Last Wish (Adam Faith)/Mr One & Only (Anita Harris)/I Haven't Got You
(Anita Harris) */Rocco's Theme (Michael Angelo) */Little Yellow Roses (Adam Faith) */
Over And Over (Bobby Shafto)/You Know What I Mean (Johnny Worth)/All These Things
(Johnny Worth)/Cutty Sark (John Barry)/Stalemate (Tony Rocco) */You're Following Me
(Peter Gordeno)/I've Just Fallen For Someone (Darren Young)/My Tears Will Turn To Laughter
(Darren Young)/Uptown (Peter Gordeno)/Coffee Grinder (Van Doran)/Caravan Of Lonely Men
(Mark Tracey)/Someone Nice Like You (Billy Cotton & Kathie Kay)/The James Bond Theme
(John Barry) */No Love But Your Love (Marion Ryan)/Down By The Riverside (Peter Gordeno)
Lover (Johnny De Little)/Away In A Manger (Nina & Frederik)/Lonely Avenue (Marty Wilde)/

Mam'selle – My Romance – Glory Of Love – Deed I Do – Say It Isn't So (Dick Kallman) */
You Can Do It If You Try (Peter Gordeno)/Ride On (Johnny De Little)/Days Of Wine & Roses
(Johnny De Little)/Unchained Melody (Johnny De Little) */The Wind & The Rain (Johnny De
Little) */Dream Maker (Tommy Steele) */Goldfinger (Shirley Bassey)
* Stereo release.

JOHN BARRY – NON SOUNDTRACK ALBUMS

N.B. All music is composed by John Barry except:-
From Russia With Love (Lionel Bart).
The James Bond Theme (Monty Norman)

For early material, an asterisk in the text denotes compositions by John Barry either solely or with other composers. Please note that reissues and compilation albums are only noted where they contain different or new tracks; or different sleeve artwork. In all cases the year quoted relates to the year the recording was first published.

1961	STRINGBEAT	UK 33	COLUMBIA 33SX 1358 (M)
	(John Barry)	UK 33	COLUMBIA SCX 3401 (S)
	Reissue: 1983 with insert and different artwork	UK 33	CHERRY RED BRED 51
	It Doesn't Matter Anymore, Sweet Talk*, Moody River,		
	There's Life In The Old Boy Yet*, A Handful Of Songs,		
	Like Waltz*, Rodeo*, Donna's Theme, Starfire,		
	Baubles, Bangles & Beads, Zapata, Rum Dee Dum Dee Dah,		
	Spanish Harlem, Man From Madrid, The Challenge*.		
1964	JOHN BARRY PLAYS GOLDFINGER	US 33	U.ARTISTS UAL 3424 (M)
	(John Barry & His Orchestra)	US 33	U.ARTISTS UAS 6424 (S)
	Goldfinger (Instrumental)*, From Russia With Love,		
	Baubles, Bangles & Beads, Blueberry Hill, Zulu Stamp*,		
	Volare, The James Bond Theme*, Cherry Pink & Apple Blossom White,		
	Spanish Harlem, Moody River, Sweet Talk*		
	March Of The Mandarins*.		
1964	ALL TIME HITS	US 33	ASCOT AM 13002 (M)
	(John Barry & His Orchestra)	US 33	ASCOT AS 16002 (S)
	Volare, Cherry Pink And Apple Blossom White,		
	There's Life In The Old Boy Yet*, Spanish Harlem,		
	Moody River, Sweet Talk*, Blueberry Hill,		
	I'll Be With You In Apple Blossom Time,		
	A Handful Of Songs, Baubles, Bangles & Beads,		
	Rodeo*, It Doesn't Matter Anymore.		
1965	JOHN BARRY PLAYS 007	UK 33	EMBER NR 5025 (M) (*)
	(John Barry Orchestra)	UK 33	EMBER STNR 5025 (S)
	Different sleeve artwork and different arrangement of	IT 33	VEDETTE VRM 36007 (M)
	Four in The Morning, plus Troubador (+)	IT 33	VEDETTE VRMS 307 (S)
	From Russia With Love, 007*, The Elizabeth Theme*	SP 33	FIDIAS EM 502 (+)
	(**), The London Theme* (**), The Loneliness Of Autumn,		
	Aliki, Fancy Dance*, Kinky, Ngenzeni**,	JA 33	GLOBE EMBER SJET 7796 (*)
	Tetha Leyanto**, Monkey Feathers *, Big Shield*.		
	** Original Zulu Stamps arranged by John Barry.		
	(**) From the original soundtrack album of Elizabeth Taylor In London.		
	(*) Reissued 1967 – Different sleeve – Bond pics		
	N.B. All recordings are new versions.		
1966	JOHN BARRY PLAYS FILM & TV THEMES	US 33	CAPITOL T 2527 (M)
	(John Barry)	US 33	CAPITOL ST 2527 (S)
	From Russia With Love, The Elizabeth Theme* (*),		
	Aliki, The London Theme* (*), Fancy Dance*,		
	The Loneliness Of Autumn, 007*, Lovers* (*),		
	Kinky, Fire Of London* (*), London Waltz* (*)		
	(*) From the original soundtrack album of Elizabeth Taylor In London.		
1966	GREAT MOVIE SOUNDS OF JOHN BARRY	UK 33	CBS SBPG 62402
	(John Barry & His Orchestra)	US 33	COLUMBIA CL 2493 (M)
		US 33	COLUMBIA CS 9293 (S)
	Thunderball, 007, Goldfinger, Mr. Kiss Kiss Bang Bang,		
	From Russia With Love, The James Bond Theme,		
	The Chase, Theme From King Rat, The Knack,		
	Seance On A Wet Afternoon, The Ipcress File,		
	Theme From Born Free.		
1966	JOHN BARRY MEETS CHAD & JEREMY	UK 33	EMBER NR 5032 (M)
	(John Barry & His Orchestra)	CA 33	CAPITOL T 6126
	From Russia With Love, 007 Theme*, Yesterday's Gone (*),		
	Lemon Tree (*), Elizabeth Theme*, The London Theme*,		
	The Loneliness Of Autumn, Aliki, Like I Love You Today (*),		
	No Tears For Johnnie (*), Fancy Dance*, Kinky.		
	(*) These tracks feature singing duo Chad (Stuart) & Jeremy (Clyde) with		
	accompaniment by John Barry & His Orchestra.		

1966	SWEET & MOODY (Ember Library Music Disc) (John Barry & His Orchestra) Loneliness Of Autumn, Fancy Dance*, Four In The Morning*, Troubadour* Includes other tracks which were not by John Barry.	UK 33	EMBER ERL 3340
1967	INCREDIBLE WORLD OF JAMES BOND (John Barry) Bond Back In Action Again, Gypsy Camp , James Bond With Bongos	US 33 US 33	U. ARTISTS UNART M 20010 (M) U. ARTISTS UNART S 21010 (S)
1967	JOHN BARRY CONDUCTS HIS GREATEST MOVIE HITS (John Barry & His Orchestra) You Only Live Twice, Theme From Born Free, Goldfinger, The Whisperers, Wednesday's Child, Space March (Capsule In Space) (*), The Girl With The Sun In Her Hair, Thunderball, Dutchman, The Wrong Box, The James Bond Theme. (*) From the film You Only Live Twice.	UK 33 US 33 US 33	CBS SS 63038 COLUMBIA CL 2708 (M) COLUMBIA CS 9508 (S)
1968	THE BEST OF BOND (John Barry) Original Soundtrack Recordings Opening Titles James Bond Is Back From Russia With Love James Bond Is Back, The Golden Horn, 007, Golden Girl, Oddjob's Pressing Engagement, Bond Back In Action Again, Thunderball, Death Of Fiona, Mr. Kiss Kiss Bang Bang, Fight At Kobe Dock Helga, Mountains & Sunsets, Bond Averts World War Three. * Best Of 007	UK 33 JA 33	U.ARTISTS UAS 29021 U. ARTISTS SR 343 *
1969	READY WHEN YOU ARE, J.B. (John Barry) Midnight Cowboy, We Have All The Time In The World, Theme from Romance For Guitar & Orchestra, Who Will Buy My Yesterdays, Fun City, The Lion In Winter, On Her Majesty's Secret Service, Theme From The Appointment, Try, The More Things Change, Afternoon, Theme From Born Free.	UK 33 US 33	CBS S 63952 COLUMBIA CS 1003
1971	JOHN BARRY REVISITED (John Barry & His Orchestra) British Pressing was originally issued in a Gatefold sleeve. Zulu Main Title Theme*, From Russia With Love, Fancy Dance*, Kinky, Four In The Morning*, Elizabeth Theme*, London Theme*, 007 Theme*, Yesterday's Gone (*), No Tears For Johnnie (*), Aliki, Monkey Feathers*, Judi Comes Back*, The Loneliness Of Autumn (Non Sapevo). (*) Chad & Jeremy with John Barry & His Orchestra.	UK 33 IT 33	EMBER SE 8008 VEDETTE SE 8008
1971	THE PERSUADERS! (John Barry) Theme From The Persuaders, Midnight Cowboy, Goldfinger, Danny Scipio Theme, 007, The Girl With The Sun In Her Hair, On Her Majesty's Secret Service, Vendetta, Thunderball, The Chase, From Russia With Love, The James Bond Theme. * Los Grandes Excitos De John Barry – Different sleeve artwork (*) Amicalement Votre – Different sleeve artwork.	UK 33 SP 33 FR 33	CBS S 64816 CBS S 64816 * CBS 466900 1 (*)
1972	THE CONCERT JOHN BARRY (The Royal Philharmonic Orchestra conducted by John Barry) John Barry At His Best Goldfinger Gatefold issue with different sleeve artwork The James Bond Suite: (Goldfinger, The James Bond Theme, From Russia With Love, Thunderball, 007, You Only Live Twice, On Her Majesty's Secret Service, Diamonds Are Forever); Born Free, Alice's Adventures In Wonderland: Suite (Curiouser & Curiouser, I've Never Been This Far Before, The Me I Never Knew); Midnight Cowboy, Mary, Queen Of Scots, The Adventurer. Leader of the R.P.O. – Erich Gruenberg, who is also the soloist on Mary, Queen Of Scots.	UK 33 JA 33	POLYDOR 2383 156 POLYDOR MP 3031
1972	THE JAMES BOND COLLECTION (10th Anniversary Issue) (John Barry) (Various Original Soundtracks 2 LP Set) Original issue initially contained booklet. With inner bag notes and different sleeve artwork James Bond Is Back, From Russia With Love, The James Bond Theme, Girl Trouble, The Golden Horn, Death Of Grant, From Russia With Love (Vocal: Matt Monro) (*); Goldfinger (Vocal: Shirley Bassey), Into Miami, Auric's Factory, Bond Back In Action Again,	UK 33 US 33 JA 33	U.ARTISTS UAD 60027/8 U. ARTISTS UXS 91 U. ARTISTS FMW 5/6

Goldfinger (Instrumental), The Death Of Goldfinger (**);
Mr. Kiss Kiss Bang Bang, 007, Thunderball (Vocal: Tom Jones),
Bond Below Disco Volante (***).
Mountains & Sunsets, Capsule In Space, A Drop In The Ocean *,
On Her Majesty's Secret Service (Main Theme),
We Have All the Time In The World (Vocal: Louis Armstrong)
Journey To Blofeld's Hideaway/This Never Happened To
The Other Fella **
Moon Buggy Ride, Bond Smells A Rat, Circus, Circus,
Diamonds Are Forever (Vocal: Shirley Bassey) ***.
(*) Selections from From Russia With Love; (**) Selections from Goldfinger;
(***) Selections from Thunderball; * Selections from You Only Live Twice;
** Selections from O.H.M.S.S.; *** Selections from Diamonds Are Forever;

1974	PLAY IT AGAIN	UK 33	POLYDOR 2383 300 *
	(Themes From Stage, Screen and Television)	UK 33	POLYDOR ACB 00204
	(John Barry)	SP 33	POLYDOR 23 83 300 (*)

Sail The Summer Winds, Walkabout, Play It Again,
Billy, The Good Times Are Coming, Lolita,
Orson Welles' Great Mysteries, Theme From Love Among
The Ruins, We Have All the Time In The World,
This Way Mary, Theme From Boom, Theme From The Glass Menagerie.
Recorded at Air Studios, London.
* Circle Of Sound release.
(*) Different cover featuring Julie Andrews.

1976	THE MUSIC OF JOHN BARRY	UK 33	CBS 22014 (S 81277/8)
	(John Barry) (2 LP Set)		

You Only Live Twice, Born Free, Goldfinger,
The Whisperers, From Russia With Love, Wednesday's
Child, Space March, The Girl With The Sun In Her Hair,
Thunderball, Dutchman, The Wrong Box, James Bond Theme,
007, Mr. Kiss Kiss Bang Bang, The Chase, King Rat,
The Knack, Seance On A Wet Afternoon, The Ipcress File,
Midnight Cowboy, Theme From Romance For Guitar & Orchestra,
On Her Majesty's Secret Service, Theme From The Appointment,
The Lion In Winter.

1976	AMERICANS	UK 33	POLYDOR 2383 405
	(John Barry)	JA 33	POLYDOR MP 3054

Yesternight Suite Interpolating By Myself*
and As Time Goes By **, Downtown Walker, Scorpio,
Social Swing, Strip Drive, Speaking Mirrors.
Recorded at Glen Glenn Sound Studios, Hollywood, November 1975.
All music composed by John Barry except:
* Composed by Arthur Schwartz/Howard Dietz.
**Composed by Herman Hupfeld.

1977	THE VERY BEST OF JOHN BARRY	UK 33	POLYDOR 2383 461
	(John Barry)		

Thunderball/007, Curiouser & Curiouser (*),
Strip Drive, We Have All The Time In The World,
Diamonds Are Forever, A Dolls House ,
Goldfinger, Theme From Love Among The Ruins,
The Adventurer, Excerpt From Yesternight Suite,
Midnight Cowboy.
(*) New version .
Music recorded at Abbey Road Studios/Air Studios, London.

1977	JOHN BARRY GRAND PRIX 20	JA 33	CBS/SONY 29AP 436E
	(John Barry & His Orchestra) (2 LP Set with booklet)		

The James Bond Theme, Goldfinger, Thunderball,
Mr. Kiss Kiss Bang Bang, You Only Live Twice,
Space March, The Ipcress File, The Chase,
Wednesday's Child, Midnight Cowboy,
From Russia With Love, 007, O.H.M.S.S.,
We Have All The Time In The World, Try,
Theme From The Persuaders!, Theme From The Appointment,
The Lion In Winter, The Knack, Born Free.

1977	ALL ABOUT 007	JA 33	U. ARTISTS FMW 39/40

The Man With The Golden Gun/Kung Fu Fight/
In Search Of Scaramanga's Island/Diamonds Are Forever
(Shirley Bassey)/Circus Circus/Moon Buggy Ride/
We Have All The Time In The World (Louis Armstrong)/
Journey To Blofeld's Hideaway-This Never Happened To The Other Fella/
On Her Majesty's Secret Service (Main Theme)/Mountains & Sunsets/
Capsule in Space/Thunderball/007/Mr. Kiss Kiss Bang Bang/
The Death Of Goldfinger/Goldfinger/Bond Back In Action Again/
From Russia With Love

1979	ALL ABOUT 007	JA 33	U. ARTISTS FMW 43/44

Tracks same as 1977 issue + Moonraker – Main Title (Shirley Bassey)

| 1979 | THE BEST OF JOHN BARRY SEVEN & ORCHESTRA | UK 33 | EMI NUTM 21 (M/S) |

1979   THE BEST OF JOHN BARRY SEVEN & ORCHESTRA   UK 33   EMI NUTM 21 (M/S)
Hit & Miss* (2), Big Guitar (1), Rodeo (1),
Big Fella* (4), Walk Don't Run (1), Bee's Knees* (1),
Ev'ry Which Way (1), Main Title Beat Girl* (3),
The Human Jungle (3), I'm Movin On (2), Zapata (4) (*),
Like Waltz* (4) (*), Black Stockings* (1),
The James Bond Theme* (3), Lost Patrol (3),
The Magnificent Seven (1), Hideaway* (1),
The Menace* (4), Never Let Go* (4), The Sharks* (4).
(1) The John Barry Seven
(2) The John Barry Seven Plus Four.
(3) The John Barry Seven & Orchestra.
(4) The John Barry Orchestra.
(*) Stereo tracks.

1980   THE BIG SCREEN HITS OF JOHN BARRY   UK 33   CBS 31862
(John Barry)
Space March (Capsule In Space), Theme From Born Free,
Theme From The Persuaders!, Midnight Cowboy,
The Ipcress File, We Have All The Time In The World,
The Lion In Winter Main Title , Goldfinger,
You Only Live Twice, Danny Scipio Theme,
The Girl With The Sun In Her Hair, The More Things Change,
Fun City, The James Bond Theme.

1981   THE VERY BEST OF JOHN BARRY   UK 33   POLYDOR 2384 120
(John Barry)   (MID 1009)
This album was a reissue of that issued in 1977.
Slightly different sleeve artwork.

1981   ALL ABOUT 007   JA 33   U. ARTISTS K22P- 4045/6
Tracks with John Barry same as 1979 issue

1982   HIT & MISS   UK 33   CHARLY CM 110
(John Barry Seven & Orchestra)
This album was a reissue of The Best Of John Barry Seven & Orchestra issued in 1979
Different sleeve artwork and notes.

1983   ALL ABOUT 007   JA 33   CBS/SONY 29AP 2649
Tracks same as 1981 + All Time High (Rita Coolidge)

1985   BOND BY BARRY   US 33   BULLDOG BDL 1036
(John Barry & His Orchestra)
This album was a reissue of the Revisited album issued in 1971.
Different sleeve artwork.

1987   MUSIC FROM THE BIG SCREEN   UK CA   DITTO DTO 10229
(John Barry)
Twin pack cassette release only.
The James Bond Theme, The Whisperers,
Mr. Kiss Kiss Bang Bang, King Rat, You Only Live Twice,
Thunderball, The Ipcress File, The Chase, Dutchman,
From Russia With Love, On Her Majesty's Secret Service,
Fun City, The Knack, We Have All The Time In The World,
Born Free, Midnight Cowboy, The Girl With The Sun In Her Hair,
The Wrong Box, The More Things Change, Goldfinger.

1988   HIT & MISS   UK 33   C5 516
(John Barry Seven)
This album was a reissue of the Hit & Miss album issued in 1982.
Different sleeve artwork and notes.

1990   AMICALEMENT VOTRE   FR 33   CBS 466 900 1
(John Barry)
Theme from The Persuaders!/Midnight Cowboy/
Goldfinger/Danny Scipio Theme/007/Girl With The Sun In Her Hair/
On Her Majesty's Secret Service/Vendetta/Thunderball/
The Chase/From Russia With Love/James Bond Theme
Reissue of The Persuaders! album issued in 1971 with different sleeve artwork.

1992   MOVIOLA   UK 33 EPIC SOUNDTRAX EPC 472490 1
(John Barry & Royal Philharmonic Orchestra)
Out Of Africa, Midnight Cowboy, Body Heat,
Somewhere In Time, Mary, Queen Of Scots,
Born Free, Dances With Wolves *, Chaplin,
The Cotton Club, Walkabout, Frances,
We Have All The Time In The World,
Moviola **
* Combination of The John Dunbar Theme & Journey To Fort Sedgewick
** Initally written for Prince Of Tides (Unused).

JOHN BARRY – COMPILATION LPs

The following albums feature various tracks by John Barry as credited. Please note that compilation albums containing one or more tracks by John Barry are not listed here unless they appear on album for the first time, or are otherwise of interest. There have been many James Bond compilation albums released in different forms in different countries over the years. The main releases have, however, already been listed. The listing of any other items would merely be repetitive. The same basis applies to the many albums, and occasionally cassette releases, which have appeared on EMI, United Artists, CBS, Polydor and other labels.
Compositions up to 1970 composed by John Barry are annotated with an asterisk. All other music is composed by John Barry.

1957	SIX FIVE SPECIAL Based on the BBC TV Series The following were recorded live by John Barry & The Seven: Let's Have A Wonderful Time*, Rock A Billy Boogie*, Every Which Way.	UK 33	PARLOPHONE PMC 1047 (M)
1958	OH BOY! Based on the ABC TV Series The following were recorded live by The John Barry Seven: When The Saints Go Marching In (*), Pancho *. (*) Arranged by John Barry. Second reissue with different sleeve artwork.	UK 33 UK 33	PARLOPHONE PMC 1072 (M) MFP 50462 (M)
1959	DRUMBEAT Based on the BBC TV Series The John Barry Seven are featured on the following live recordings: Bees Knees* (*), Little John*, Say Mama (**), C'Mon Everybody (**), Rebel Rouser, Believe What You Say (**), Mad Mab*, Good Rockin' Tonight (*). (*) With Bob Miller & The Millermen. (**)with Adam Faith. I Vibrate with Adam Faith	UK 33 UK EP	PARLOPHONE PMC 1101 (M) FONTANA TFE 17146
1960	SATURDAY CLUB Compilation of artists who appeared on the BBC Radio Series John Barry Seven play Saturday's Child.	UK 33	PARLOPHONE PMC 1130 (M)
1960	BLACKPOOL NIGHTS Compilation of artists who appeared at Blackpool during the 1960 Summer Season. John Barry Seven plays Twelfth Street Rag. Adam Faith sings What Do You Want (*). (*) Accompaniment directed by John Barry.	UK 33	COLUMBIA 33SX 1244 (M)
1960	FINGS AIN'T WOT THEY USED T'BE Based on the Musical; Book by Frank Norman. Music & Lyrics by Lionel Bart. Musical Direction by Tony Osborne Big Time (*), Carve Up (*). (*) Adam Faith with John Barry & His Orchestra.	UK 33 UK 33	HMV CLP 1358 (M) HMV CSD 1298 (S)
1960	CHAPPELL RECORDED MUSIC Music Library Disc with John Barry & His Orchestra: Mood One*, Mood Two*, Mood Three*, Mood Four (1 4)* (C 673A) (C673B) (C676A) (C676B) N.B. All tracks were previously released by Chappell on 78 r.p.m. discs.	UK 33	CHAPPELL 672-677 (M)
1960	CHAPPELL RECORDED MUSIC Music Library Disc with John Barry & His Orchestra: Smoky Blues* (C 681B). Previously released by Chappell on 78 r.p.m. disc.	UK 33	CHAPPELL 678-682 (M)
1973	16 ALL TIME ORCHESTRAL CHARTBUSTERS John Barry Seven & Orchestra: The James Bond Theme (*) (*) The first stereo release of the James Bond Theme.	UK 33	ONE UP OU 2023
1976	THE GREAT FILM COMPOSERS Features various composers including: Born Free (*) , The Whisperers (**) (*) John Barry & Royal Philharmonic Orchestra (**) Orchestra conducted by John Barry	UK 33	POLYDOR 2489 123
1986	ORIGINAL TV HITS OF THE SIXTIES John Barry: The Human Jungle (*) Limited Collector's Edition. A later pressing had different sleeve artwork. (*) This was the original arrangement as used in the TV Series -	UK 33	FILMTRAX MOMENT 105
1992	BEST OF JAMES BOND – 30th ANNIVERSARY COLLECTION Includes Mister Kiss Kiss Bang Bang sung by Dionne Warwick Previously unreleased.	UK 33	EMI BOND 007

DISCOGRAPHY
PART TWO

Where composer credits are given, that of the music composer is quoted prior to the lyricist(s).

KEY

AUS = Australia	BL = Belgium	BR = Brazil
CA = Canada	CH = Chile	FR = France
GR = Germany	NL = Holland	IT = Italy
JA = Japan	SA = South Africa	SI = Singapore
SP = Spain	UK = Britain	US = America

All undermentioned EPs and 12" singles were issued with picture covers unless stated. Those singles issued with picture covers are annotated (P) unless otherwise stated in the main text.
For early LP releases the different Mono/Stereo catalogue numbers are quoted and are annotated by (M) or (S) respectively.
LPs/CDs listed in this filmography are those for the complete film score. Compilation albums have been listed in Part 1 and will not be included here unless specific tracks, contained therein, have a special relevance to this section.
All UK and US versions are quoted, where applicable, but pressings from other countries are only listed if they contain extra music, different sleeve artwork or are of special interest (i.e. Japanese pressings). Reissues and Cassettes are ignored for the same reasons.
All tracks feature (accompaniments by) John Barry (Orchestra) unless stated.
If the background score to a particular film was not commercially recorded for LP or CD release an annotation appears to the right hand side of the text – COMMERCIALLY UNRECORDED.

FILMS & TELEVISION SCORES/MUSICALS

YEAR	TITLE	MUSIC/OTHER CREDITS	RECORD DETAILS
1959	BEAT GIRL (US Title: WILD FOR KICKS)	Music composed and arranged by John Barry Played by John Barry & His Orchestra Featuring The John Barry Seven Adam Faith: I Did What You Told Me * Shirley Ann Field: It's Legal * Adam Faith: Made You (*) All songs by John Barry & Trevor Peacock except: It's Legal by John Barry & Hyam Maccoby. Adam Faith: Beat Girl Song on album but not used in film.	UK 33 COLUMBIA 33SX 1225 (M) UK EP COLUMBIA SEG 8138 * UK 45 PARLOPHONE R 4665 (*) UK CD PLAY IT AGAIN PLAY 001 (M)
1960	NEVER LET GO (Original Title: MOMENT OF TRUTH)	Johnny Comes Marching Home * - Composed by John Barry/John Maitland (a.k.a. Lionel Bart) sung by Adam Faith.	UK 45 COLUMBIA DB 4480 UK 45 PARLOPHONE R 4665 * COMMERCIALLY UNRECORDED
1961	WHAT A WHOPPER!	Music composed by Laurie Johnson Music arranged by John Barry * The Time Has Come What A Whopper! (Unrecorded) Songs by Adam Faith. Lyrics by Les Vandyke.	UK 45 PARLOPHONE R 4837 * COMMERCIALLY UNRECORDED
1961	A MATTER OF WHO	Music by Edwin Astley Title theme composed by Bob Russell John Barry Seven appeared in the film playing: Main Titles/Mayfair party sequence	UK 45 COLUMBIA DB 4699 COMMERCIALLY UNRECORDED
1961	FALLING IN LOVE	TV Documentary (ATV) transmitted 31.5.61. Written by John McGrath and narrated by Michael Flanders.	COMMERCIALLY UNRECORDED
1961	GIRL ON A ROOF	TV Play (BBC) Written by Stewart Douglas John Barry Seven performed the following numbers: Skid Row/Mad Mab/Saturday's Child/ Not Guilty (Trevor Peacock)/Walk Don't Run (John Smith)/ Kid's Stuff/Black Stockings/Bees Knees/ I Want You Baby . With Ray Brookes: Flea Brain/I Want You Baby. With Johnnie De Little: I Want You Baby/ I Did What You Told Me (Barry/Peacock). All items composed by John Barry unless stated. Orchestrations: John Barry Transmitted – 16.2.61.	COMMERCIALLY UNRECORDED
1962	THE COOL MIKADO	Adapted from the Gilbert & Sullivan opera: The Mikado. Music composed & conducted by Martin Slavin John Barry Seven appeared playing: Tit Willow Twist	UK 33 PARLOPHONE PMC 1194 (M)
1962	DR. NO	Music composed by Monty Norman Orchestrated by Burt Rhodes Conducted by Eric Rodgers The James Bond Theme played by John Barry & His Orchestra Songs by The Byron Lee All Chinese Band:- Underneath The Mango Tree/ Kingston Calypso/Jump Up. (*) 1st Stereo release. * The James Bond Theme only	UK 33 U. ARTISTS (S) ULP 1097 (S/M)* US 33 U. ARTISTS UAL 4108 (M) * US 33 U. ARTISTS UAS 5108 (S) * UK EP U. ARTISTS UEP 1010* UK 33 ONE UP OU 2023 (*) UK 45 COLUMBIA DB 4898 SA 45 COLUMBIA DSA 447 US 45 UNITED ARTISTS UA 581 JA 45 ODEON OR 1057 (P) UK 45 CBS WB 730 (P)

1962	THE AMOROUS PRAWN (US Title: THE PLAY GIRL & THE WAR MINISTER)	The Lolly Theme * Reissue	UK 45 COLUMBIA DB 4941 UK 45 CHERRY RED CHERRY 67 (P) * COMMERCIALLY UNRECORDED
1962	MIX ME A PERSON	Music & Lyrics: Johnny Worth Musical arrangements: John Barry Musical Advisor: Muir Mathieson La Bamba (Unrecorded) and Mix Me A Person sung by Adam Faith * ; Composed by Les Vandyke; With Johnny Keating & His Orchestra	UK 45 PARLOPHONE R 4930 * COMMERCIALLY UNRECORDED
1962	THE L SHAPED ROOM	Music from Brahm's No.1 piano concerto Played by Peter Catlin & The Sinfonia Of London Conducted by Muir Mathieson. 2 Jazz sequences composed by John Barry	COMMERCIALLY UNRECORDED
1963	IT'S ALL HAPPENING	Music/Musical producer: Philip Green Lyrics: Norman Newell Musical recordings by EMI John Barry arranged 4 numbers:- * Johnnie De Little: The Wind & The Rain ** Tommy Steele: The Dream Maker/ Egg & Chips ** Demo release b/w Maximum Plus sung by Tommy Steele & Marion Ryan.	UK 33 COLUMBIA 33SX 1537 (M) UK 33 COLUMBIA SCX 3486 (S) UK 45 COLUMBIA DB 7044 * UK 45 COLUMBIA DB 7070 **
1963	ZULU	Original music composed & conducted by John Barry. Narration: Richard Burton. * Reissued in Stereo Enhanced Mono US release contained different artwork LPs contain 6 original Zulu stamps arranged by John Barry (4 composed by Barry) ** Reissue (+ other Ember tracks) (*) – Extra music Single releases: Monkey Feathers/Zulu Stamp	UK 33 EMBER NR 5012 * US 33 U. ARTISTS UAL 4116 (M) US 33 U. ARTISTS UAS 5116 (S) UK 33 SILVA SCREEN FILM 022 ** UK 45 EMBER S 185 (P) SA 45 HMV 45 SAB 2036 JA 45 GLOBE JET 1403 (P) UK CD S. SCREEN FILM CD 022 (*)
1963	FROM RUSSIA WITH LOVE	Orchestral music composed & conducted by John Barry. Alan Haven features (although uncredited) on the opening titles Different tracks and sleeve artwork * Matt Monro sings From Russia With Love Lyrics: Lionel Bart Accompaniment by Johnnie Spence Two different picture covers From Russia With Love/007 007 From Russia With Love/007 007 Music recorded at CTS Studios, London. (*) 3" CD Single	UK 33 U. ARTISTS (S) ULP 1052 US 33 U. ARTISTS UAL 4114 (M) US 33 U. ARTISTS UAS 5114 (S) UK EP U. ARTISTS UEP 1011 FR EP U. ARTISTS 36043 US 45 U. ARTISTS UA 863 UK 45 PARLOPHONE R 5068 * JA 45 ODEON OR 1057 (P) * UK 45 EMBER S 181 (P) UK 45 EMBER S 243 (P) US 45 MERCURY 77261 IT 45 VEDETTE VRN 34059 (P) JA EP CBS/SONY SONE 70090 (P) UK CD EMI CZ 550 US CD EMI USA CDP 7 95344 2 FR CD CBS 655356 1 (*)
1963	THE PARTY'S OVER	Music & Lyrics by John Barry Annie Ross sings Time Waits For No Man * Theme only	UK CD EMI 8 35046 2 (EMS 1555) * COMMERCIALLY UNRECORDED
1963	ELIZABETH TAYLOR IN LONDON	TV Documentary Transmitted 6.10.63 (USA – CBS) Transmitted 24.12.63. (UK – BBC) Music composed by John Barry Arranged & conducted by Johnnie Spence Narrated by Elizabeth Taylor (*) Extra track: The Churchill Speech (**) Elizabeth Theme – LP version * Elizabeth/London Theme	UK 33 COLPIX PXL 459 (MONO) US 33 COLPIX (S)CP 459 (M/S) (*) UK 45 EMBER S 183 * IT 45 VEDETTE VRN 34059 (P) (**) UK CD PLAY IT AGAIN PLAY 002
1964	SEANCE ON A WET AFTERNOON		UK 45 U. ARTISTS UP 1060 COMMERCIALLY UNRECORDED
1964	A JOLLY BAD FELLOW (US Title: THEY ALL DIED LAUGHING)	Alan Haven: A Jolly Bad Fellow	UK 45 U. ARTISTS UP 1057 UK CD EMI 8 35046 2 (CDEMS 1555) COMMERCIALLY UNRECORDED
1964	MAN IN THE MIDDLE	Music by Lionel Bart/John Barry Arranged & conducted by John Barry * Man In The Middle (No More)/ Barney's Blues (*) Man In The Middle (No More)	UK 33 STATESIDE SSL 10087 US 33 20th CENTURY TFM 3128 (M) US 33 20th CENTURY TFS 4128 (S) UK EP STATESIDE SE 1021 (*) UK 45 STATESIDE SS 296 * US 45 20th CENTURY FOX 472 *
1964	GOLDFINGER	Music by John Barry Lyrics by Leslie Bricusse/Anthony Newley * Contains less music than UK release Music recorded at CTS Studios, London (*) Different tracks and sleeve artwork ** Shirley Bassey: Goldfinger	UK 33 U. ARTISTS SULP 1176 US 33 U. ARTISTS UAL 4117 (M) * US 33 U. ARTISTS UAS 5117 (S) * UK EP U. ARTISTS UEP 1012 FR EP U. ARTISTS 36057 (*) JA EP CBS/SONY SONE 70090 (P)

		Gold Disc award	UK 45 U. ARTISTS UP 1068
		Grammy nomination	US 45 U. ARTISTS 791
			UK 45 COLUMBIA DB 7360 **
			US 45 U. ARTISTS UA 790 **
			GR 45 COLUMBIA DW 6362 **
			JA 45 ODEON OR 1188 (P) **
			US 45 COLUMBIA 4-43801
		Goldfinger/Death Of Goldfinger	JA 45 HIT 1879 (P)
		Goldfinger (Instrumental)/James Bond	NL 45 U. ARTISTS UA 23. 008
		Back In Action	UK CD EMI CZ 557
			US CD EMI USA CDP 7 95345-2
1964	MULOORINA	Short (27 minutes) for B.P. Co	COMMERCIALLY UNRECORDED
1965	IPCRESS FILE	Different sleeve artwork	UK 33 CBS SBPG 62530
			US 33 DECCA DL 79124
		Danger Immediate	FR EP CBS EP 6207
		A Man Alone *	UK 45 CBS 201747 *
			IT 45 CBS 1747 (P) *
			US 45 COLUMBIA 4-43320 *
		A Man Alone (Jazz/Latin)	US 45 DECCA 31815
		Music recorded at CTS Studios, London	JA CD MVCM 22046
1965	MISTER MOSES		COMMERCIALLY UNRECORDED
1965	KING RAT		UK 33 FONTANA STL 5302
			US 33 MAINSTREAM 56061 (M)
			US 33 MAINSTREAM S 6061 (S)
		King Rat March (Parts 1 & 2)	US 45 MAINSTREAM S 633
		King Rat March (Parts 1 & 2)	FR 45 PATHE DISQUES VOGUE INT 80028 (P)
			US CD LEGACY JK 57894
1965	THE KNACK... And How To Get It		UK 33 U. ARTISTS ULP 1104 (M)
		Different sleeve artwork	US 33 U. ARTISTS UAL 4129 (M)
		The Knack sung by Johnnie De Little *	US 33 U. ARTISTS UAS 5129 (S)
		Le Knack: Et Comment L'Avoir	FR EP U. ARTISTS 36062
		Composed by John Barry/Leslie Bricusse	UK 45 CBS 201790 *
		Solo Jazz Organ: Alan Haven	US 45 COLUMBIA 4-43360 *
		The Knack (Vocal)/Main Theme	IT 45 CBS 1960 (P) *
		The Knack (Vocal)/Main Theme	NL 45 CBS 1960 (P) *
		Alan Haven with Acc. directed by John Barry	UK 45 FONTANA TF 590
		The Knack (Main Theme)	US CD RHINO R2 72240
		With dialogue excerpts/film trailer	US/UK CD RYKO RCD 10718
1965	BE MY GUEST	Incidental Music by Malcolm Lockyer	
		Gotta Get Away Now by John Barry/Michael Pratt	
		Sung by Joyce Blair	COMMERCIALLY UNRECORDED
1965	FOUR IN THE MORNING	Contains music and dialogue	UK 33 EMBER NR 5029
		Different sleeve artwork	US 33 ROULETTE OSS 805
		Original music composed & conducted	UK CD PLAY IT AGAIN PLAY 002 *
		by John Barry. * Excludes dialogue.	
1965	THUNDERBALL	Different sleeve artwork	UK 33 U. ARTISTS SULP 1110
		* Contains different arrangement of:	US 33 U. ARTISTS UAL 4132 (M) *
		Mr. Kiss Kiss Bang Bang	US 33 U. ARTISTS UAS 5132 (S)
		Thunderball sung by Tom Jones (*)	UK EP U. ARTISTS UEP 1015
		Composed by John Barry/Don Black	UK 45 DECCA F. 12292 (*)
		Mr. Kiss Kiss Bang Bang originally sung	UK 45 PARROT 9801 (*)
		over the main titles but removed -	JA EP CBS/SONY SONE 70090 (P)
		Composed by John Barry/Leslie Bricusse	JA 45 LONDON HIT 572 (P) (*)
		Music recorded at CTS, Studios, London	UK CD EMI CZ 556
			US CD EMI MANHATTAN CDP 7 90628 2
		Thunderball Suite/Mr. Kiss Kiss Bang	US CD EMI USA 7 98560 2
		Sung by Shirley Bassey/Dionne Warwick	
1965	SOPHIA LOREN IN ROME	TV Documentary (ABC TV)	US 33 COLUMBIA OL 6310 (M)
		Sophia Loren sings The Secrets Of Rome	US 33 COLUMBIA OS 2710 (S)
		Music and lyrics by John Barry. * 6 cuts	US 33 COLUMBIA CSP 172 *
		The Secrets Of Rome (Vocal/Instrumental) (*)	US 45 COLUMBIA 4-43170 (*)
			JA 45 CBS LL-830-C (P) (*)
		The Secrets Of Rome (Vocal)	GR CD COLUMBIA CDL 483531 2
			US CD PENDULUM PEG 023
1965	PASSION FLOWER HOTEL	Stage Musical	UK 33 CBS SBPG 62598
		Music: John Barry/Lyrics: Trevor Peacock	UK 45 CBS 201822 *
		Orchestra directed by Richard Holmes	UK 45 CBS 201823 **
		* The Syndicate/What A Question	UK CD SONY WEST END SMK 66175
		** New version of I Love My Love	US CD COLUMBIA WK 36640 2
		sung by Jeremy Clyde	
1965	ONE MAN AND HIS BANK	Short for Midland Bank	COMMERCIALLY UNRECORDED
1966	THE WRONG BOX	* Cancelled release	UK 33 FONTANA STL 5387 *
			US 33 MAINSTREAM 56088 (M)

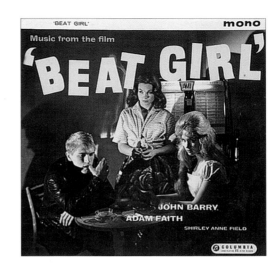

AN ORIGINAL TELEVISION
SOUNDTRACK RECORDING

COLPIX
RECORDS

ELIZABETH
TAYLOR
IN
LONDON

HER MAJOR
RECORDING
DEBUT

MUSIC COMPOSED BY
JOHN BARRY
ARRANGED AND
CONDUCTED BY
JOHNNIE SPENCE

HI FIDELITY

STEREO

Original Television Sound Track Recording

SOPHIA LOREN
IN ROME
COMPOSED & CONDUCTED
BY JOHN BARRY

stereo

ZULU · ORIGINAL SOUND TRACK · UNITED ARTISTS UAS 5114

ZULU

ORIGINAL
MOTION PICTURE
SOUND TRACK
& THEMES

COMPOSED AND
CONDUCTED BY
JOHN BARRY

UNITED
ARTISTS

S/6066

STEREO

MAINSTREAM

ORIGINAL SOUND TRACK RECORDING

THE WRONG BOX

MUSIC COMPOSED AND CONDUCTED BY
JOHN BARRY

COLUMBIA PICTURES Present
BRYAN FORBES'
PRODUCTION OF
THE WRONG BOX

JOHN MILLS · RALPH RICHARDSON
MICHAEL CAINE
PETER COOK · DUDLEY MOORE · NANETTE NEWMAN
TONY HANCOCK and PETER SELLERS

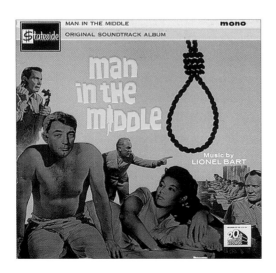

Stateside

MAN IN THE MIDDLE

mono

ORIGINAL SOUNDTRACK ALBUM

man
in the
middle

Music by
LIONEL BART

SE-4368

Sounds Great in STEREO

ORIGINAL SOUND TRACK RECORDING
Columbia Pictures and Carl Foreman present
BORN FREE
Produced by Sam Jaffe and Paul Radin
A Columbia Pictures Release in Panavision and Columbia Color

MGM
RECORDS

Music Composed and Conducted by John Barry

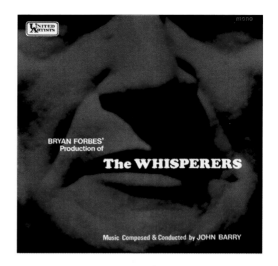

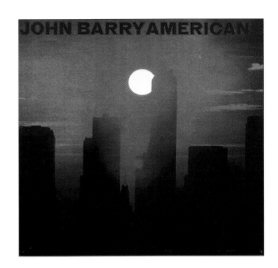

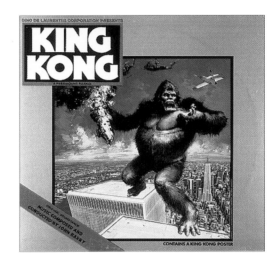

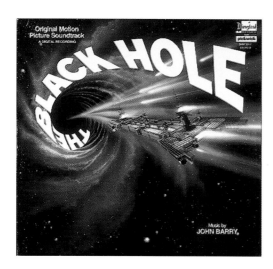

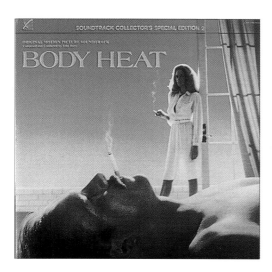

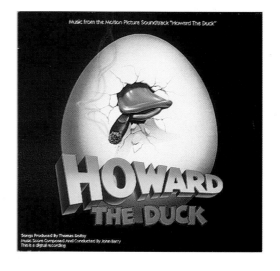

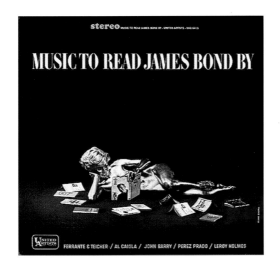

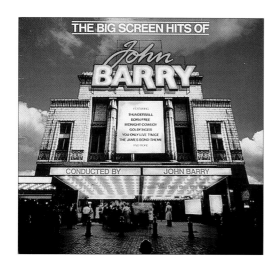

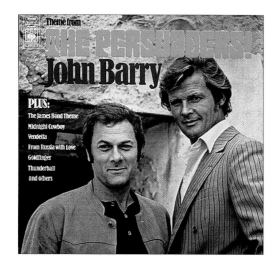

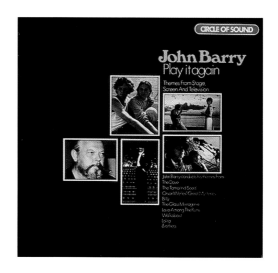

READY WHEN YOU ARE, J.B.

JOHN BARRY
PLAYS HIS
GREAT MOVIE HITS

ON HER MAJESTY'S SECRET SERVICE
MIDNIGHT COWBOY
THE LION IN WINTER
THEME FROM "ROMANCE FOR GUITAR AND ORCHESTRA"
WHO WILL BUY MY YESTERDAYS
FUN CITY
WE HAVE ALL THE TIME IN THE WORLD
TRY
THE MORE THINGS CHANGE
AFTERNOON
THEME FROM "BORN FREE"
THEME FROM "THE APPOINTMENT"

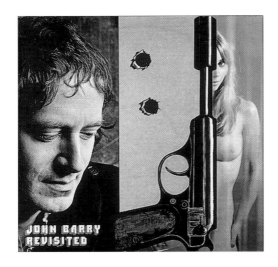

JOHN BARRY
REVISITED

Los grandes éxitos de
John Barry
Los persuasores
Tema de James Bond
Al servicio secreto de su Majestad
Desde Rusia con amor
Goldfinger / 007
La chica con el sol en sus cabellos
Vendetta / La caza
Midnight cowboy
Thunderball
The Danny Scipio theme

007 Special 10th Anniversary Edition
JAMES BOND COLLECTION
The Original Motion Picture Soundtracks From....

DR. NO...
THUNDERBALL...
FROM RUSSIA WITH LOVE...
ON HER MAJESTY'S SECRET SERVICE...
GOLDFINGER...
YOU ONLY LIVE TWICE...
DIAMONDS ARE FOREVER...

John Barry
Play it again

Tema original del film
'LA SEMILLA DEL TAMARINDO'

Música
compuesta y dirigida
por
JOHN BARRY

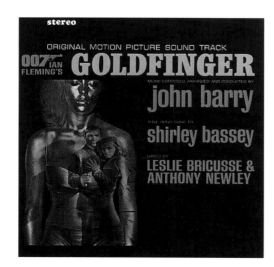

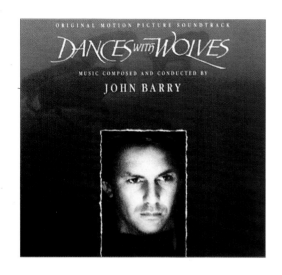

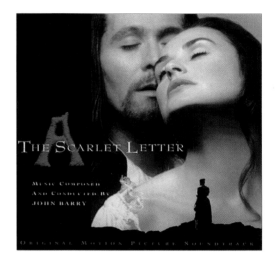

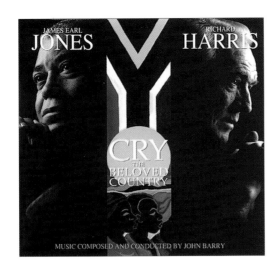

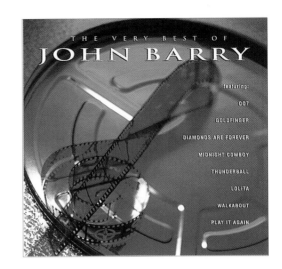

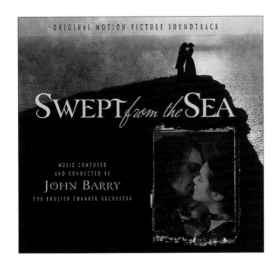

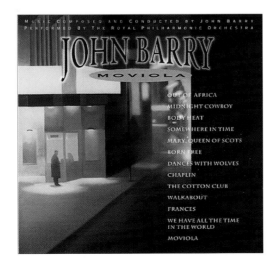

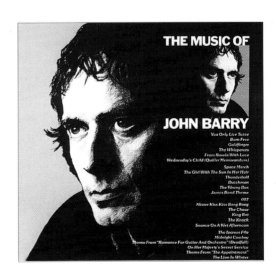

			US 33 MAINSTREAM S 6088 (S) US CD LEGACY/COLUMBIA CK 66139 *
1966	THE CHASE	The Chase (Main Title)/Saturday Night Philosopher * Alternate version of The Chase (Main Title) Music Recording: Eric Tomlinson	UK 33 CBS SBPG 62665 US 33 COLUMBIA OL 6860 (M) US 33 COLUMBIA OS 2960 (S) US CD PENDULUM PEG 027 US 45 COLUMBIA 4-43544 US CD VARESE VSD 5229 US CD COLUMBIA CK 44376 *
1966	BORN FREE	Music by John Barry Lyrics by Don Black. Repressing Gatefold issue with dialogue and poster (One sided). Gatefold issue with booklet * Born Free sung by Lois Lane – not arranged by John Barry Born Free sung by Matt Monro (*) ** Nacida Libre (Original arrangement) Academy Awards for Best Song and Best Score. Three Grammy Nominations (Song of the Year/Original Score/ Instrumental Arrangement)	UK 33 MGM CS 8010 UK 33 MGM 2315 031 US 33 DISNEYLAND ST 3803 * JA 33 MGM MMF 1014 SP EP MGM 63544 (*) US 45 COLUMBIA 4-43801 UK 45 CAPITOL CL 15346 (*) US 45 CAPITOL 5623 (*) JA 45 CAPITOL CR 1508 (P) (*) SP 33 CAPITOL ST 19006 ** CH EP CAPITOL 2031 ** SP 45 CAPITOL CSL 21297 (P) ** JA EP CBS/SONY SONE 70103 (P) JA 45 POLYDOR DPQ 6069 (P)
1966	THE QUILLER MEMORANDUM	Music by John Barry/Lyrics by Mack David Different sleeve artwork on US release Matt Monro sings Wednesday's Child * (*) Wednesday's Child (**) Ven Mi Amor; Spanish version sung by Matt Monro Adapted by A. Puig Domenech	UK 33 CBS SBPG 62869 US 33 COLUMBIA OL 6660 (M) US 33 COLUMBIA OS 3060 (S) UK 45 CAPITOL CL 15477 * UK 45 CBS 202451 (*) US 45 COLUMBIA 4-43951 (*) GR/IT 45 CBS 2451 (P) (*) JA 45 CBS LL-1019-C (P) SP 45 CAPITOL J 006-80 541 (P) (**) US CD VARESE VSD 5218
1967	YOU ONLY LIVE TWICE	Music by John Barry Lyrics by Leslie Bricusse Reissue: Different sleeve artwork * Contains end title vocal which also appears on some original foreign pressings although not always credited. This replaced the second part of Twice Is The Only Way To Live ** Fight At Kobe Dock – Helga (Edited) (*) Arranged and conducted by Billy Strange; Vocal: Nancy Sinatra Julie Rogers: You Only Live Twice (Unused)	UK 33 U. ARTISTS SULP 1171 US 33 U. ARTISTS UAL 4155 (M) US 33 U. ARTISTS UAS 5155 (S) UK 33 SUNSET SLS 50365 GR 45 U. ARTISTS 35912 (P) ** UK 45 CBS 2825 US 45 COLUMBIA 4-44167 UK 45 REPRISE RS 20595 (*) US 45 REPRISE 0595 (*) UK CD EMI CZ 559 * US CD EMI MANHATTAN CDP 7 90626 2 * US CD EMI USA 7 98560 2
1967	DUTCHMAN	Theme	UK 33 CBS SS 63038 US 33 COLUMBIA CL 2708 (M) US 33 COLUMBIA CS 9508 (S)
1967	THE WHISPERERS	Different sleeve artwork *Troubador: Used as source music With dialogue excerpts/film trailer	UK 33 U. ARTISTS SULP 1168 US 33 U. ARTISTS UAL 4161 (M) US 33 U. ARTISTS UAS 5161 (S) UK 33 POLYDOR 2489 123 UK 45 U. ARTISTS UP 1068 * US/UK CD RYKO RCD 10720
1968	DEADFALL	Music by John Barry Lyrics by Jack Lawrence Limited souvenir album -one sided includes Theme for Romance For Guitar... *Shirley Bassey: My Love Has Two Faces Theme from Romance For Guitar & Orchestra – Soloist: Renata Tarrago (guitar) with London Philharmonic Orchestra conducted by John Barry. ** Includes Male vocal (3.32)/Instrumental Demo (3.18) of: My Love Has Two Faces	UK 33 STATESIDE SSL 10263 US 33 20th CENTURY S 4203 US 33 20th CENTURY FOX DF-A UK 45 U. ARTISTS UP 2254 * UK CD EMI BASSEY 1 (8 31236 2) * US CD RETROGRADE FSM 80124 2 **
1968	PETULIA	* Not used in the film Petulia/Highway 101 *	US 33 WARNER/7 ARTS WS 1755 FR 33 VOGUE WB CLPW 1548 US 45 WARNER/7 ARTS 7230
1968	BOOM		UK 33 MCA MUPS 360
1968	THE LION IN WINTER	Orchestrations: Bobby Richards With Voices of Accademia Monteverdiana Princess Alias sings: Allons Gai Gai/ The Christmas Wine * * Lyrics by James Goldman	UK 33 CBS 70049 US 33 COLUMBIA OS 3250 UK 45 CBS 3935 ** UK 45 COLUMBIA 4-44721 ** US CD VARESE VSD 5217

		** The Lion In Winter (Parts 1 & 2)	US CD LEGACY/COLUMBIA CK 66133
		** Organist: Alan Haven	JA 33 CBS/SONY SONX 60109 (*)
		Academy Award: Best Original Score	JA EP CBS/SONY SONE 70103 (P)
		Anthony Asquith Memorial Award – Original film music.	
		(*) Different back cover.	
1969	O.H.M.S.S.	Music by John Barry	UK 33 U. ARTISTS UAS 29020
		Lyrics by Hal David	US 33 U. ARTISTS UAS 5204
		*All The Time In The World :Louis Armstrong	UK 45 U. ARTISTS UP 35059 *
		Do You Know How Christmas Trees Are	US 45 U. ARTISTS 50617 *
		Grown: Nina**	IT 45 U. ARTISTS UA 3172 (P) *
		O.H.M.S.S./All The Time In The World (*)	SP 45 U. ARTISTS UP 067153 *
		Who Will Buy My Yesterdays (**)	GR 45 U. ARTISTS 35059 (P) *
		(Based on a theme used in the film)	UK 45 CBS 4680 (*)
		Music recorded at CTS Studios, London	US 45 COLUMBIA 4-45062 (*)
		Produced by Phil Ramone	UK 45 CBS 4681 **
			SI 45 CBS 2-594 (P)
			JA EP CBS/SONY SONE 70090 (P)
			JA 45 CBS/SONY CBSA 82039 (P)
			JA 45 U. ARTISTS HIT 1706 (P) *
			UK 33 CBS 63952 (**)
			US 33 COLUMBIA CS 1003 (**)
			UK CD EMI CZ 549
			US CD EMI MANHATTAN CDP 7 90618 2
1969	THE APPOINTMENT	Le Rendez-Vous (Main Theme)/Le Cafe *	FR 45 MGM 61629 (P)
		Orchestrations: Don Walker	JA 45 DM 1186 (P)
		* Not used in the film	UK 33 CBS 63952
			JA EP CBS/SONY SONE 70103 (P)
			COMMERCIALLY UNRECORDED
1969	MIDNIGHT COWBOY	Musical supervision: John Barry	UK 33 U. ARTISTS UAS 29043
		Harmonica: Jean Toots Thielemans	US 33 U. ARTISTS UAS 5198
		Midnight Cowboy/Fun City (Originals)	UK 45 U. ARTISTS UP 634 (P)
		Midnight Cowboy/Fun City**	UK 45 CBS 4468 **
		Nilsson: Everybody's Talkin' (*)	US 45 COLUMBIA 4-44891 **
		Arranged & conducted by George Tipton,	
		Composed by Fred Neil	UK 45 RCA 1876 (*)
			US 45 RCA 0161 (*)
		Golden Disc award	JA EP CBS/SONY SONE 70103 (P)
		Grammy Award – Best instrumental theme	UK CD PREMIER PRMCD 6
			US CD EMI MANHATTAN CDP 7 48409 2
1970	THE LAST VALLEY	With The Voices of Accedemia	UK 33 PROBE SPB 1027
		Monteverdiana (*)	US 33 DUNHILL DSX 50102
		The Last Valley/Main Title Theme (*)	UK 45 PROBE PRO 518
		Inside Cinema version with voiceover	UK 45 PROBE SPSR 339
1970	MURPHY'S WAR	Musical themes and supervision by J. Barry	US CD *
		Additional music composed and conducted	
		by Ken Thorne. * The Film Music Of Ken Thorne. Vol.2 -	
		Promotional CD – no catalogue number.	
1970	MONTE WALSH	Music by John Barry	UK 45 PROBE 512
		Lyrics by Hal David	US 45 DUNHILL 45-D- 4253 (P)
		Mama Cass Elliot: The Good Times Are	JA 45 HR 2674 (P)
		Comin' * .	US CD MCA MCAD 31147 *
		Music produced by Phil Ramone	COMMERCIALLY UNRECORDED
		Supervising Music Editor: Gene Feldman	
1970	WALKABOUT	Music by John Barry	
		Produced by Phil Ramone	COMMERCIALLY UNRECORDED
1971	DIAMONDS ARE FOREVER	Music by John Barry	UK 33 U. ARTISTS 29216
		Lyrics by Don Black	US 33 U. ARTISTS UAS 5220
		Different sleeve artwork	FR/IT 33 U. ARTISTS UAS 29216
		Diamonds Are Forever	GR 45 U. ARTISTS UA 35912 (P)
		Shirley Bassey – Diamonds Are Forever *	UK 45 U. ARTISTS UP 35293 *
		As above	US 45 U. ARTISTS 50845 *
		* * Includes British & Italian versions of:	GR 45 U. ARTISTS 35293 (P)
		Diamonds Are Forever	IT 45 U. ARTISTS 35293 (P) **
		(Una Cascata Di Diamanti Lyrics by	JA 45 MCA D 1151 (P)
		Boncompagni)	UK 45 POLYDOR 2058 216
		Ivor Novello Award	JA 45 KING/U. ARTISTS HIT 1950 (P)*
			UK CD CZ 554
			US CD EMI USA CDP 7 96209 2
1971	FOLLOW ME	Music by John Barry	JA 33 MCA MUPS 5137
	(US Title: THE PUBLIC EYE)	Lyrics by Don Black	UK 45 POLYDOR 2058 275
		Film includes – Universal fanfare	JA 45 MCA D 1178 (P)
		Follow, Follow sung by Thelma Keating	
1971	MARY, QUEEN OF SCOTS		UK 33 MCA MUPS 441
		Vanessa Redgrave sings Vivre Et Mourir	US 33 DECCA DL 79186
		Lyrics by Mary, Queen Of Scots	AUS 33 DECCA DL 79186 (*)

		This Way Mary	UK 45 POLYDOR 2058 216
		This Way Mary/Mary Queen Of Scots	UK 45 COLUMBIA DB 8860 (**)
		(*) Reissue with one extra track (2 parts)	JA 45 MCA D 1151 (P)
		(**) 2 songs based on themes from the film:	
		Lyrics by Don Black – Sung by Matt Monro	
		Academy Award nomination	
1971	THEY MIGHT BE GIANTS	Music composed & supervised by John Barry Arranged, orchestrated and conducted by Ken Thorne.	COMMERCIALLY UNRECORDED
1971	LOLITA, MY LOVE	Stage musical based on novel Lolita	US 33 COLUMBIA S-30519 **
		Music by John Barry	US EP MEDIASOUND MSP 117 (**)
		Lyrics by Alan Jay Lerner	US EP MEDIASOUND MSP 118 (*)
		3 vocals: Uncredited session singers (*)	
		2 vocals/2 instrumentals: Uncredited session singers (**)	
		** Cancelled album	COMMERCIALLY UNRECORDED
1972	ALICE'S ADVENTURES IN WONDERLAND	Music by John Barry	UK 33 WARNER K 56009
		Lyrics by Lewis Carroll (3); Don Black (8)	US 33 WARNER BS 2671
		Recording Engineer: John Richards	US EP RAINBOW PRO 543
		Recorded at CTS Studios, London	
1973	A DOLL'S HOUSE	Theme	UK 33 POLYDOR 2383 461
1973	LOVE AMONG THE RUINS	TV Movie	UK 33 POLYDOR 2383 300
		Music by John Barry/Lyrics by Don Black	COMMERCIALLY UNRECORDED
		Love Among The Ruins sung by Laurence Olivier	
1973	THE GLASS MENAGERIE	TV Movie	UK 33 POLYDOR 2383 300
			COMMERCIALLY UNRECORDED
1974	THE DOVE	Music by John Barry	US ABC ABDP 852
		Lyrics by Don Black	UK 45 POLYDOR 2058 472 *
		* Lyn Paul sings Sail The Summer Winds	UK 45 POLYDOR 2814 016 **
		** Promotional issue with voice over	
		Music Scoring Mixer: John Richards	
1974	THE MAN WITH THE GOLDEN GUN		UK 33 U. ARTISTS UAS 29671
		Music by John Barry/Lyrics by Don Black	US 33 U. ARTISTS UA LA 358-G
		Different sleeve artwork	IT 33 U. ARTISTS 29671
		Man With The Golden Gun sung by Lulu (*)	UK 45 CHELSEA 2005 015 (*)
			US 45 CHELSEA CH 3009 (*)
		Music by John Barry/Lyrics by Don Black	IT 45 CHELSEA 2005 015 (P)(*) *
		* Same sleeve as German issue	JA 45 CHELSEA DM-1085 (P) (*)
		Music recorded at CTS Studios, London	UK CD EMI CZ 552
			US CD EMI MANHATTAN CDP 7 90619 2
1974	THE TAMARIND SEED	Music by John Barry/Lyrics by Don Black	JA 45 POLYDOR DPQ 6019
		Wilma Reading sings Play It Again	UK 45 PYE 7N 45380 *
		* Arranged by Barrie Guard	COMMERCIALLY UNRECORDED
1974	DAY OF THE LOCUST	Music scored & conducted by John Barry	UK 33 DECCA PFS 4339
		Engineer: John Norman	US 33 LONDON PS 912
			JA 45 LONDON FM 1101 (P)
1974	BILLY	Stage musical based on Billy Liar	UK 33 CBS 70133
		Music by John Barry; Lyrics by Don Black	UK 45 RCA LPBO 5025 *
		* Michael Crawford sings I Missed The Last	UK 45 CBS S 2622 **
		Rainbow/Lady From L.A. – Different	UK CD COLUMBIA 472818 2
		arrangements to Original Cast recordings	
		** Michael Crawford sings Some Of Us Belong	
		To The Stars – Arranged by Keith Mansfield	
1976	ROBIN & MARIAN	Promotional issue with 4 page booklet	US 33 PRO 4345
		* John Bursts In/The End	US CD BIG SCREEN 9 24503 2 *
1976	KING KONG	* With poster	UK 33 REPRISE K 54090 *
		** Includes Kong's Cry (with poster)	US 33 REPRISE MS 2260 *
		Andy Williams sings Are You In There (*)	JA 33 TAM YX 7032 **
		- Song based on main theme -	US 45 COLUMBIA 3-10471 (*)
		Composed, arranged and cond & prod by	JA 45 TAM YT 4010 (P) (*)
		John Barry/David Pomeranz	IT 45 CBS 5019 (P) (*)
		Music Editor: Kenneth. J. Hall	IT CD MASK MK 702
		Recording/Mixing Engineer: Dan Wallin	
		(*) Are You In There/(Disco version)	
1976	ELEANOR & FRANKLIN	TV Movie (Part 1)	US 45 CASABLANCA NB 887
		Disco version of main theme:	
		The White House Years	
		Composed, arranged, orchestrated & produced	
		by John Barry	
		Emmy nominaton	COMMERCIALLY UNRECORDED

1976	THE DEEP	(*) With poster. ** Blue vinyl release Donna Summer sings Down Deep Inside John Barry: Theme from "The Deep" Donna Summer sings Down Deep Inside Down Deep Inside (A Love Song) sung by Donna Summer – Lyrics by Donna Summer Music Editor: Ken Hall Recording Engineer: Danny Wallin	UK 33 CASABLANCA CAL 2018 (*) US 33 CASABLANCA NBLP 7060** (*) GR 33 CASABLANCA NB 7024 ** UK 45 CASABLANCA CAN 111 US 12 CASABLANCA NBD 20104 US 45 CASABLANCA 887 FR 45 CASABLANCA CB 140 297 (P) IT 45 CASABLANCA CA 503 (P)
1977	THE WHITE BUFFALO	Music Editor: Dan Carlin	COMMERCIALLY UNRECORDED
1977	FIRST LOVE	Most of John Barry's score was removed Music soundtrack supervised by Joel Sill Music editor: Milton Lustig	COMMERCIALLY UNRECORDED
1977	THE BETSY	Music Editor: Else Blangsted	COMMERCIALLY UNRECORDED
1977	THE WHITE HOUSE YEARS	 TV Movie (Part 2) Emmy Award Nomination (Also see Eleanor & Franklin above)	US 45 CASABLANCA NB 887 COMMERCIALLY UNRECORDED
1977	WAR BETWEEN THE TATES	TV Movie	COMMERCIALLY UNRECORDED
1977	THE GATHERING	TV Movie	COMMERCIALLY UNRECORDED
1977	YOUNG JOE, THE FORGOTTEN KENNEDY	TV Movie	COMMERCIALLY UNRECORDED
1978	THE GAME OF DEATH (a.k.a. BRUCE LEE'S GAME OF DEATH)	Music & Lyrics by John Barry Colleen Camp sings Will This Be The Song I'll Be Singing Tomorrow (*) Game Of Death/Will This Be The Song..	JA 33 TAM YX 7037 JA 45 TAM YT 4033 (P) (*) UK CD SILVA SCREEN FILMCD 123
1978	STARCRASH	Vocal on Italian film print: Cher Winz Supervising Music Editor: Ken Hall Music publisher: Claude Carrere International	IT 33 DURIUM D. AI 30314 FR 33 CARRERE 67333 GR 33 POLYDOR 2374 138 UK CD SILVA SCREEN FILMCD 085
1978	THE CORN IS GREEN	TV Movie	COMMERCIALLY UNRECORDED
1979	HANOVER STREET	Music by John Barry; Conducted by Harry Rabinowitz Music Editor: Ken Hall	COMMERCIALLY UNRECORDED
1979	MOONRAKER	Music by John Barry/Lyrics by Hal David * Shirley Bassey sings: Moonraker (Main/End Titles) Supervising Sound Engineer: Dan Wallin Music recorded at Studio Davout, Paris	UK 33 U. ARTISTS UAG 30247 US 33 U. ARTISTS UALA 971 1 UK 45 U. ARTISTS UP 602 * US 45 U. ARTISTS UA X1308-Y * UK CD EMI CZ 551 US CD EMI MANHATTAN CDP 7 90620 2
1979	THE BLACK HOLE	Digital recording Orchestrations: Al Woodbury Music Editor: Helen Sneddon Music Scoring Mixer: Dan Wallin * Music, dialogue and sound effects with storybook	UK 33 PICKWICK SHM 3017 US 33 DISNEYLAND/BUENA VISTA DS 5008 US 33 DISNEYLAND 3821 * US 45 DISNEYLAND 381 (P) *
1979	NIGHT GAMES	Music Editor: Ken Hall Music Mixer: Dan Wallin	UK CD SILVA SCREEN FILMCD 123
1979	WILLA	TV Movie Music Editor: Ken Hall	COMMERCIALLY UNRECORDED
1980	TOUCHED BY LOVE	Elvis Presley music adapted by John Barry Music Editor: Clif Kohlweck Music Scoring Mixer: Dan Wallin	COMMERCIALLY UNRECORDED
1980	SOMEWHERE IN TIME	Original Music composed/conducted by John Barry. Roger Williams plays Theme From Somewhere In Time Rhapsody On A Theme By Paganini - Piano solo by Chet Swiatkowski Music Editor: Ken Hall Recording/Mixing Engineer: Dan Wallin Mastered at Whitney Recording Studios, Glendale, CA (*) 24 Karat Gold issue	UK 33 MCA MCF 3333 US 33 MCA 5154 UK 45 MCA 1195 (P) UK CD MCA DMCF 3333 US CD MCA MCAD 5154 US CD MCAD 10954 (*)
1980	INSIDE MOVES	Inside Moves/Love Theme Engineer: Dennis Sands Music Editor: Ken Wilhout Music recorded at Group IV Recording, Hollywood	UK 33 WARNER K 56901 US 33 FULL MOON FMH 3506 JA 45 WARNER P 1510 W (P) COMMERCIALLY UNRECORDED

1980	RAISE THE TITANIC	Main Theme Music Editor: Ken Hall Music recorded at Glen Glenn Sound	JA 45 SEVEN SEAS K07S 9003 (P) COMMERCIALLY UNRECORDED
1981	LEGEND OF THE LONE RANGER	Original Music by John Barry Narration/Lyrics: Dean Pitchford Merle Haggard sings The Man In The Mask Music Editor; Clif Kohlweck Music recorded in Paris	US 33 MCA 5212
1981	BODY HEAT	Limited issue Orchestrations: Al Woodbury Music Editor: Clifford. C. Kohlweck Music Scoring Mixer/Recording Engineer: Dan Wallin. Music recorded at Record Plant Scoring (*) Scheduled catalogue number * 45rpm Audiophile release which re-appeared in 1988 as bootleg in the original sleeve.	US 33 SOUTHERN CROSS LXSE-1002 * US CD SOUTHERN CROSS LXCD 5 (*) US CD SOUTHERN CROSS SCSE CD-1
1981	BELLS (a.k.a. MURDER BY PHONE/THE CALLING/HELL'S BELLS)	Music orchestrated by John Barry and performed by Jonathan Elias/John Peterson	COMMERCIALLY UNRECORDED
1982	HAMMETT	Solo piano: Michael Lang Solo clarinetist: Ronny Lang Chinese Music consultant: Lucia Hwong Music Editor: Robert. Q. Lovett Music Recorded at Group IV Recording Engineer: Dennis Sands	COMMERCIALLY UNRECORDED
1982	FRANCES	Piano: Chet Swiatkowski Orchestrations: Al Woodbury Music Editors: Michael Clifford/Ken Hall Recording Engineer: Dan Wallin Music recorded at Record Plant Scoring * Limited Gold issue	US 33 SOUTHERN CROSS SCRS 1001 BL/FR 33 MILAN A 205 US CD SOUNDTRACK COLLECTOR'S SPECIAL EDITIONS SCSE CD-5-G*
1982	SVENGALI	TV Movie Music by John Barry Songs by John Barry/Don Black Produced by Phil Ramone Music Editor: Lou Cerborino	COMMERCIALLY UNRECORDED
1983	HIGH ROAD TO CHINA	Music Editor: Michael Clifford Music Scoring Mixer: Dan Wallin Different sleeve artwork * Limited Gold issue	UK 33 A & R FILM 001 UK 33 SILVA SCREEN FILM 001 US 33 SOUTHERN CROSS SCAR 5003 US CD SOUTHERN CROSS SCSE CD-2 US CD S. CROSS SCSE CD-2-G *
1983	THE GOLDEN SEAL	Main Themes by John Barry Music scored by Dana Kaproff Lyrics by Don Black * Glen Campbell sings Letting Go Music Editor: Clifford Kohlweck Orchestrations: Al Woodbury Recording Engineer: John Richards Music recorded at Olympic Studios, London	UK 33 COMPLEAT CLTLP 351 US 33 COMPLEAT CSTR 6001 UK 45 COMPLEAT CLT 3 (P) * US 45 COMPLEAT CP 113 * JA 45 VICTOR VIPX 1770 (P) *
1983	OCTOPUSSY	Music by John Barry Lyrics by Tim Rice Rita Coolidge sings All Time High Music/song produced by Phil Ramone Music Scoring Mixer: John Richards Music recorded at CTS Studios, London * All Time High/Extended Instrumental (*) Contains excerpts from All Time High ** Digitally remastered. Contains dialogue excerpts/Original Theatrical Trailer	UK 33 A & M AMLX 64967 US 33 A & M SP 4967 UK 45 A & M AM 007 (P) * IT 45 A & M AMS 9286 (P) * US 45 A & M AM 2551 (P) * FR/BL 45 A & M AMS 9713 (P) * UK 45 SCANLITE BOND 1 (P) (*) IT CD A&M 394967 2 US CD A&M 394 967 2 UK/US RYKO RCD 10705 **
1983	MIKE'S MURDER	Music composed & conducted by John Barry Additional music composed by Joe Jackson Music Supervisor: Becky Shargo Music Editors: Clif Kohlweck/John La Salandra Music Mixer: Dan Wallin	COMMERCIALLY UNRECORDED
1984	UNTIL SEPTEMBER	Music Editor: Clifford Kohlweck Recording Engineer: John Richards Film score recorded at CTS Studios, London	US 33 VARESE STV 81226 SP 33 VARESE VINILO VS 1004 UK CD SILVA SCREEN FILMCD 085
1984	THE COTTON CLUB	Original music composed & conducted by John Barry Music Supervisor: John Barry Music Consultant: Jerry Wexler Arrangements/Transcriptions: Bob Wilber Vocal/Dance arrangements: Joyce Brown	IT/UK 33 GEFFEN GEF 70260 US 33 GEFFEN GHS 24062 US 12 GEFFEN PRO A 2239 (P) * UK 45 GEFFEN A 6256 (P) JA 45 GEFFEN 07SP 871 (P) (*) UK CD GEFFEN CDGEF 70260

		Music Editor: Norman Hollyn	US CD GEFFEN GEFD 2406 2
		Assistant Music Editor: Patrick Mullins	COMMERCIALLY UNRECORDED
		Trumpet solo: Dave Brown	
		Clarinet/Alto sax: Bob Wilber	
		Arranger/Orchestrator/Associate	
		Music Supervisor: Sy Johnson	
		Additional Orchestrations: Al Woodbury	
		Music Recreations: Bob Wilber	
		Recording Engineer: Tom Jung	
		Recorded & Mixed at A & R Studios, NYC and	
		Clinton Recording Studios, NYC	
		* Promo.	
		(*) – The Mooche/Dixie Kidnaps Vera	
1985	A VIEW TO A KILL	Music composed & conducted	UK 33 PARLOPHONE BOND 1 (EJ 24 0349 1)
		by John Barry	
		Duran Duran sing A View To A Kill	US 33 CAPITOL SJ 12413
		Produced by Bernard Edwards,	GR 12 CAPITOL 1 CK 052 20 0630 *
		Jason Corsaro, Duran Duran.. (Promo)	US 12 CAPITOL SPRO 9391
			UK 45 PARLOPHONE DURAN 007 (P)
		Lyrics by Duran Duran	UK 45 PARLOPHONE DURAN G007 (P) **
		Music Scoring Mixer: Dick Lewzey	
		Music Editor: Allan Killick	US 45 CAPITOL B 5475 (P)
		Solo flute: Susan Milan	FR 45 CAPITOL 2006 307 (P)
		Orchestrator: Nicholas Raine	JA 45 TOSHIBA-EMI EMS 17546 (P)
		Cancelled release	UK CD CAPITOL CDP 7 46519 2
			JA CD TOSHIBA/EMI CP32-5076 (EJ-2403491)
		* Contains different edits of the song	
		** Special sleeve – Limited issue	
		Music recorded at CTS, Studios, London	
		BMI Award 1986	
1985	JAGGED EDGE	Synthesizer: Jonathan Elias	UK 33 TER 1107
		Music Engineer: Tom Jung	US 33 VARESE STV 81252
		CD Club issue	US CD VARESE BCL 6001
1986	OUT OF AFRICA	Original music composed & conducted by	UK 33 MCA MCF 3310
		John Barry	US 33 MCA 6158
		Melissa Manchester/Al Jarreau sing:	UK 12 MCA MCAT 1038
		The Music Of Goodbye composed by	UK 45 MCA 1038 (P)
		John Barry/Alan & Marilyn Bergman	US 45 MCA 52784 (Vocal)
		Arranged & produced by Robbie Buchanan	JA 45 MCA P-2091 (P)
		Music Editor: Clif Kohlweck	FR/BL 45 WEA MCA 258736 7 (P)
		Recording Engineers: Nicholas Basich/	UK CD MCA DMCF 3310
		Mike Novitch. Music research: Alan Smyth	US CD MCA MCAD 6158
		Music Scoring Mixer: Dan Wallin	US CD MCA MCAD 11311 **
		Music recorded at Record Plant, Studio M	
		African Music Advisor: George. W. Senoga Zake	
		US releases do not contain vocal	
		** 24 Karat Gold issue	
		Academy Award (Best Original Score)	
		BAFTA Nomination	
		Golden Globe Award	
		Grammy Award	
		Best Score (London Film Critics)	
		BMI Award (1986)	
1986	MY SISTER'S KEEPER	Electronic Realisation: John Barry/Jonathan Elias	
	(Originally titled MONDAY, TUESDAY, WEDNESDAY)	Synthesizer performed by Jonathan Elias	
		Synthesizer performed by Jonathan Elias	
		Music Editor: George Craig	
		Music recorded at Magno Sound	COMMERCIALLY UNRECORDED
1986	PEGGY SUE GOT MARRIED	Original score composed & conducted	UK 33 TER 1126 *
		by John Barry. Music Editor: George Craig	US 33 VARESE STV 81295
		Underscore recorded at Clinton Recording,	US CD VARESE VCD 47275
		New York. Produced for the film by John Barry	
		Mixdown: Joel Moss at Record Plant, L.A.	
		Engineer: Ed Rak	
		* Different sleeve artwork	
1986	HOWARD THE DUCK	Music score composed & conducted	UK 33 MCA MCF 3342
	(a.k.a.HOWARD....A NEW BREED OF HERO)	by John Barry	US 33 MCA 6173 *
		Original songs produced by Thomas Dolby	
		Additional music by Sylvester Levay	
		Music Scoring Mixer: Dan Wallin	
		Assistant Music Editor: Louise Aubacky	
		Music recorded at Record Plant, Studio M, L.A., California.	
		* With poster	
1986	THE GOLDEN CHILD	Most of John Barry's score was removed	UK 33 CAPITOL EST 2030
		from the film. Orchestrations: Al Woodbury	US 33 CAPITOL SJ 12544
		Music Score: Michael Columbier	US 45 CAPITOL B 5654 (P) *
		Music Editing: Seque Music	JA 45 CAPITOL ECS 17687 (P) *
		Music Scoring Mixer: Dan Wallin	UK CD CAPITOL CDP 7 46658 2
		Recording Engineers: Dan Wallin/Frank Wolf	COMMERCIALLY UNRECORDED

Supervising Music Editor: Jeff Carson
Ann Wilson sings: The Best Man In The World -
John Barry/Ann Wilson/Nancy Wilson/Sue Ennis
Produced by Ron Nevinson
Music score recorded at Record Plant Scoring, L.A.
* Contains Best Man In The World (Vocal/Instrumental)
Albums/CDs contain only one theme by John Barry:
The Wisdom Of The Ages

1987	THE LIVING DAYLIGHTS	a-ha sing The Living Daylights Composed by John Barry/Pal Waktaar Produced by Jason Corsaro/A-ha & J. Barry Orchestra arranged/conducted by John Barry The Pretenders For 007 sing: If There Was A Man */Where Has Everybody Gone (*) Composed by John Barry/Chrissie Hynde Produced by John Barry/Paul O' Duffy Music Editor: Alan Killick Engineer/Music Scoring Mixer: Dick Lewzey Orchestrations: Nicholas Raine Music recorded at CTS Studios, London (p) Picture disc (g) Gatefold sleeve (**) Contains extended version of song (xx) Contains The Living Daylights (Instrumental) Reissue with extra music/film trailer	UK 33 WARNER WX 111 (925 616 1) US 33 WARNER 25616 1 UK 12 WARNER W 8305 T (P) (**) (xx) UK 12 WARNER W 8305 TP (**) (xx) (P) UK 45 WARNER W 8305 (P) (xx) UK 45 WARNER W 8305 V (P) (xx)(g) US 45 WARNER 7-28305 (P) (xx) UK 12 REAL YZ 149TX (P) * (*) UK 45 REAL YZ 149 (P) * US 45 WARNER 7-28259 (P) * UK CD WARNER 925616 2 US CD WARNER 25616 2 US/UK CD RYKO RCD 10725
1987	HEARTS OF FIRE	Original score by John Barry Music Director: Beau Hill Music Editor: William Diver Synthesizer Realisations: Jonathan Elias	 COMMERCIALLY UNRECORDED
1988	MASQUERADE	Orchestrations: Al Woodbury Music Editor: Clifford Kohlweck Music Scoring Mixer: John Richards Music recorded at Evergreen Studios	 COMMERCIALLY UNRECORDED
1990	DANCES WITH WOLVES	Fire Dance: Peter Buffett Traditional Music: The Porcupine Singers * John Dunbar Theme/Dances With Wolves Re-recorded versions produced by John Barry & David Foster -Inspired by The John Dunbar Theme/Journey To Fort Sedgewick; The Pawnee Attack/The Buffalo Hunt Orchestrations: Greig McRitchie Music Supervisor: John Coinman Music Editor: Clif Kohlweck Music Scoring Mixer: Shawn Murphy Scoring Recordist: Susan McLean Recorded at Columbia Studios, Los Angeles (*) 24 Karat Gold edition. Contains Fire Dance	UK 33 EPIC 467591 1 BR 33 EPIC 188154 UK 45 EPIC 656796 7 (P) * US 45 EPIC 35-73841 * UK 45CD EPIC 656796 2 * UK CD EPIC 467591 2 US CD EPIC ASSOC ZK 46982 US CD EPIC ZK 66817 (*) *
1992	RUBY CAIRO	Kristina Nichols sings The Secrets Of My Heart * Composed by John Barry/Cynthia Haagens & Graeme Clifford * Music performed by Kim Bullard * Flamenco guitar: Doug MacAskill * Recording Engineer: Kim Bullard * Produced by Kim Bullard/Gerry Tolmain Ruby Cairo Theme – Flamenco performed by Ottmar Liebert/Luna Negra Arranged and Produced by Ottmar Leibert Orchestrations: Greig McRitchie Recording Engineer: Shawn Murphy Music recorded at Sony Pictures Studio. (*) Main Theme.	 JA CD SONY SRCS 6618 JA 45CD SONY SRDS 8248 (*)
1992	CHAPLIN	Performed by The English Chamber Orchestra Recording Engineer: Shawn Murphy Recorded at EMI, Abbey Road Studio London Includes re-recorded music from City Lights/ The Honeysuckle & The Bee/Salt Lake City Episode by Charles Chaplin	BR 33 EPIC SOUNDTRAX 188 290 UK CD EPIC EPC 472602 2 US CD EPIC SOUNDTRAX EK52986 2
1993	INDECENT PROPOSAL	Piano solo: Michael Lang Lisa Stansfield sings In All The Right Places Composed by John Barry/Lisa Stansfield/ Ian Devaney/Andy Morris Produced by Ian Devaney/Andy Morris Executive Producer: John Barry Instrumental suite – 5 selections Recording Engineer/Mixer: Shawn Murphy Music Supervisor: Kathy Nelson	BR 33 MCA 1708080 UK 12 MCA MCST 1780 ** UK 45 MCA MCS 1780 (P) UK CD MCA MCD 10863 US CD MCA MCAD 10795 GR CD45 MCA MCD 30796 *

Music Editor: Clif Kohlweck
* Includes In All The Right Places (Instrumental)
** Includes Soul Mix – Not arranged by John Barry
Orchestra Manager: Nathan Kaproff
Recorded at Sony Pictures Studio, Culver City, Ca.

1993	MY LIFE	Solo Piano: Michael Lang Orchestra Manager: Nathan Kaproff Music Editor: Clif Kohlweck Recording Engineer: Shawn Murphy Recorded at Sony Scoring Stage	UK CD EPIC EPC 475510 2 US CD EPIC SOUNDTRAX EK 57683
1994	THE SPECIALIST	Solo Alto Sax: Ronny Lang Solo Piano: Michael Lang Music Scoring Mixer: Shawn Murphy Music Editor: Clif Kohlweck Orchestra Manager: Nathan Kaproff Orchestrations: Greig McRitchie Recorded at Sony Scoring Stage * Songs album – Includes Did You Call Me?/ The Specialist played by The Royal Philharmonic Orchestra	UK CD EPIC 477810 2 US CD EPIC SOUNDTRAX EK 66370 UK CD CRESCENT MOON/EPIC SOUNDTRAX 477666 2 * US CD CRESCENT MOON/EPIC SOUNDTRAX EK 66384 *
1995	THE SCARLET LETTER	Performed by The English Chamber Orchestra Orchestrations: Nic Raine Title sequence & native American instrumentation by Peter Buffett. Assistant Music Editor: Shannon Erbe Recording Engineer/Scoring Mixer: John Kurlander Music Supervisor: Happy Walters Recorded at EMI Abbey Road Studio, London	UK CD EPIC EPC 483577 2 US CD EPIC SOUNDTRAX EK 67431
1995	ACROSS THE SEA OF TIME	IMAX Film Performed by The English Chamber Orchestra Recording Engineer: Shawn Murphy Recorded at EMI Abbey Road Studio, London	US CD EPIC SOUNDTRAX EK 67355
1995	CRY THE BELOVED COUNTRY	Performed by The English Chamber Orchestra Recording Engineer: Shawn Murphy Recorded at EMI Abbey Road Studio, London	US CD EPIC SOUNDTRAX EK 67354
1997	SWEPT FROM THE SEA (UK title: Amy Foster)	Performed by the English Chamber Orchestra Recording Engineer: John Richards Recorded at EMI Abbey Road Studio, London Music Editor: Clif Kohlweck.	US CD LONDON 458 793 2
1998	MERCURY RISING	Music recorded and mixed by John Richards at at Sony Scoring Stage/O'Henry Sound Studios. Music Contractor: Nathan Kaproff	US/UK CD VARESE VSD 5925

TELEVISION THEMES

N.B. Please refer to the Compilation/Collection LPs/CDs above for additional releases.

1960	JUKE BOX JURY	BBC Series (Hit & Miss)	UK 45 COLUMBIA DB 4414 Used from 13.2.60.
1962	THE BETRAYERS	ATV TV Play	COMMERCIALLY UNRECORDED
1962	LOOK NORTH	Local BBC News Programme (Lost Patrol)	UK 45 COLUMBIA DB 4806 AUS 45 COLUMBIA DO-4380
1962	DATELINE	London News Programme (Cutty Sark)	UK 45 COLUMBIA DB 4806 AUS 45 COLUMBIA DO-4380
1963	THE FOUR CORNERS	Australian Series (Lost Patrol)	AUS 45 COLUMBIA DO -4380 (The Four Corners Theme)
1963	THE HUMAN JUNGLE	ABC Series Composed by Bernard Ebbinghouse Arranged by John Barry Played by John Barry & Orchestra Original arrangement – * Mono/** Stereo	UK 45 COLUMBIA DB 7003 (P) UK 33 FILMTRAX MOMENT 105 * UK CD PLAY IT AGAIN PLAY 006 **
1965	THE NEWCOMERS	BBC Serial (Fancy Dance)	UK 45 EMBER S 178 UK CD PLAY IT AGAIN PLAY 010
1966	VENDETTA	BBC Series (2 Themes) (Vendetta/Danny Scipio Theme)	UK 45 CBS 202390

1971	THE PERSUADERS!	ITC Series Mono/Stereo versions (X) Amicalement Votre Picture Disc Promo	UK 45 CBS 7469 * US 45 EPIC 5-10865 FR CD CBS 466900 2 (X) FR CD45 COLUMBIA PRO 731 FR CD45 CBS 655356 1 (*) FR 45 CBS SPECIAL MARKETING 655356 7 (X) **
		(*) 3" disc. ** Reissue with different sleeve artwork	
1972	THE ADVENTURER	ITC Series With The Royal Philharmonic Orchestra	UK 45 POLYDOR 2058 275 UK 33 POLYDOR 2383 156
1973	ORSON WELLES GREAT MYSTERIES	 Anglia Series	JA 45 POLYDOR DPQ 6069 (P) UK 33 POLYDOR 2383 300
1988	USA TODAY ON TV (Previously Titled: USA TODAY; THE TELEVISION SHOW)	USA Daily News Programme Themes & Incidental Music	COMMERCIALLY UNRECORDED

OTHERS

1960s	DISCS-A-GO-GO	(Starfire)	See: Part 1 – John Barry Singles
1979	WILDTRACK	BBC Nature Series (Florida Fantasy) The above theme was also used for several Rugby/Cricket programme on TV & Radio including:	See Part 2 – Midnight Cowboy (1969)
	RUGBY SPECIAL TEST MATCH SPECIAL	BBC TV Series BBC Radio Series	As above As above

RADIO THEMES

| 1960 | EASYBEAT | Played by Bert Weedon
With Instrumental Accompaniment | UK 45 TOP RANK JAR 517
UK CD EMI CDB 7 52042 2 (CC 217) |

UK TELEVISION COMMERCIALS

1963	INGERSOLL	Flexi disc issued with 8 page promotional A4 booklet to promote Ingersoll Watches (Ingersoll Trendsetters) Contains uncredited female vocal.	UK 45 LYNTONE LYN 378
1967	SUNSILK	 (The Girl With The Sun In Her Hair) Lyrics by Don Black * Re-recording (30 secs) (Sunny Girl) ** Flexi containing Original arrangement	UK 45 CBS 2825 US 45 COLUMBIA 4-44167 UK 33 CBS LSP 15019 * NL 45 KANT 1 (P) **
1992	KODAK GOLD II	Used to promote Kodak Gold II film during the Olympic Games 1992	COMMERCIALLY UNRECORDED

OTHER SIXTIES UK TV COMMERCIALS

ACRILAN CARPETS
ARIEL
AUSTIN CARS
BALLITO STOCKINGS
CASTROL
CHIVERS JELLIES
DULUX PAINTS
FABLON
GAY FRUIT
HEARTS CROWN CUP
IZAL TOILET PAPER
KRAFT SAUCE
All commercially unrecorded.

MILK MARKETING BOARD
MORRIS CARS
NESTLE'S MILO
PLAYERS BATCHELOR CIGARETTES
PRO-PLUS
ROWNTREE'S BLACK MAGIC
SUNCAP
TRIANG TOYS
VIDOR BATTERIES
WHITE HORSE WHISKY
WOOL
YARDLEY

USA TELEVISION COMMERCIALS

1965	WHITE OWL CIGARS		COMMERCIALLY UNRECORDED
1968	EASTERN AIRLINES	2nd Summer only Award – Best Music for a Commercial	COMMERCIALLY UNRECORDED
1982	LINCOLN TOWN CARS		COMMERCIALLY UNRECORDED

$\mathscr{A}$CKNOWLEDGEMENTS

The authors give special thanks to the following people who contributed to the production of this book:

Malcolm Addey
David Arnold
John Barry
BASCA
BFI
Don Black
Alan Bown
Royal S. Brown
Ley Bricknell
Christina Brouder
John Burgess
Jon Burlingame
Martyn Crosthwaite
Ronald Curry MBE
Mike d'Abo
Vic Flick
Bryan Forbes
Mo Foster
Norman Fowler
Fiona Fullerton
Alexander Gleason
John Glen
Ken Golder
Bob Graham
Guy Hamilton
Andrea Hess
Robert Hoshowsky
Dave Howell
John Hudson
Peter Hunt
Simon Jones
Bob Kingston
Jeffrey Kruger
Vic Lewis
Dick Lewzey
Don Lusher
Gered Mankowitz
Sid Margo
Brian Matthew
Scott Minty
Trevor Peacock
Les Reed

Dave Richmond
Graham Rye
John Scott
Meg Simmonds
Tom Soter
David Stoner
Alan Taylor and Dave Burke of Pipeline
Eric Tomlinson
David Toop
Terry Walstrom
Chrissie Wilde
John Williams
Johnny Worth
Dougie Wright
Terence Young

Picture sources
Black and white
Pic Photos: 101 (top), 103, 104 (bottom), 105, 106, 107, 119, 121, 125, 130, 160, 161 (top), 162 (left), 181, 182; Terry O'Neil: 188–189; Courtesy of the Board of Trustees of the V & A Picture Library: 12, 19 (top), 50 (left), 54, 58, 74, 179, 180; Publicity Photos: 28, 30,59; CTS Studios: 101 (bottom); Rex Features: 16, 25 (top), 38, 40, 45, 60, 64; Bob Graham: 75, 81; Ken Golder: 11; Steve Cassidy: 72; Mirror Syndication: 11 (bottom right), 14, 19 (bottom right), 117; BFI: 68 (top right), 71, 102 (right), 112, 113, 128, 158, 161 (bottom), 162 (right); Redferns: 25 (bottom), 26 (top); York & County Press: 10, 104 (top); BBC Picture Archives: 19 (Middle right), 24 (bottom), 26

(bottom), 68 (bottom); BASCA: 194 (bottom); Stephen Woolston: 94; Flair Photography: 23, 24 (top), 48; Pictorial Press: 51; Getty Images: 68 (top left), 124; Alan Bown: 78, 84 (bottom); Antony Medley Photography: 194 (top); Gered Mankowitz: 73, 82, 83, 86; Camera Press: 196.

Every reasonable effort has been made to ascertain and acknowledge the ownership of copyrighted material included in this volume. Any errors or omissions that have inadvertently occurred will be rectified in subsequent editions provided notification is sent to the publisher.

Colour
Credits for the colour images are included in the captions.

INDEX